CONTENTS

Dear Friend,

Just desserts—that's what we have in store for you. And what an array! Look through the book—the range is wide, and there are recipes perfect for any mood, any occasion. Maybe you'll choose a tender layer cake, crowned with swirls of deep dark chocolate frosting...a fruit cobbler, bubbling with juicy goodness... a luscious made-in-advance ice-cream pie...showy, spectacular flaming crepes ...hearty gingerbread, rich with spices...flavorful fruit with a silken custard sauce ...warm-from-the-oven pudding.

Whatever you choose—old favorite or new idea—keep a few basic guidelines in mind. If your meal is hearty, you'll be wise to choose a light dessert. Rich desserts are best after less-filling meals or for a dessert-and-coffee party. Many of the recipes in this book can be made ahead of time—they're ideal for rush-hour meals or when you have guests. And our quick-to-make desserts are a real boon for those days (most days?) when time is short.

Remember that desserts are more than sheer enjoyment; they're good energy foods and can add nutritional value to the diet if they contain milk, eggs or fruit. Finally, an important tip: All our cake recipes include high altitude directions when necessary (based on testing at 5000 feet). When a recipe calls for a cake mix, be sure to check the package directions for high altitude information.

Generate some sunshine and give today a happy ending—create a special dessert for people special to you.

Cordially,

Betty Crocker

Betty Crocker's
DESSERTS
COOKBOOK

Golden Press / New York

Western Publishing Company, Inc.
Racine, Wisconsin

Director of Photography
George Ancona

Fourth Printing, 1978
Copyright © 1977, 1974 by General Mills, Inc., Minneapolis, Minnesota.

Printed in the U.S.A. by Western Publishing Company, Inc.
Published by Golden Press, New York, New York.

Library of Congress Catalog Card Number: 74-81984.

Golden® and Golden Press® are trademarks of
Western Publishing Company, Inc.

Nostalgic Naturals

Mmm—what smells so good?
Childhood memories are made of the good smells
of home—and here they are again in these
hearty desserts. Shortcakes, gingerbreads,
custards and puddings—these content the heart
and help carry sound nutrition through
to the end of the meal!

Cake-type Desserts

Fancy party cakes may take the prize for glamor, but there's something soul-satisfying about such homey cake-desserts as gingerbread, upside-down cake or old-fashioned strawberry shortcake. You'll find these basic favorites here, along with new delights we've dreamed up. Lemon Upside-down Gingerbread, Strawberry Shortcake Royale and Peach Butter-Almond Shortcake could make a party out of any evening. Friendly tip: These desserts are all at their best served warm. So plan ahead! Bake a cake-dessert as part of an energy-saving oven meal.

PINEAPPLE UPSIDE-DOWN CAKE

2 tablespoons butter or margarine
¼ cup brown sugar (packed)
1 can (8¼ ounces) sliced pineapple, drained
1½ cups biscuit baking mix
½ cup granulated sugar
1 egg
½ cup milk or water
2 tablespoons shortening
1 teaspoon vanilla

Heat oven to 350°. Melt butter in oven in square pan, 8×8×2 inches, or round layer pan, 9×1½ inches. Sprinkle brown sugar evenly over butter. Arrange pineapple slices on sugar mixture.

Blend remaining ingredients in large mixer bowl on low speed ½ minute, scraping bowl frequently. Beat 4 minutes on medium speed, scraping bowl occasionally. Pour batter evenly over fruit in pan.

Bake until wooden pick inserted in center comes out clean, 35 to 40 minutes. Invert pan on heatproof serving plate; leave pan over cake a few minutes. Serve warm, and if you like, with sweetened whipped cream.

9 servings.

High Altitude (5000 feet): Heat oven to 375°. Add 2 tablespoons flour and increase liquid to ⅔ cup.

Pictured on page 5: Ingredients for Mexican Bread Pudding (page 20)

Substitutions
One can (13½ ounces) crushed pineapple, drained, or 1 can (13½ ounces) pineapple tidbits, drained, can be substituted for the sliced pineapple.

Variations
APRICOT UPSIDE-DOWN CAKE: Substitute 1 can (about 17 ounces) apricot halves, drained, for the pineapple.

CRANBERRY UPSIDE-DOWN CAKE: Substitute 1 jar (14 ounces) cranberry-orange relish or 1 package (10½ ounces) frozen cranberry-orange relish, thawed, for the pineapple.

PEACH UPSIDE-DOWN CAKE: Substitute 1 can (about 17 ounces) peach slices, drained, for the pineapple.

SPICED APPLE UPSIDE-DOWN CAKE: Substitute 1 jar (14 ounces) spiced apple rings, drained, for the pineapple. Cut apple rings in half and arrange in parallel rows over sugar mixture.

UPSIDE-DOWN CAKE DELUXE

Bake Pineapple, Apricot or Peach Upside-down Cake as directed at left except—reserve syrup from fruit. Prepare Fruit Sauce (below). Spoon Fruit Sauce over each serving, and if desired, top with sweetened whipped cream.

9 servings.

Fruit Sauce
⅓ cup brown sugar (packed)
1 tablespoon cornstarch
1 cup reserved pineapple, apricot or peach syrup (if necessary, add enough water to measure 1 cup)
2 tablespoons butter or margarine
½ teaspoon lemon juice

Mix sugar and cornstarch in saucepan. Stir in fruit syrup. Heat to boiling, stirring constantly. Boil and stir over medium heat 1 minute. Remove from heat; stir in butter and lemon juice. Serve warm.

BANANA UPSIDE-DOWN CAKE

¼ cup butter or margarine
½ cup brown sugar (packed)
2 or 3 medium bananas, cut into ½-inch
  slices
1 package (18.5 ounces) yellow, devils food
  or spice cake mix
Eggnog Sauce (below) or sweetened
  whipped cream

Heat oven to 350°. Melt butter in oven in square pan, 8×8×2 or 9×9×2 inches, or round layer pan, 9×1½ inches. Sprinkle sugar evenly over butter. Arrange banana slices in rows on sugar mixture.

Prepare cake mix as directed on package. Pour 3 cups batter evenly over bananas in pan. Pour remaining batter into greased and floured round layer pan, 8 or 9×1½ inches.

Bake upside-down cake until wooden pick inserted in center comes out clean, 35 to 45 minutes. Bake remaining batter as directed on package.* Invert upside-down cake on heatproof serving plate; leave pan over cake a few minutes. Serve warm, with Eggnog Sauce.

9 servings.

Eggnog Sauce
Beat 2 egg yolks until thick and lemon colored. Beat in ½ cup confectioners' sugar and 1 to 2 tablespoons rum or sherry flavoring. In chilled bowl, beat ½ cup chilled whipping cream until stiff; fold into egg yolk mixture. Serve immediately or refrigerate until needed.

Variation
MINCEMEAT UPSIDE-DOWN CAKE: Decrease butter to 1 tablespoon; omit brown sugar and bananas. Spread 1½ cups prepared mincemeat and ½ cup chopped nuts over melted butter. Prepare cake mix and bake as directed above. Serve with sweetened whipped cream or Hard Sauce (page 36).

* Freeze round layer for other use.

LEMON UPSIDE-DOWN GINGERBREAD

¼ cup butter or margarine
½ cup brown sugar (packed)
1 lemon
1 package (14.5 ounces) gingerbread mix

Heat oven to 350°. Melt butter in oven in square pan, 9×9×2 inches. Sprinkle sugar evenly over butter. Cut lemon into 9 very thin slices (about ⅛ inch thick); quarter each slice. Arrange lemon slices in pan.

Prepare gingerbread mix as directed on package except—decrease water to ¾ cup; pour batter evenly over fruit in pan. Bake until wooden pick inserted in center comes out clean, 30 to 35 minutes. Invert pan on heatproof serving plate; leave pan over cake a few minutes. Serve warm, and if desired, with sweetened whipped cream.

9 servings.

Variations
APPLE UPSIDE-DOWN GINGERBREAD: Substitute 2 cups thinly sliced pared apples (about 2 medium) for the lemon. Overlap in 3 rows in pan.

APRICOT UPSIDE-DOWN GINGERBREAD: Substitute 1 can (about 17 ounces) apricot halves, drained, for the lemon.

PEAR UPSIDE-DOWN GINGERBREAD: Substitute 1 can (16 ounces) pear halves, drained, for the lemon. Cut each half into 4 lengthwise slices. If desired, add maraschino cherry halves or pecan halves.

NOTE

Here's a tip for the thrifty! Don't throw away that delicious syrup you drain from canned or frozen fruits when you use them for an upside-down cake. Let it play a second role—as part of the liquid in gelatin desserts, as an extra dimension in fruit drinks and party punches. Or include it in the Fruit Sauce recipe you'll find on page 6. This sauce is superb served over ice cream, cake or gingerbread.

GINGERBREAD

2¼ cups all-purpose flour* or cake flour
⅓ cup sugar
1 cup dark molasses
¾ cup hot water
½ cup shortening
1 egg
1 teaspoon baking soda
1 teaspoon ginger
1 teaspoon cinnamon
¾ teaspoon salt
Whipped Cream Topping (below), Caramel
   Fluff Topping (page 71) or applesauce

Heat oven to 325°. Grease and flour square pan, 9×9×2 inches. Measure all ingredients except toppings into large mixer bowl. Blend ½ minute on low speed, scraping bowl constantly. Beat 3 minutes on medium speed, scraping bowl occasionally. Pour batter into pan.

Bake until wooden pick inserted in center comes out clean, about 50 minutes. Serve warm, with one of the toppings.

9 servings.

* Do not use self-rising flour in this recipe.

High Altitude (5000 feet): For all-purpose flour, heat oven to 350°. Increase flour to 2½ cups and hot water to ¾ cup plus 2 tablespoons.

Whipped Cream Topping
In chilled bowl, beat 1 cup chilled whipping cream and 3 tablespoons granulated or confectioners' sugar.

2 cups.

To vary, fold in one of the following:

- [ ] 1 teaspoon grated orange or lemon peel
- [ ] 1 teaspoon vanilla
- [ ] ½ teaspoon rum flavoring
- [ ] ½ cup prepared mincemeat
- [ ] ½ cup finely crushed peanut brittle

APRICOT GINGERBREAD DESSERT

Bake Gingerbread as directed at left or on 1 package (14.5 ounces) gingerbread mix. Mix 1 cup apricot preserves, 1 tablespoon grated lemon peel and 2 tablespoons lemon juice. Cut warm gingerbread into squares. Top with vanilla ice cream and apricot sauce.

9 servings.

GINGER PEACHY SHORTCAKE

1 package (14.5 ounces) gingerbread mix
1 cup chilled whipping cream
¼ cup sugar
1 teaspoon instant coffee (optional)
4 cups sweetened sliced fresh peaches or
   1 can (29 ounces) sliced peaches, drained

Bake gingerbread mix as directed on package. In chilled bowl, beat whipping cream, sugar and coffee. Cut warm gingerbread into squares; split each square in half. Fill and top with whipped cream and peaches.

9 servings.

GINGERBREAD WITH LEMON SAUCE

Bake Gingerbread as directed at left or on 1 package (14.5 ounces) gingerbread mix. Beat 1 package (8 ounces) cream cheese, softened, and ¼ cup milk until fluffy. Prepare Lemon Sauce (page 12).

Cut warm gingerbread into 12 pieces; split each piece in half. Fill each with about ½ tablespoon of the cream cheese mixture. Top with remaining cream cheese mixture and warm Lemon Sauce.

12 servings.

PEAR FUDGE SHORTCAKE

1½ cups biscuit baking mix
⅓ cup sugar
1 egg
½ cup cold water
½ cup semisweet chocolate pieces or 2 ounces
  semisweet chocolate, melted and cooled
2 tablespoons shortening
1 teaspoon vanilla
½ teaspoon ginger
Pear Topping (below)

Heat oven to 350°. Grease and flour square pan, 8 × 8 × 2 inches, or round layer pan, 9 × 1½ inches. Blend all ingredients except Pear Topping in large mixer bowl on low speed ½ minute, scraping bowl frequently. Beat 4 minutes on medium speed. Pour into pan.

Bake until wooden pick inserted in center comes out clean, 30 to 35 minutes. Serve warm, with Pear Topping.

Pear Topping

¼ cup sugar
2 teaspoons cornstarch
1 can (16 ounces) pear halves, drained
  (reserve syrup)
2 teaspoons lemon juice
½ teaspoon ginger
2 teaspoons butter or margarine

In saucepan, combine sugar, cornstarch, pear syrup, lemon juice, ginger and butter. Cook, stirring constantly, until mixture thickens and boils. Boil and stir 1 minute. Stir in pear halves and heat.

STRAWBERRY SHORTCAKE

1 quart fresh strawberries
1 cup sugar
2 cups all-purpose flour*
2 tablespoons sugar
3 teaspoons baking powder
1 teaspoon salt
⅓ cup shortening
1 cup milk
Butter or margarine, softened
Sweetened whipped cream

Slice strawberries; sprinkle with 1 cup sugar and let stand 1 hour.

Heat oven to 450°. Grease round layer pan, 8 × 1½ inches. Stir together flour, 2 tablespoons sugar, the baking powder and salt. Cut in shortening thoroughly until mixture is crumbly. Stir in milk just until blended. Pat dough in pan.

Bake until golden brown, 15 to 20 minutes. Split layer crosswise while hot. Spread with butter; fill and top with whipped cream and sweetened berries.

8 servings.

* If using self-rising flour, omit baking powder and salt.

Variation

INDIVIDUAL STRAWBERRY SHORTCAKES: Decrease milk to ¾ cup. Gently smooth dough into a ball on lightly floured cloth-covered board. Knead 20 to 25 times. Roll or pat dough with floured hands to ½-inch thickness; cut with floured 3-inch biscuit cutter. Place 1 inch apart on ungreased baking sheet. Bake until golden brown, 10 to 12 minutes.

6 shortcakes.

NOTE

For custard sauce in a hurry, prepare 1 package (about 3½ ounces) regular vanilla pudding and pie filling as directed except—increase the milk to 3 cups. Cover and refrigerate.

STRAWBERRY SHORTCAKE ROYALE

Creamy Stirred Custard (page 15)
1½ cups biscuit baking mix
½ cup sugar
1 egg
½ cup milk or water
2 tablespoons shortening
1 teaspoon rum flavoring or vanilla
4 cups sweetened sliced strawberries or
  2 packages (10 ounces each) frozen sliced
  strawberries, thawed

Prepare custard; cover and refrigerate. Heat oven to 350°. Grease and flour square pan, 8×8×2 inches. Blend baking mix, sugar, egg, milk, shortening and flavoring in large mixer bowl on low speed ½ minute, scraping bowl frequently. Beat 4 minutes on medium speed. Pour into pan.

Bake until wooden pick inserted in center comes out clean, 30 to 35 minutes. Cool slightly; cut into squares. Split squares; fill and top with sweetened berries. Pour custard over each serving.

9 servings.

High Altitude (5000 feet): Heat oven to 375°. Add 2 tablespoons flour and increase liquid to ⅔ cup.

Variations
BROWN SUGAR SHORTCAKE ROYALE: Substitute ½ cup brown sugar (packed) for the granulated sugar. Spoon 4 cups sweetened sliced fresh peaches, strawberries or raspberries between and over top; top with custard or sweetened whipped cream.

RASPBERRY SHORTCAKE ROYALE: Substitute 4 cups sweetened fresh raspberries or 2 packages (10 ounces each) frozen raspberries, thawed, for the strawberries.

PEACH BUTTER-ALMOND SHORTCAKE

4⅔ cups biscuit baking mix
⅓ cup granulated sugar
⅓ cup butter or margarine, melted
1 cup milk
2 tablespoons butter or margarine, softened
½ cup brown sugar (packed)
½ cup slivered almonds
Almond Whipped Cream (below)
4 cups sweetened sliced fresh peaches

Heat oven to 400°. Stir baking mix, granulated sugar, ⅓ cup butter and the milk to a soft dough. Gently smooth dough into a ball on floured cloth-covered board. Knead 8 to 10 times.

Divide dough in half. Pat each half in an ungreased round layer pan, 9×1½ inches. Spread each with 1 tablespoon butter; sprinkle each with ¼ cup brown sugar and ¼ cup almonds.

Bake until light brown, 15 to 20 minutes. Remove from pans; cool slightly. Fill layers with half of the Almond Whipped Cream and sliced peaches. Top servings with remaining whipped cream and peaches.

8 to 10 servings.

Almond Whipped Cream
In chilled bowl, beat 1 cup chilled whipping cream, 3 tablespoons sugar and ½ teaspoon almond extract until soft peaks form.

Variation
BERRY BUTTER-ALMOND SHORTCAKE: Substitute 1½ quarts fresh strawberries for the peaches. Slice strawberries and sprinkle with 1 cup granulated sugar; let stand 1 hour.

Note: If fresh fruit is not available, 4 to 6 cups drained canned or thawed frozen fruit can be substituted. Try combinations too: half peaches and raspberries or a combination of strawberries and blueberries.

Peach Butter-Almond Shortcake (page 10)

Plantation Cake (page 12)

Strawberry Shortcake Royale (page 10)

PLANTATION CAKE

⅔ cup shortening
½ cup brown sugar (packed)
2 cups all-purpose flour*
¼ teaspoon salt
⅔ cup water
⅔ cup light molasses
¾ teaspoon baking soda
Lemon Sauce (below)
Cream Cheese Topping (below)

Heat oven to 350°. Grease square pan, 8×8×2 inches. Beat shortening and sugar in small mixer bowl 5 minutes on high speed, scraping bowl occasionally. Mix in flour and salt. Press half of the sugar mixture evenly in bottom of pan.

Mix water, molasses and soda; pour half over sugar mixture in pan. Sprinkle with half of the remaining sugar mixture. Pour remaining molasses mixture over top; sprinkle with remaining sugar mixture. Bake 35 to 40 minutes. Serve warm, with Lemon Sauce and Cream Cheese Topping.

9 servings.

Lemon Sauce
½ cup sugar
1 tablespoon cornstarch
1 cup water
1 tablespoon butter or margarine
1 tablespoon grated lemon peel
1 tablespoon lemon juice

Mix sugar and cornstarch in small saucepan. Gradually stir in water. Cook over medium heat, stirring constantly, until mixture thickens and boils. Boil and stir 1 minute. Remove from heat; stir in remaining ingredients. Serve warm or cool.

About 1 cup.

Cream Cheese Topping
Beat 2 packages (3 ounces each) cream cheese, softened, and 2 to 3 tablespoons milk until smooth and creamy.

* Do not use self-rising flour in this recipe.

CRANBERRY CAKE

2 cups biscuit baking mix
½ cup sugar
2 tablespoons shortening, melted
⅓ cup milk
1 egg
2 cups fresh or frozen cranberries
Lemon Butter Sauce (below)

Heat oven to 350°. Grease and flour square pan, 9×9×2 inches, or 6-cup ring mold. Mix baking mix, sugar, shortening, milk and egg. Beat ½ minute. Fold in cranberries. Spread batter in pan.

Bake until cake is golden brown and wooden pick inserted in center comes out clean, about 35 minutes. Serve warm, with Lemon Butter Sauce.

9 to 12 servings.

Lemon Butter Sauce
Combine ½ cup butter or margarine, 1 cup sugar and ¾ cup half-and-half in saucepan. Cook over low heat, stirring constantly, until smooth. Stir in 1 teaspoon grated lemon peel. Serve warm.

TRIPLE FUDGE CAKE

1 package (about 3¾ ounces) chocolate
   regular pudding and pie filling
1 package (18.5 ounces) devils food cake mix
½ cup semisweet chocolate pieces
½ cup coarsely chopped nuts

Heat oven to 350°. Grease and flour oblong pan, 13×9×2 inches. In large saucepan, cook pudding and pie filling as directed on package for pudding. Stir cake mix into hot pudding. Beat 2 minutes on medium speed or 300 strokes by hand. Pour batter into pan; sprinkle with chocolate pieces and nuts. Bake 35 to 40 minutes. Serve warm.

High Altitude (5000 feet): Heat oven to 375°. Cook pudding as directed on package except—add 2 tablespoons milk. Continue as directed above.

APPLE-NUT CAKE WITH VELVET RUM SAUCE

¼ cup shortening
1 egg
2 tablespoons water
1 cup sugar
1 cup all-purpose flour*
1 teaspoon baking soda
½ teaspoon salt
½ teaspoon nutmeg
2 cups chopped pared apple (about 2 medium)
½ cup chopped nuts
Velvet Rum Sauce (below)

Heat oven to 350°. Grease 9-inch pie pan or square pan, 8×8×2 inches. Measure all ingredients except apple, nuts and sauce into large mixer bowl. Blend ½ minute on low speed, scraping bowl constantly. Beat 2 minutes on medium speed, scraping bowl occasionally. Fold in apple and nuts. Spread batter in pan.

Bake until wooden pick inserted in center comes out clean, 40 to 45 minutes. Serve warm, with Velvet Rum Sauce.

* If using self-rising flour, omit soda and salt.

Velvet Rum Sauce

½ cup butter or margarine
1 cup sugar
½ cup light cream (20%) or 1 can (about 6 ounces) evaporated milk
2 tablespoons rum or 1 teaspoon rum flavoring
1 teaspoon nutmeg

Combine all ingredients in medium saucepan. Heat to boiling over low heat, stirring constantly. Serve warm.

1¼ cups.

DATE PUDDING

3 eggs
1 cup sugar
¼ cup all-purpose flour*
1 teaspoon baking powder
¼ teaspoon salt
2½ cups cut-up dates
1 cup chopped nuts
Sweetened whipped cream

Heat oven to 350°. Grease square pan, 9×9×2 inches. Beat eggs until light and fluffy. Gradually add sugar, beating until mixture is thick. Stir together flour, baking powder and salt. Mix into egg-sugar mixture. Stir in dates and nuts. Pour into pan. Bake 30 minutes. While warm, cut into squares and serve with whipped cream.

9 to 12 servings.

* If using self-rising flour, decrease baking powder to ½ teaspoon.

CHOCOLATE-APPLESAUCE CAKE

1 package (18.5 ounces) devils food cake mix
¾ cup canned applesauce
¼ teaspoon baking soda
⅓ cup finely chopped nuts
1 cup chilled whipping cream
¼ cup sugar
1 cup canned applesauce
½ teaspoon nutmeg

Prepare cake mix as directed on package except —use ¼ cup less water; add ¾ cup applesauce and the soda before beating. Fold nuts into batter. Bake cake as directed. Cool.

In chilled bowl, beat whipping cream and sugar until stiff. Fold in 1 cup applesauce and the nutmeg; frost cake. Refrigerate.

PINEAPPLE-GLAZED CAKE

1 package (18.5 ounces) yellow or white
cake mix
1 can (13½ ounces) crushed pineapple
½ cup brown sugar (packed)
Sweetened whipped cream

Bake cake mix in oblong pan, 13×9×2 inches, as directed on package. In small saucepan, heat pineapple (with syrup) and sugar to boiling. With sharp knife, mark 1-inch squares on cake, cutting ½ inch deep. Spoon hot pineapple mixture over hot cake. Cool. Serve with whipped cream.

LEMON CAKE DESSERT

3 cups biscuit baking mix
¾ cup granulated sugar
1 package (3 ounces) lemon-flavored gelatin
4 eggs (about ¾ cup)
½ cup water
⅓ cup salad oil
1½ cups confectioners' sugar
½ cup lemon juice
Ice cream or sweetened whipped cream

Heat oven to 350°. Grease and flour oblong pan, 13×9×2 inches. Blend all ingredients except confectioners' sugar, lemon juice and ice cream in large mixer bowl ½ minute on low speed, scraping bowl frequently. Beat 4 minutes on medium speed, scraping bowl occasionally. Pour batter into pan.

Bake until wooden pick inserted in center comes out clean, 25 to 30 minutes. Cool 5 minutes. Mix confectioners' sugar and lemon juice. Make many holes in top of cake with fork; pour lemon mixture evenly over top. Serve with ice cream.

ROCKY ROAD CAKE

1 package (18.5 ounces) any chocolate
flavor cake mix
1 package (15.4 ounces) chocolate fudge
frosting mix
½ cup chopped toasted almonds
1 cup miniature marshmallows

Bake cake mix in oblong pan, 13×9×2 inches, as directed on package. Cool. Prepare frosting mix as directed on package. Stir in almonds and marshmallows. If too stiff to spread, stir in few drops water. Spread over cake.

TOASTED MARSHMALLOW CAKE

1 package (18.5 ounces) devils food cake
mix
12 large marshmallows
½ cup brown sugar (packed)
½ cup chopped nuts

Prepare cake mix as directed on package; pour batter into greased and floured oblong pan, 13×9×2 inches. Cut marshmallows crosswise in half and arrange in rows over batter in pan. Mix brown sugar and nuts; sprinkle over top.

Bake until wooden pick inserted in center comes out clean, 40 to 45 minutes. (If marshmallows are browning too quickly, cover cake with aluminum foil.) Serve warm.

BROILED HONEY-COCONUT CAKE

Bake 1 package (18.5 ounces) yellow cake mix in oblong pan, 13×9×2 inches, as directed. Drizzle ½ cup honey over hot cake; sprinkle with 1 cup flaked coconut.

Set oven control at broil and/or 550°. Place cake with top 5 inches from heat. Broil until coconut is toasted, about 3 minutes. Serve warm.

Custards and Puddings

Cost-conscious and nutrition-minded—that's you when you star one of these in your mealtime plans. Try our offbeat Brown Rice Pudding or Pineapple-Pecan Bread Pudding as your next stellar attraction.

BAKED CUSTARD

2 eggs or 4 egg yolks, slightly beaten
⅓ cup sugar
¼ teaspoon salt
½ teaspoon vanilla
2 cups milk, scalded
Nutmeg

Heat oven to 350°. Blend eggs, sugar, salt and vanilla. Gradually stir in milk. Pour into five 6-ounce custard cups. Sprinkle with nutmeg. Place cups in baking pan on oven rack; pour very hot water into pan to within ½ inch of tops of cups.

Bake until knife inserted halfway between center and edge comes out clean, 40 to 50 minutes. Remove cups from water. Serve warm or cold, in custard cups—or refrigerate and unmold on dessert plates.

5 servings.

Variations

BUTTERSCOTCH CUSTARD: Substitute brown sugar (packed) for the granulated sugar.

COFFEE CUSTARD: Dissolve 1 teaspoon instant coffee in scalded milk before adding to egg mixture.

MOLDED GLAZED CUSTARD: Use 3 eggs or 6 egg yolks. Before pouring custard mixture into cups, spoon 2 teaspoons of *one* of the following into each cup: maple-flavored syrup, pineapple ice-cream topping, caramel sauce or honey. After baking, cool slightly, refrigerate about 3 hours and unmold on dessert plates.

CREAMY STIRRED CUSTARD

3 eggs, slightly beaten
⅓ cup sugar
Dash of salt
2½ cups milk
1 teaspoon vanilla

Blend eggs, sugar and salt in top of double boiler. Gradually stir in milk. Place enough hot water in bottom part of double boiler so that top part does not touch water. Cook over medium heat, stirring constantly, until mixture just coats a metal spoon, about 20 minutes. (Water in double boiler should not boil.)

Remove top of double boiler from heat; stir vanilla into custard. Place top of double boiler in cold water until custard is cool. (If custard curdles, beat with rotary beater until smooth.) Cover and refrigerate 2 to 3 hours. Serve plain or as a sauce over fresh fruit or cake.

6 servings.

Variation

FLOATING ISLAND: Substitute 2 whole eggs plus 2 egg yolks for the 3 eggs; reserve whites. Refrigerate custard until thoroughly chilled, about 3 hours.

Heat oven to 350°. Butter and sugar six 6-ounce custard cups. Beat reserved egg whites and ⅛ teaspoon cream of tartar until foamy. Beat in ¼ cup sugar, 1 tablespoon at a time; continue beating until stiff and glossy. Stir in ¼ teaspoon vanilla. Spoon meringue into cups, pressing mixture gently in cups to remove air pockets. Place cups in oblong pan, 13×9×2 inches; pour very hot water (1 inch deep) into pan.

Bake until light brown, 20 to 25 minutes. Remove cups from water; unmold in dessert dishes. Cool slightly and refrigerate. Just before serving, spoon custard around meringue. If desired, garnish with strawberries, raspberries or orange sections.

6 servings.

LEMON PUDDING CAKE

2 eggs, separated
1 teaspoon grated lemon peel
¼ cup lemon juice
1 cup milk
1 cup sugar
¼ cup all-purpose flour*
¼ teaspoon salt

Heat oven to 350°. Beat egg whites until stiff peaks form; set aside. Beat egg yolks. Blend in lemon peel, juice and milk. Add sugar, flour and salt; beat until smooth. Fold into whites. Pour into ungreased 1-quart casserole. Place casserole in pan of very hot water (1 inch deep).

Bake 45 to 50 minutes. Serve warm or cool, and if desired, with sweetened whipped cream.

6 servings.

* If using self-rising flour, omit salt.

High Altitude (5000 feet): Increase milk to 1 cup plus 2 tablespoons.

Variation
LIME PUDDING CAKE: Substitute 1½ teaspoons grated lime peel and ¼ cup lime juice for the lemon peel and juice.

BUTTERSCOTCH-GINGER PUDDING CAKE

Prepare 1 package (14.5 ounces) gingerbread mix as directed except—sprinkle 1½ cups brown sugar (packed) over batter in pan; slowly pour 1½ cups lukewarm water over sugar. Bake as directed. While gingerbread is hot, cut into squares; invert each square on dessert plate and spoon sauce from pan over each serving. If desired, serve with sweetened whipped cream.

9 servings.

HOT FUDGE SUNDAE CAKE

1 cup all-purpose flour*
¾ cup granulated sugar
2 tablespoons cocoa
2 teaspoons baking powder
¼ teaspoon salt
½ cup milk
2 tablespoons salad oil
1 teaspoon vanilla
1 cup chopped nuts (optional)
1 cup brown sugar (packed)
¼ cup cocoa
1¾ cups hottest tap water
Favorite ice cream

Heat oven to 350°. In ungreased square pan, 9×9×2 inches, stir together flour, granulated sugar, 2 tablespoons cocoa, the baking powder and salt. Mix in milk, oil and vanilla with fork until smooth. Stir in nuts. Spread evenly in pan. Sprinkle with brown sugar and ¼ cup cocoa. Pour *hot* water over batter. Bake 40 minutes. While warm, spoon into dessert dishes and top with ice cream. Spoon sauce from pan over each serving.

9 servings.

* If using self-rising flour, omit baking powder and salt.

High Altitude (5000 feet): Use oblong pan, 13×9×2 inches, and bake 25 minutes.

Variations
BUTTERSCOTCH SUNDAE CAKE: Omit nuts; add 1 package (6 ounces) butterscotch pieces (1 cup). Decrease brown sugar to ½ cup and the ¼ cup cocoa to 2 tablespoons.

MALLOW SUNDAE CAKE: Omit nuts; add 1 cup miniature marshmallows.

PEANUTTY SUNDAE CAKE: Omit nuts; stir in ½ cup peanut butter and ½ cup chopped peanuts.

RAISIN SUNDAE CAKE: Omit nuts; add 1 cup raisins.

Hot Fudge Sundae Cake (page 16)

BROWN RICE PUDDING

½ cup uncooked regular or quick-cooking
  brown rice
3 tablespoons honey
1 tablespoon butter or margarine
¼ teaspoon cinnamon
¾ cup milk
¼ cup raisins (optional)
Light cream
Honey or brown sugar

Cook brown rice as directed on package. Stir in 3 tablespoons honey, the butter, cinnamon, milk and raisins. Heat to boiling. Reduce heat; cook over low heat, stirring occasionally, until thickened to desired consistency, 10 to 15 minutes. Serve warm, with cream and honey.

3 or 4 servings.

NOTE

A few facts and figures about rice: It's an excellent source of energy—and of some B vitamins as well. The calorie cost? Just 115 calories per ½-cup serving of cooked rice.

Regular white rice is either the short-grain or long-grain variety. The short grain is less expensive, and is fine for puddings and creamy desserts. Parboiled (converted) rice has been specially processed to preserve its nutritive value but needs a slightly longer cooking time than the regular white. Precooked (instant) rice is commercially cooked, rinsed, dried and packaged. It's a real quick-fixer! Brown rice comes to you with only the outer hull removed—so it's very nutritious, with a nice nutty flavor and chewy texture. (Brown rice is a key ingredient in the recipe above—delicious!)

Why do some of our recipes call for scalded milk? Scalding reduces the baking time for custards and custard-type desserts. To scald milk, heat it to just below the boiling point. Remove from heat when tiny bubbles form at edge of pan.

CUSTARD-RICE PUDDING

½ cup water
½ cup uncooked instant rice
3 eggs, slightly beaten
½ cup sugar
2 teaspoons vanilla
¼ teaspoon salt
2½ cups milk, scalded
½ cup raisins (optional)
Cinnamon

Heat oven to 350°. Heat water to boiling in small saucepan. Remove from heat; stir in rice. Cover and let stand 5 minutes.

Blend eggs, sugar, vanilla and salt. Slowly stir in milk. Stir in rice and raisins. Pour into ungreased 1½-quart casserole; sprinkle with cinnamon. Place casserole in square pan, 9×9×2 inches; pour very hot water (1¼ inches deep) into pan.

Bake until knife inserted halfway between edge and center comes out clean, about 70 minutes. Remove casserole from water. Serve pudding warm or cold.

6 to 8 servings.

GLORIFIED RICE

1 cup cooked regular white or brown rice, cooled
⅓ cup sugar
1 can (13½ ounces) crushed pineapple, drained
½ teaspoon vanilla
⅓ cup miniature marshmallows
2 tablespoons drained chopped maraschino cherries
1 cup chilled whipping cream

Mix rice, sugar, pineapple and vanilla. Stir in marshmallows and cherries. In chilled bowl, beat whipping cream until stiff. Fold into rice mixture.

6 to 8 servings.

OLD-FASHIONED RICE PUDDING

⅔ cup uncooked regular rice
1⅓ cups water
2 eggs or 4 egg yolks
½ cup sugar
¼ teaspoon salt
½ teaspoon vanilla or 1 tablespoon grated
   orange peel
2 cups milk
½ cup raisins
Nutmeg

Stir together rice and water in saucepan. Heat to boiling, stirring once or twice. Reduce heat; cover and simmer 14 minutes without removing cover or stirring. All water should be absorbed.

Heat oven to 325°. Beat eggs in ungreased 1½-quart casserole. Stir in sugar, salt, vanilla, milk, hot rice and the raisins. Sprinkle with nutmeg. Bake, stirring occasionally, until knife inserted halfway between edge and center comes out clean, 50 to 60 minutes. Serve pudding warm or cold. If you like, serve with cream, Lingonberry Sauce (page 48) or Cinnamon-Blueberry Sauce (page 141).

6 to 8 servings.

QUICK RICE AND RAISIN PUDDING

1 cup uncooked instant rice
1 cup milk or water
3 tablespoons sugar
½ teaspoon salt
¼ teaspoon cinnamon or nutmeg
¼ cup raisins
Light cream

Combine all ingredients except cream in saucepan. Heat to rolling boil, stirring constantly. Remove from heat; cover and let stand, stirring occasionally, 12 to 15 minutes. Serve warm, with cream.

4 servings.

DELUXE BREAD PUDDING

4 slices bread
2 tablespoons butter or margarine, softened
⅓ cup brown sugar (packed)
½ teaspoon cinnamon
⅓ cup raisins
3 eggs, slightly beaten
⅓ cup granulated sugar
1 teaspoon vanilla
Dash of salt
2½ cups milk, scalded

Heat oven to 350°. Toast bread slices lightly; trim crusts. Spread slices with butter; sprinkle with brown sugar and cinnamon. Cut each slice into 4 pieces. Arrange pieces sugared sides up in greased 1½-quart casserole; sprinkle with raisins. Blend eggs, granulated sugar, vanilla and salt. Slowly stir in milk. Pour mixture over bread.

Place casserole in square pan, 9×9×2 inches; pour very hot water (1 inch deep) into pan. Bake until knife inserted halfway between edge and center comes out clean, 65 to 70 minutes. Remove casserole from hot water. Serve pudding warm or cold.

6 to 8 servings.

DATE BETTY

1 package (14 ounces) date bar mix
1¼ cups hot water
1 tablespoon lemon juice
1 egg
⅓ cup coarsely chopped nuts

Heat oven to 375°. Grease square pan, 8×8×2 inches. Stir together Date Filling from date bar mix, hot water and lemon juice. Pour into pan. Mix crumbly mix and egg; drop by teaspoonfuls onto date filling mixture. Sprinkle with nuts. Bake 30 minutes. Serve warm, and if desired, with light cream.

6 to 8 servings.

PINEAPPLE-PECAN BREAD PUDDING

½ cup butter or margarine, softened
1 cup sugar
½ teaspoon cinnamon
4 eggs
1 can (13½ ounces) crushed pineapple, well
    drained
2 cups ½-inch bread cubes (about 3 slices)
¼ cup chopped pecans

Heat oven to 325°. Beat butter, sugar and cinnamon in large mixer bowl 1 minute on medium speed, scraping bowl constantly. Add eggs; beat on high speed, scraping bowl occasionally, until mixture is light and fluffy, about 2 minutes. Fold in pineapple, bread cubes and pecans. Pour into greased 1½-quart casserole. Bake until knife inserted in center comes out clean, 40 to 45 minutes. Serve pudding warm or cold.

4 to 6 servings.

MEXICAN BREAD PUDDING

6 slices bread, toasted
6 ounces shredded Cheddar cheese (about
    1½ cups)
½ cup raisins
¼ cup salted peanuts
2 cups maple-flavored syrup
1 teaspoon cinnamon
2 tablespoons butter or margarine
Milk

Heat oven to 350°. Cut each toast slice into 4 pieces. Arrange 8 toast pieces in single layer in ungreased 1½-quart casserole; sprinkle half of the cheese, raisins and peanuts over toast. Repeat; top with remaining toast. Heat syrup, cinnamon and butter over medium heat just to boiling; pour over toast. Bake uncovered until syrup is absorbed, about 30 minutes. Cool slightly. Serve with milk.

6 to 8 servings.

CINNAMON TOAST-APPLE DESSERT

6 slices whole wheat or white bread
Butter or margarine, softened
⅓ to ½ cup sugar
½ teaspoon cinnamon
1 can (16 ounces) applesauce (2 cups)
⅓ cup raisins
¼ cup maple-flavored syrup
Light cream

Heat oven to 350°. Trim crusts from bread slices; spread slices with butter. Cut each slice into 4 pieces. Mix sugar and cinnamon; sprinkle 2 tablespoons sugar mixture in ungreased square pan, 8 × 8 × 2 inches.

Arrange half of the bread in pan, buttered sides up; sprinkle with 2 tablespoons sugar mixture. Cover with applesauce; sprinkle raisins on applesauce. Top with remaining bread; sprinkle with remaining sugar mixture. Pour syrup over top. Bake until golden brown, about 30 minutes. Serve warm, with cream.

6 servings.

APPLESAUCE DELICIOUS

1 can (16 ounces) applesauce (2 cups)
5 slices white bread
Butter or margarine, softened
⅓ cup sugar
1 teaspoon cinnamon
Light cream

Heat oven to 350°. Spread applesauce in ungreased 9-inch glass pie pan. Cut bread slices diagonally in half. Spread both sides of slices with butter. Arrange halves on top of applesauce, overlapping edges. Mix sugar and cinnamon; sprinkle over bread in pan. Bake until slightly crusty, about 20 minutes. Serve warm, with cream.

6 servings.

Super-Specials

Dine in state—introduce your guests
to these sophisticates whenever you want
to establish a really lavish atmosphere.
Add a little dazzle to everyday dinners, too!
Let your love shine through
with one of these sparklers
—made just to make this day special.

Fondues

Such an entertaining way to entertain! Serve our luscious Chocolate or Caramel Fondue after a card game, or for an evening dessert and coffee party. Same principle as the original Swiss cheese classic: You dunk delicious morsels into a creamy mixture kept warm over very low heat (to prevent scorching). If you don't have a fondue pot, a small heavy saucepan or heatproof dish will do. Dessert fondues are informal yet sophisticated—also quite simple, if you make the sauce ahead of time. Take your pick of our assorted dippers: strawberries, pineapple chunks, ladyfingers. Whatever you choose, have fun with fondues!

CARAMEL FONDUE

¼ cup sugar
1 cup whipping cream
1 tablespoon cornstarch
¼ cup sugar
Dippers (right)
Granola, chopped nuts or cookie coconut
   (optional)

Melt ¼ cup sugar in small saucepan over medium heat, stirring constantly, until sugar turns golden brown; remove from heat. Add cream (mixture will steam and sugar will harden). Cook over low heat, stirring constantly, until mixture is smooth.

Mix cornstarch and ¼ cup sugar; stir into cream mixture. Boil and stir until thickened, about 1 minute. Pour into fondue pot or chafing dish; keep warm over very low heat.

Guests select choice of Dippers and place on dessert plates; then, with fondue forks or bamboo skewers, they dip each one into caramel sauce and roll each in granola.

4 to 6 servings.

Note: If you prefer, double the recipe. Any remaining sauce is delicious as an ice-cream topping.

Pictured on page 21: Crepes Suzette (page 25)

CHOCOLATE FONDUE

12 ounces milk chocolate, semisweet chocolate pieces or sweet cooking chocolate
¾ cup light cream
1 to 2 tablespoons orange-flavored liqueur, kirsch, brandy, white crème de menthe or 2 teaspoons instant coffee or ¼ teaspoon cinnamon
Dippers (below)

Heat chocolate and cream in heavy saucepan over low heat, stirring constantly, until chocolate is melted and mixture is smooth. Remove from heat; stir in liqueur. Pour into fondue pot or chafing dish to keep warm.

Guests select choice of Dippers and place on dessert plates; then, with fondue forks or bamboo skewers, they dip each one into chocolate mixture. If mixture becomes too thick, stir in small amount of cream. If desired, Dippers can be rolled in granola, chopped peanuts, chopped salted cashews or cookie coconut after coating with chocolate mixture.

6 to 8 servings.

Dippers
Choose two to five of the following:
☐ Fresh strawberries
☐ Banana slices*
☐ Pineapple chunks
☐ Mandarin orange segments
☐ Fresh orange sections
☐ Apple wedges*
☐ Grapes
☐ Melon balls
☐ Maraschino cherries
☐ Angel food cake cubes
☐ Pound cake cubes
☐ Ladyfingers
☐ Miniature cream puffs
☐ Miniature doughnuts
☐ Marshmallows

* Dip in lemon or pineapple juice to prevent discoloration of fruit.

WHITE ALMOND FONDUE

12 ounces white almond bark coating
⅓ cup light cream
1 to 2 tablespoons orange-flavored liqueur,
    kirsch, brandy, white crème de menthe or
    2 teaspoons instant coffee or ¼ teaspoon
    cinnamon
Dippers (page 22)

Heat almond bark and cream in heavy saucepan over low heat, stirring constantly, until almond bark is melted and mixture is smooth. Remove from heat; stir in liqueur. Pour into fondue pot or chafing dish to keep warm.

Guests select choice of Dippers and place on dessert plates; then, with fondue forks or bamboo skewers, they dip each one into almond mixture. If mixture becomes too thick, stir in small amount of cream. If desired, each Dipper can be rolled in granola, chopped peanuts, chopped salted cashews or cookie coconut after it is coated with almond mixture.

6 to 8 servings.

Variation
ALMOND-SOUR CREAM FONDUE: Decrease light cream to ¼ cup; add ¼ cup dairy sour cream.

QUICK CHOCOLATE FONDUE

Heat 1 can (16.5 ounces) chocolate frosting in saucepan over low heat, stirring frequently. Pour into fondue pot or chafing dish to keep warm. Guests select choice of Dippers (page 22) and place on dessert plates; then, with fondue forks or bamboo skewers, they dip each one into chocolate frosting.

Variations
CHOCOLATE-ALMOND FONDUE: Stir ½ teaspoon vanilla and ¼ teaspoon almond extract into frosting.

CHOCOLATE-MINT FONDUE: Stir ½ teaspoon mint extract into frosting.

Crepes and Cream Puffs

If you've thought it takes genius to make crepes—the tender-thin pancakes with the French connection—take heart. Dainty cream puffs needn't be difficult, either. Start with our clear basic recipes, then go on to such impressive works as Crepes Chantilly or Brandied Apricot Crepes—or even a cream puff Christmas tree!

CREPES

1½ cups all-purpose flour*
1 tablespoon sugar
½ teaspoon baking powder
½ teaspoon salt
2 cups milk
2 eggs
½ teaspoon vanilla
2 tablespoons butter or margarine, melted

Measure flour, sugar, baking powder and salt into bowl. Stir in remaining ingredients. Beat with rotary beater until smooth.

Lightly butter 6-, 7- or 8-inch skillet; heat over medium heat until butter is bubbly. For each crepe, pour a scant ¼ cup of the batter into skillet; immediately rotate skillet until thin film of batter covers bottom. Cook until light brown. Run wide spatula around edge to loosen; turn and cook other side until light brown. Stack crepes, placing waxed paper or paper towel between them. Keep crepes covered to prevent them from drying out.

If desired, spread applesauce, sweetened strawberries, currant jelly, raspberry jam or fruit-flavored yogurt thinly on warm crepes; roll up. (Be sure to roll crepes so the most attractive side is on the outside.) Sprinkle with confectioners' sugar.

12 to 16 crepes.

* If using self-rising flour, omit baking powder and salt.

CREPES CHANTILLY

Crepes (page 23)
¾ cup chilled whipping cream
¼ cup granulated or confectioners' sugar
¾ cup sliced fresh strawberries

Prepare crepes. In chilled bowl, beat whipping cream and sugar until stiff. Fold in strawberries. Spoon about 2 tablespoons of the strawberry mixture on each crepe; roll up. Place 2 crepes seam sides down on each dessert plate; dust with confectioners' sugar.

6 to 8 servings.

BANANA CREPES

Crepes (page 23)
½ cup brown sugar (packed)
¼ cup light cream (20%)
¼ cup light corn syrup
2 tablespoons butter or margarine
½ teaspoon cinnamon
2 firm bananas
¾ cup chilled whipping cream

Prepare crepes. Combine sugar, light cream, corn syrup, butter and cinnamon in small saucepan. Cook over low heat 5 minutes, stirring occasionally. Slice bananas thinly on the diagonal into hot sauce; stir carefully until slices are well coated. In chilled bowl, beat whipping cream until stiff.

Place 3 or 4 banana slices on each crepe. Top with about 2 tablespoons of the whipped cream; roll up. Place 2 crepes seam sides down on each dessert plate; spoon warm sauce over crepes.

6 to 8 servings.

BRANDIED APRICOT CREPES

Crepes (page 23)
1 package (8 ounces) cream cheese, softened
¼ cup sugar
¼ cup butter or margarine, softened
1 tablespoon brandy or 1 teaspoon vanilla
1 teaspoon grated lemon peel
Apricot Sauce (below)
¼ cup toasted slivered almonds

Prepare crepes. Heat oven to 350°. Blend cheese, sugar, butter, brandy and lemon peel in small mixer bowl; beat on medium speed until light and fluffy, about 2 minutes. Spread 1 to 2 tablespoons cheese mixture on each crepe; roll up. Arrange crepes seam sides down in ungreased baking dish, 11¾ × 7½ × 1¾ inches. Heat uncovered 10 minutes.

Place 2 crepes seam sides down on each dessert plate; spoon Apricot Sauce over crepes and sprinkle with almonds.

6 to 8 servings.

Apricot Sauce
Mix ⅔ cup apricot jam, 2 tablespoons orange juice and 1 tablespoon butter or margarine in small saucepan. Heat, stirring constantly, until smooth. Remove from heat. Stir in 1 tablespoon brandy if desired. Serve warm.

About 1 cup.

NOTE

Crepes on call, whenever you want! Serve these elegant little pancakes even on a busy-bustle day. The secret? Make crepes ahead, then refrigerate or freeze them. Stack 6 to 8 of them together, with a layer of waxed paper between crepes. Wrap and refrigerate for several days. For long-term storage, wrap, label and freeze. When ready to use, thaw (wrapped) at room temperature about 3 hours. These versatile wonders freeze well, but should not be kept for more than 3 months.

CREPES SUZETTE

Crepes (page 23)
⅔ cup butter or margarine
¾ teaspoon grated orange peel
⅔ cup orange juice
¼ cup sugar
⅓ cup brandy
⅓ cup orange-flavored liqueur

Prepare crepes. Heat butter, orange peel, juice and sugar to boiling in 10-inch skillet, stirring occasionally. Boil and stir 1 minute. Reduce heat and simmer. Heat brandy and liqueur in small saucepan, but do not boil.

Fold crepes into fourths; place in hot orange sauce and turn once. Arrange crepes around edge of skillet. Pour warm brandy mixture into center of skillet and ignite. Spoon flaming sauce over crepes. Place 2 crepes on each dessert plate; spoon warm sauce over crepes.

6 servings.

CHERRY CREPES FLAMBE

Crepes (page 23)
1 cup dairy sour cream
⅓ cup brown sugar (packed)
1 can (21 ounces) cherry pie filling
¼ cup orange-flavored liqueur or brandy

Prepare crepes. Heat oven to 350°. Blend sour cream and sugar. Spoon 1 tablespoon of the sour cream mixture on each crepe; roll up. Place crepes seam sides down on ovenproof platter or in baking dish, 11¾ × 7½ × 1¾ inches. Heat 5 minutes.

Heat pie filling in chafing dish or small saucepan until warm. Heat liqueur in small long-handled pan just until warm. Ignite and pour flaming liqueur over pie filling. Place 2 crepes seam sides down on each dessert plate; spoon pie filling over crepes.

6 to 8 servings.

CHERRY BLINTZES

Crepes (page 23)
1 cup dry cottage cheese
½ cup dairy sour cream
1 to 2 tablespoons sugar
½ teaspoon grated lemon peel
1 teaspoon vanilla
¼ cup butter or margarine
1 cup dairy sour cream
Quick Cherry Sauce (below) or Tart Cherry
    Sauce (page 141)

Prepare crepes except—brown only on one side. Blend cottage cheese, ½ cup sour cream, the sugar, lemon peel and vanilla. Spoon about 1½ tablespoons of the cheese mixture on browned side of each crepe. Fold sides of crepe up over filling until edges meet in center; roll up from open end.

Melt butter in skillet over medium heat until bubbly. Place blintzes seam sides down in skillet. Cook until golden brown, turning once. Top each with a rounded tablespoon of sour cream and about 3 tablespoons of the warm cherry sauce.

12 servings.

Quick Cherry Sauce
1 can (21 ounces) cherry pie filling
1 teaspoon lemon juice
¼ teaspoon cinnamon

Heat pie filling, lemon juice and cinnamon over medium heat, stirring occasionally, until bubbly.

CREAM PUFFS

1 cup water
½ cup butter or margarine
1 cup all-purpose flour
4 eggs
Whipped Cream Fillings (below)
Confectioners' sugar

Heat oven to 400°. Heat water and butter to rolling boil in 1-quart saucepan. Stir in flour. Stir vigorously over low heat until mixture forms a ball, about 1 minute. Remove from heat. Add eggs; beat until smooth. Drop dough by scant ¼ cupfuls 3 inches apart onto ungreased baking sheet.

Bake until puffed and golden, 35 to 40 minutes. Cool. Cut off tops of puffs; pull out any filaments of soft dough. Fill puffs with one of the Whipped Cream Fillings. Replace tops; dust with confectioners' sugar. Serve immediately or refrigerate.

10 to 12 puffs.

Whipped Cream Fillings

SWEETENED WHIPPED CREAM: In chilled bowl, beat 1 cup chilled whipping cream, ¼ cup confectioners' sugar and ½ teaspoon vanilla. Basic recipe can be varied by the addition of one of the following. Enough filling for 6 puffs.

COFFEE WHIPPED CREAM: Add 1½ teaspoons instant coffee before beating.

FRENCH WHIPPED CREAM: Omit sugar; fold in ¼ cup crème de cacao after beating.

HAWAIIAN WHIPPED CREAM: Fold in ⅓ cup crushed pineapple, well drained, ⅓ cup chopped toasted almonds and ⅓ cup flaked coconut after beating.

SPICED WHIPPED CREAM: Add ½ teaspoon cinnamon or nutmeg or ¼ teaspoon ginger before beating.

STRAWBERRY CHANTILLY CREAM: Fold in 1 cup sliced fresh strawberries after beating.

TEA WHIPPED CREAM: Add 2 tablespoons instant tea before beating.

Variations

ICE-CREAM PUFFS: Fill puffs with 1 pint French vanilla, peppermint or coffee ice cream. Top with chocolate sauce if desired. Enough filling for 6 puffs.

SPICED PEACH PUFFS: Prepare Cream Puffs (left) except—add 1 teaspoon nutmeg with the water and butter. Fill baked puffs with sweetened whipped cream and sliced peaches.

STRAWBERRY-CARDAMOM PUFFS: Prepare Cream Puffs (left) except—add 1 teaspoon cardamom with the water and butter. Fill baked puffs with Strawberry Chantilly Cream (left).

CHOCOLATE ECLAIRS: Drop dough by scant ¼ cupfuls onto ungreased baking sheet; with spatula, shape each into finger about 4½ inches long and 1½ inches wide. Fill baked éclairs with Sweetened Whipped Cream (left). Spread Chocolate Glaze (below) over tops. Serve immediately or refrigerate.

12 éclairs.

Chocolate Glaze

Melt 1 ounce unsweetened chocolate and 1 teaspoon butter or margarine in small saucepan over low heat. Remove from heat; blend in 1 cup confectioners' sugar and 2 tablespoons hot water. Beat until smooth.

NOTE

Cream puff preplanning help: to freeze unbaked, place mounds of dough in freezer, uncovered. Freeze until solid, about 4 hours. Then store in freezer bags in freezer. Will keep up to 1 month. To bake, heat oven to 400°. Bake frozen puffs 3 inches apart on ungreased baking sheet. Bake until puffed and golden, 45 to 50 minutes. To freeze baked puffs, wrap and label; they'll keep well up to 3 months. Thaw unwrapped at room temperature about 30 minutes.

CREAM PUFF CHRISTMAS TREE

1¼ cups water
⅔ cup butter or margarine
1¼ cups all-purpose flour
5 eggs
2 cups chilled whipping cream
⅓ cup green crème de menthe or crème de menthe syrup
Chocolate Glaze (page 87)

Heat oven to 400°. Heat water and butter to rolling boil in 2-quart saucepan. Stir in flour. Stir vigorously over low heat until mixture forms a ball, about 1 minute. Remove from heat. Add eggs; beat until smooth. Drop dough by slightly rounded teaspoonfuls onto ungreased baking sheet. Bake until puffed and golden, 25 to 30 minutes. Cool thoroughly.

In chilled bowl, beat whipping cream until stiff; fold in crème de menthe. Cut a small slit in each puff. Fill decorators' tube with whipped cream mixture. Insert tip of decorators' tube in slit and fill each puff with cream mixture. Refrigerate filled puffs until ready to use.

Cut a 9-inch circle from aluminum foil; place on plate. Dip bottom of each puff in Chocolate Glaze; place around edge of foil circle (use about 11 puffs). Place about 6 puffs in a circle inside the first circle; fill in center with a few puffs. Continue to dip remaining puffs in glaze and layer to form a cone shape. Drizzle remaining glaze down side of puff tree. (If necessary, stir few drops hot water into glaze until desired consistency.) Refrigerate tree until ready to serve. To serve, use 2 forks to separate puffs; place 3 or 4 puffs on each plate.

About 16 servings.

Place a second circle of cream puffs inside the outer circle.

Cream Puff Christmas Tree

STRAWBERRY PUFF REVEL

Petits Choux (below)
1 pint vanilla ice cream
1 cup chilled whipping cream
2 tablespoons confectioners' sugar
1 package (10 ounces) frozen strawberries,
  thawed

Bake Petits Choux. Cool. Cut off tops of puffs; pull out any filaments of soft dough. Fill puffs generously with ice cream. Replace tops; freeze at least 1 hour.

In chilled bowl, beat whipping cream and sugar until stiff. Remove puffs from freezer. Alternate layers of puffs, whipped cream and strawberries (with syrup) in 1½- to 2-quart glass serving bowl.

8 to 10 servings (3 puffs each).

Petits Choux
½ cup water
¼ cup butter or margarine
½ cup all-purpose flour
2 eggs

Heat oven to 400°. Heat water and butter to rolling boil in 1-quart saucepan. Stir in flour. Stir vigorously over low heat until mixture forms a ball, about 1 minute.

Remove from heat. Add eggs; beat until smooth. Drop dough by slightly rounded teaspoonfuls onto ungreased baking sheet. Bake until puffed and golden, 25 to 30 minutes. Cool.

About 30 puffs.

Variation
CHOCOLATE PUFF REVEL: Substitute Chocolate Sauce (below) for the strawberries.

Chocolate Sauce
Heat ¼ cup light cream (20%) and ¾ bar (4-ounce size) sweet cooking chocolate over low heat until chocolate is melted. Beat until smooth; cool.

FLAMING DESSERTS

Festivity is what these are all about. There's no dessert quite so ooh-and-aah as one that's made with liquor and brought to the table aflame. Yet you don't have to be a French chef to make one of the special occasion treats in this section. With just a bit of practice you'll soon be wowing people with a famous dessert like Cherries Jubilee. We include this favorite here—with instructions for warming, then igniting, the liquor. (Most popular choices are 80-proof rum, kirsch or brandy—but any liquor containing 40-proof alcohol will do.) For a simpler flaming dessert, soak sugar cubes in lemon, orange, rum or brandy extract; place cubes around dessert, then light up and watch the sparkle reflected in admiring eyes! What foods are suitable for flaming? Ice cream, of course; fresh, frozen or canned fruits; steamed puddings; even crepes. So be a show-off and let your talents shine with our Peaches Flambé or Strawberries Jubilee—dazzling, delightful, deluxe!

PEACHES FLAMBE

¼ cup apricot jam
3 tablespoons sugar
½ cup water
4 large fresh peaches or 1 can (28 ounces)
  sliced peaches, drained
1 teaspoon lemon juice
¼ cup brandy
1 quart vanilla ice cream

Simmer jam, sugar and water in chafing dish or attractive skillet over low heat until mixture is syrupy, about 5 minutes. Peel and slice peaches; add to syrup and cook over low heat until almost tender, about 3 minutes. (If using canned peaches, cook only long enough to heat through.) Stir in lemon juice.

Heat brandy just until warm in small long-handled pan; ignite and pour flaming over peaches. Stir; spoon over each serving of ice cream.

6 to 8 servings.

CHERRIES JUBILEE

1 can (16 ounces) pitted dark sweet cherries,
  drained (reserve ¼ cup syrup)
¼ cup rum
¾ cup currant jelly
1 teaspoon grated orange peel
¼ cup brandy
1 quart vanilla ice cream

Combine reserved syrup and the rum; pour over cherries and refrigerate about 4 hours.

At serving time, melt jelly in chafing dish or attractive skillet over low heat. Stir in cherry mixture and orange peel. Cook, stirring constantly, until mixture simmers.

Heat brandy just until warm in small long-handled pan; ignite and pour flaming over cherries. Stir; spoon over each serving of ice cream.

6 to 8 servings.

FLAMING ORANGES

¼ cup butter or margarine
⅓ cup brown sugar (packed)
1 teaspoon grated orange peel
2 cans (11 ounces each) mandarin orange
  segments, drained
¼ cup white rum

Heat butter, sugar and orange peel in chafing dish or attractive skillet over medium heat, stirring constantly, until mixture is bubbly. Add orange segments; cook until fruit is heated through, about 2 minutes.

Heat rum just until warm in small long-handled pan; ignite and pour flaming over orange segments. Stir; spoon over vanilla ice cream or serve with Ginger Alaska Jubilee (page 64).

6 to 8 servings.

BANANAS FLAMBE

½ cup butter or margarine
⅔ cup brown sugar (packed)
1 teaspoon cinnamon
4 firm bananas
⅓ cup rum, brandy or orange-flavored
  liqueur
1 quart vanilla ice cream
6 to 8 maraschino cherries (with stems)

Melt butter and sugar with cinnamon in chafing dish or attractive skillet. Cook over medium-high heat, stirring occasionally, until golden brown, about 3 minutes. Cut bananas diagonally into ½-inch slices; add to syrup and heat through, carefully turning slices to coat.

Heat rum just until warm in small long-handled pan; ignite and pour flaming over bananas. Stir; spoon over each serving of ice cream. Garnish each serving with a cherry.

6 to 8 servings.

STRAWBERRIES JUBILEE

1 package (16 ounces) frozen strawberries,
  thawed and drained (reserve syrup)
2 teaspoons cornstarch
2 to 3 tablespoons brandy

Blend reserved strawberry syrup and cornstarch; heat over medium heat, stirring frequently, until thick and clear. Remove from heat; stir in strawberries. Pour into chafing dish to keep warm.

Heat brandy just until warm in long-handled ladle or small pan. Ignite and pour flaming over strawberry mixture in chafing dish. Stir; spoon over vanilla ice cream or serve with Strawberry Alaska Jubilee (page 64).

6 to 8 servings.

Soufflés

Company for dinner? Soufflé for dessert! Hot? Bake Orange Soufflé Deluxe—serve fast, before it falls. Cold? Make Lemon Soufflé ahead of time and chill.

ORANGE SOUFFLE DELUXE

3 tablespoons butter or margarine
3 tablespoons flour
¾ cup milk
¼ cup sugar
5 eggs, separated
¼ cup orange-flavored liqueur
¼ teaspoon cream of tartar
¼ cup sugar

Extend depth of a 2-quart soufflé dish 3 inches above dish with band of double thickness aluminum foil; secure by tying with string. Butter dish and foil; sprinkle with sugar.

Move oven rack to lowest position. Heat oven to 375°. Melt butter in saucepan over low heat. Blend in flour. Cook over low heat, stirring constantly, until mixture is smooth and bubbly. Remove from heat. Stir in milk. Heat to boiling, stirring constantly. Boil and stir 1 minute. Remove from heat. Stir in ¼ cup sugar. Gradually stir at least half of the hot mixture into egg yolks. Blend into hot mixture in saucepan. Cool slightly; stir in liqueur.

Beat egg whites and cream of tartar in large mixer bowl until foamy. (Egg whites should be at room temperature for best volume.) Gradually beat in ¼ cup sugar; continue beating until stiff and glossy. Do not underbeat. Fold egg yolk mixture into meringue. Carefully turn into soufflé dish.

Bake until puffy and golden brown, 40 to 45 minutes. Run knife around inside of foil band and remove band. *Serve immediately.*

6 servings.

BRANDIED CHERRY CHEESECAKE SOUFFLE

3 eggs, separated
¼ teaspoon cream of tartar
¼ cup granulated sugar
1 teaspoon grated lemon peel
1½ cups dairy sour cream
¼ cup granulated sugar
⅓ cup all-purpose flour
⅛ teaspoon salt
Confectioners' sugar
Brandied Cherry Sauce (below)

Extend depth of 6-cup soufflé dish 2 inches above dish with band of triple thickness aluminum foil; secure foil by taping or fastening with paper clips. Butter dish and foil; sprinkle with granulated sugar. (A buttered and sugared 2-quart casserole can be used instead of soufflé dish and foil band.)

Heat oven to 350°. Beat egg whites and cream of tartar in large mixer bowl until foamy. Gradually beat in ¼ cup granulated sugar; continue beating until stiff and glossy. Do not underbeat.

Beat egg yolks thoroughly in small mixer bowl. Stir in lemon peel and sour cream. Mix ¼ cup granulated sugar, the flour and salt; stir into sour cream mixture. Fold sour cream mixture into meringue. Carefully turn into soufflé dish.

Bake until knife inserted halfway between center and edge comes out clean, about 40 minutes. Run knife around inside of foil band and carefully remove band. Dust soufflé with confectioners' sugar. *Serve immediately,* with Brandied Cherry Sauce.

6 to 8 servings.

Brandied Cherry Sauce
Drain 1 can (16 ounces) pitted dark sweet cherries; reserve ¾ cup syrup. Mix 1 tablespoon sugar and 1 tablespoon cornstarch in saucepan. Stir in reserved cherry syrup. Cook, stirring constantly, until mixture thickens and boils. Boil and stir 1 minute. Cool; stir in 1 tablespoon brandy or 1½ teaspoons brandy flavoring and the cherries.

Orange Soufflé Deluxe (page 30)

Chill pan in bowl of ice and water, stirring occasionally, just until mixture mounds slightly, 20 to 30 minutes. If mixture becomes too thick, place pan in bowl of hot water; stir constantly until mixture is proper consistency.

Gently fold gelatin mixture into meringue.

Just before serving, remove foil band from Grasshopper Soufflé.

GRASSHOPPER SOUFFLE

½ cup sugar
2 envelopes unflavored gelatin
¼ teaspoon salt
1¼ cups water
6 eggs, separated
⅓ cup green crème de menthe
⅓ cup white crème de cacao
½ cup sugar
1½ cups chilled whipping cream

Extend depth of 6-cup soufflé dish 2 inches above dish with band of triple thickness aluminum foil; secure foil by folding ends together, taping or fastening with paper clips. (A 2-quart casserole can be used instead of soufflé dish and foil band.)

Mix ½ cup sugar, the gelatin, salt and water in saucepan. Beat egg yolks slightly; stir into gelatin mixture. Cook over medium heat, stirring constantly, just until mixture boils. Remove from heat. Stir in crème de menthe and crème de cacao. Chill *just* until mixture mounds slightly (see photo).

Beat egg whites until foamy in large mixer bowl. Gradually beat in ½ cup sugar; continue beating until stiff and glossy. Do not underbeat. Fold gelatin mixture into meringue.

In chilled bowl, beat whipping cream until stiff. Fold whipped cream into meringue mixture. Carefully turn into soufflé dish. Refrigerate until set, about 8 hours.

Just before serving, remove foil band. Garnish with sweetened whipped cream and shaved chocolate or chocolate curls if desired.

10 to 12 servings.

Variations

BRANDY ALEXANDER SOUFFLE: Substitute ⅓ cup dark crème de cacao and ⅓ cup brandy for the crème de menthe and white crème de cacao.

VELVET FUDGE SOUFFLE: Increase water to 1¾ cups; omit crème de menthe and crème de cacao. Stir 1 package (12 ounces) semisweet chocolate pieces into gelatin mixture with egg yolks. If desired, serve with Brandy Sauce (page 127).

LEMON SOUFFLE

¾ cup sugar
2 envelopes unflavored gelatin
¼ teaspoon salt
¾ cup lemon juice (3 to 4 lemons)
1 cup water
6 eggs, separated
2 teaspoons grated lemon peel
¾ cup sugar
1½ cups chilled whipping cream
Raspberry-Currant Sauce (page 141) or
    chopped pistachio nuts

Extend depth of 6-cup soufflé dish as directed for Grasshopper Soufflé (page 32).

Mix ¾ cup sugar, the gelatin, salt, lemon juice and water in saucepan. Beat egg yolks slightly; stir into gelatin mixture. Cook over medium heat, stirring constantly, just until mixture boils. Remove from heat. Stir in grated peel. Chill just until mixture mounds slightly (see photo on page 32).

Beat egg whites until foamy in large mixer bowl. Gradually beat in ¾ cup sugar; continue beating until stiff and glossy. Do not underbeat. Fold gelatin mixture into meringue.

In chilled bowl, beat whipping cream until stiff. Fold whipped cream into meringue mixture. Carefully turn into soufflé dish. Refrigerate until set, about 8 hours.

Just before serving, remove foil band. Serve with Raspberry-Currant Sauce or garnish by pressing chopped nuts around side.

10 to 12 servings.

Variation

LIME SOUFFLE: Substitute ¾ cup lime juice (about 6 limes) and 2 teaspoons grated lime peel for the lemon juice and peel. Add 4 drops green food color with the lime peel. Garnish top with sweetened whipped cream and lime twist if desired.

APRICOT SOUFFLE

1 cup dried apricots
1¼ cups water
½ cup sugar
1 envelope unflavored gelatin
⅛ teaspoon salt
¾ cup water
3 eggs, separated
¼ cup sugar
1½ cups chilled whipping cream

Extend depth of 4-cup soufflé dish 2 inches above dish with band of triple thickness aluminum foil; secure foil by folding ends together, taping or fastening with paper clips.

Heat apricots and 1¼ cups water to boiling in small saucepan. Reduce heat; cover and simmer until tender, about 15 minutes. Drain off ¼ cup liquid and reserve. Place apricots and remaining liquid in blender. Blend on medium speed until pureed, about 2 minutes, or press apricots through sieve into small bowl.

Mix ½ cup sugar, the gelatin, salt, reserved apricot liquid and ¾ cup water in saucepan. Beat egg yolks slightly; stir into gelatin mixture. Cook over medium heat, stirring constantly, just until mixture boils. Remove from heat. Stir in apricot puree. Chill just until mixture mounds slightly (see photo on page 32).

Beat egg whites until foamy in large mixer bowl. Beat in ¼ cup sugar, 1 tablespoon at a time; continue beating until stiff and glossy. Do not underbeat. Fold gelatin mixture into meringue.

In chilled bowl, beat whipping cream until stiff. Fold whipped cream into meringue mixture. Carefully turn into soufflé dish. Refrigerate until set, about 8 hours.

Just before serving, remove foil band. If desired, garnish with sweetened whipped cream and cluster of dried apricots.

8 to 10 servings.

Steamed Puddings

Old-fashioned steamed pudding—remember that spicy aroma? These hearty-type puddings have been around a long time. For English Christmas feasting, they were made with raisins, but called Plum Pudding. Still great for holidays—and other days, too! Steamed puddings can be a happy part of your regular meal-planning—serve warm, with sauce or whipped cream. Or make them ahead of time and reheat. Try our Down East Pudding, Steamed Date Pudding or Steamed Apple-Ginger Pudding—they'll be welcome at your table all year 'round.

STEAMED DATE PUDDING

½ cup hot water
1 package (14 ounces) date bar mix
2 eggs
½ cup finely chopped nuts
½ teaspoon mace
½ teaspoon cinnamon
¼ teaspoon nutmeg
Hard Sauce (page 36) or Whipped Cream
    Sauce (right)

Grease well a 3-cup ovenproof glass bowl. Stir together water and Date Filling from date bar mix. Mix in crumbly mix, eggs, nuts, mace, cinnamon and nutmeg. Pour into bowl; cover with aluminum foil.

Place rack in saucepan; pour water into pan up to level of rack. Heat to boiling. Place bowl of pudding on rack. Cover saucepan. Keep water boiling over low heat to steam pudding until wooden pick inserted in center comes out clean, about 2 hours. (If it is necessary to add water during steaming, lift lid and quickly add boiling water.)

Lift cover away from you to prevent scalding; remove bowl. Remove foil and let pudding stand about 5 minutes before removing from bowl. Cut into wedges; serve warm, with Hard Sauce.

8 servings.

PLUM DUFF

2 eggs
1 cup brown sugar (packed)
½ cup shortening
2 cups cut-up cooked prunes, drained
1 cup all-purpose flour*
1 teaspoon baking soda
1 teaspoon salt
Whipped Cream Sauce (below) or Best
    Sauce (page 36)

Grease well a 1½-quart mold. Beat eggs thoroughly; mix in sugar, shortening and prunes. Stir in flour, soda and salt. Pour into mold; cover with aluminum foil.

Place mold on rack in large kettle; pour in enough boiling water to reach halfway up mold. Cover kettle. Keep water boiling over low heat to steam pudding until wooden pick inserted in center comes out clean, 2½ to 3 hours.

Lift cover away from you to prevent scalding; remove mold. Remove foil and let pudding stand 5 minutes. Unmold on serving platter; serve hot, with Whipped Cream Sauce.

10 servings.

* If using self-rising flour, omit soda and salt.

Whipped Cream Sauce
In chilled bowl, beat 1 cup chilled whipping cream until stiff. Beat 1 cup confectioners' sugar, 2 egg yolks and 1 teaspoon vanilla; fold into whipped cream. Serve immediately or refrigerate up to 2 hours.

About 2 cups.

Note

Steamed puddings, as their name implies, are at their best served warm. But you can still make them ahead of time. Just wrap them, then refrigerate or freeze. If frozen, thaw before reheating. To reheat, wrap in aluminum foil; heat in a 350° oven 45 to 60 minutes.

STEAMED APPLE-GINGER PUDDING

1 package (14.5 ounces) gingerbread mix
1 cup applesauce
¼ cup water
1 cup raisins

Grease ten 6-ounce custard cups or three 2½-cup cans. Blend gingerbread mix (dry), applesauce and water in large mixer bowl. Beat 2 minutes on medium speed, scraping bowl frequently. Stir in raisins. Pour batter into cups.

Place rack in Dutch oven or roasting pan; pour water into pan up to level of rack. Heat to boiling. Place filled cups on rack (water should not touch cups). Cover Dutch oven. Keep water boiling over low heat to steam pudding until wooden pick inserted in center comes out clean, cups 30 minutes, cans 1½ hours. Remove pudding from cups. (Or, if using cans, remove pudding; slice.) Serve warm, and if desired, with Hard Sauce (page 36), Whipped Cream Sauce (page 34) or warm applesauce.

10 servings.

NOTE

What equipment do you need for steaming puddings? There's a wide assortment of steamers and molds available on the market. Look for them in shops that feature specialty cooking equipment, or check the gourmet section of your favorite department or housewares store. But you don't need special utensils. You can use any large kettle or Dutch oven. Just make sure it has a tight-fitting lid. Place a wire rack, trivet or vegetable steamer-basket inside it to hold the pudding about 1 inch above the kettle bottom. A perforated foil pan, inverted, will work too. The traditional turk's-head mold, heatproof bowls, gelatin molds, custard cups, jelly glasses or coffee cans— all of these can be used as molds for steaming. Always grease the mold generously and fill ½ to ⅔ full (to allow for expansion). Cover the mold with aluminum foil or with a lid.

ENGLISH PLUM PUDDING

1 cup all-purpose flour*
1 teaspoon baking soda
1 teaspoon salt
1 teaspoon cinnamon
¾ teaspoon mace
¼ teaspoon nutmeg
2 cups currants
1½ cups cut-up raisins
¾ cup finely cut-up citron
⅓ cup each cut-up candied orange and
   candied lemon peel
½ cup chopped walnuts
1½ cups soft bread crumbs
2 cups ground suet (½ pound)
1 cup brown sugar (packed)
3 eggs, beaten
⅓ cup currant jelly
¼ cup fruit juice
Hard Sauce or Best Sauce (page 36)

Grease well a 2-quart ring mold or turk's head mold. Stir together flour, soda, salt, cinnamon, mace and nutmeg in large bowl. Mix in fruits, nuts and bread crumbs. Mix suet, sugar, eggs, jelly and fruit juice in another bowl. Mix into flour-fruit mixture. Pour into mold; cover with aluminum foil.

Place rack in Dutch oven; pour water into pan up to level of rack. Heat to boiling. Place filled mold on rack. Cover Dutch oven. Keep water boiling over low heat to steam pudding until wooden pick inserted in center comes out clean, about 4 hours. (If it is necessary to add water during steaming, lift lid and quickly add boiling water.)

Lift cover away from you to prevent scalding; remove mold. Remove foil. Unmold on serving platter; cut into slices and serve hot, with Hard Sauce.

16 servings.

* If using self-rising flour, decrease soda to ½ teaspoon.

DOWN EAST PUDDING

1 cup boiling water
1 cup cut-up raisins or chopped cranberries
2 tablespoons shortening
1 egg, well beaten
½ cup sugar
½ cup molasses
1½ cups all-purpose flour*
1 teaspoon baking soda
1 teaspoon salt
Best Sauce, Hard Sauce (below) or
    Whipped Cream Sauce (page 34)

Grease well a 1½-quart mold. Pour boiling water over raisins and shortening. Mix egg, sugar and molasses; stir in fruit mixture. Stir in flour, soda and salt. Pour into mold; cover with aluminum foil.

Place mold on rack in large kettle; pour in enough boiling water to reach halfway up mold. Cover kettle. Keep water boiling over low heat to steam pudding until wooden pick inserted in center comes out clean, about 2 hours.

Lift cover away from you to prevent scalding; remove mold. Remove foil and let pudding stand 5 minutes. Unmold on serving platter; serve hot, with Best Sauce.

8 servings.

* If using self-rising flour, omit soda and salt.

Best Sauce
Beat ½ cup confectioners' sugar and ½ cup butter or margarine, softened, in small saucepan until smooth and creamy. Beat ½ cup chilled whipping cream in chilled bowl until stiff. Fold whipped cream into sugar-butter mixture. Heat, stirring occasionally, until sauce boils. Serve immediately.

1½ cups.

Hard Sauce
Beat ½ cup butter or margarine, softened, 1 cup confectioners' sugar and 2 teaspoons vanilla until smooth. For a fluffier sauce, beat 1 egg white until stiff peaks form; blend into sauce and refrigerate.

MERINGUES AND TORTES

Leaf through this section to find a treasure trove—from simple one-layer desserts to elegant multilayered creations. Our meringues and tortes are versatile, too, with a range that includes cake, meringue or pastry bases put together with whipped cream, pudding or fruit fillings. Whether it's a snowy meringue or a rich chocolate torte that captures your fancy (maybe both!), we know you'll find a favorite here.

STRAWBERRY SNOWCAP

½ cup butter or margarine, softened
¼ cup brown sugar (packed)
1 cup all-purpose flour*
½ cup chopped pecans
3 egg whites
¼ teaspoon cream of tartar
¾ cup granulated sugar
½ teaspoon vanilla
2 cups fresh strawberries
½ cup granulated sugar
1 quart strawberry ice cream

Heat oven to 400°. With hands, mix butter, brown sugar, flour and pecans. Press mixture evenly in ungreased square pan, 9 × 9 × 2 inches. Bake until light brown, about 12 minutes. Crumble baked crust with spoon; cool.

Reduce oven temperature to 325°. Grease round layer pan, 9 × 1½ inches. Beat egg whites and cream of tartar until foamy. Beat in ¾ cup granulated sugar, 1 tablespoon at a time; continue beating until stiff and glossy. Do not underbeat. Fold in vanilla and crumb mixture. Pour into pan. Bake until light brown, about 35 minutes. Cool.

Sprinkle strawberries with ½ cup granulated sugar; let stand 1 hour. Cut meringue into wedges. Serve with scoops of ice cream, topped with strawberries.

6 to 8 servings.

* Do not use self-rising flour in this recipe.

DUCHESS MERINGUES

Individual Meringue Shells (page 40)
1 cup chilled whipping cream
1½ cups confectioners' sugar
1½ teaspoons vanilla
1 package (10 ounces) frozen raspberries or
*   strawberries, thawed*
Almond Praline (below)

Heat oven to 275°. Prepare Individual Meringue Shells as directed except—fill decorators' tube with meringue; use rosette point to make sixteen 2-inch meringues on brown paper. Or swirl meringue by heaping tablespoonfuls onto brown paper.

Bake 30 minutes. Turn off oven; leave meringues in oven with door closed 1 hour. Remove from oven and cool.

In chilled bowl, beat whipping cream, sugar and vanilla until stiff. For each serving, put flat sides of 2 meringues together with about 2 heaping tablespoonfuls whipped cream mixture. Refrigerate about 3 hours.

Heat raspberries. Sprinkle Almond Praline over meringues; serve with warm raspberries.

8 servings.

Almond Praline
Heat oven to 275°. Mix ½ cup coarsely chopped almonds, 1 unbeaten egg white and 2 tablespoons sugar. Spread on ungreased baking sheet. Bake until golden brown and dry, 25 to 30 minutes. Cool and crumble.

NOTE

This delightful dessert could almost make a party out of any dinner. Our recipe calls for frozen raspberries or strawberries, but you can vary the fruit to suit your fancy. How about mixed fruit or sliced peaches for a pretty change of pace? Another nice variation: Flavor the whipped cream mixture for the filling with ¾ teaspoon almond extract instead of vanilla.

Meringue should be beaten until it stands in stiff glossy peaks.

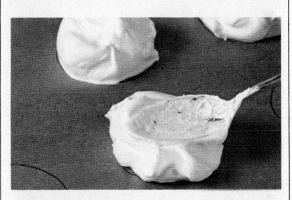

Shape meringues with the back of a spoon.

Duchess Meringue

Chocolate Pastry Torte (page 42)

Angel Meringue Torte (page 39)

Cloud Seven Torte (page 42)

ANGEL MERINGUE TORTE

6 egg whites
½ teaspoon cream of tartar
¼ teaspoon salt
1½ cups sugar
½ teaspoon vanilla
½ teaspoon almond extract
1 cup chilled whipping cream or 1 envelope
   (about 2 ounces) dessert topping mix
Cranberries Jubilee (below) or sweetened
   sliced strawberries

Heat oven to 450°. Butter bottom only of 9-inch springform pan or tube pan, 10×4 inches. Beat egg whites, cream of tartar and salt in large mixer bowl on medium speed until foamy. Beat in sugar, 2 tablespoons at a time; continue beating until stiff and glossy. Beat in vanilla and almond extract. Spread evenly in pan.

Place in oven; immediately turn off oven. Leave pan in oven at least 8 hours. Run knife around torte to loosen; invert on serving plate. In chilled bowl, beat whipping cream until stiff. (If using dessert topping mix, prepare as directed on package.) Frost torte with whipped cream. Refrigerate several hours. Cut into wedges and serve with Cranberries Jubilee.

12 servings.

Cranberries Jubilee
¾ teaspoon grated orange peel
½ cup orange juice
½ cup water
2 cups sugar
2 cups cranberries
2 tablespoons water
2 teaspoons cornstarch
¼ cup brandy

Stir together orange peel, juice, ½ cup water and the sugar in medium saucepan. Heat to boiling; boil 5 minutes. Stir in cranberries. Heat to boiling; boil rapidly 5 minutes. Mix 2 tablespoons water and the cornstarch; stir into cranberry mixture. Cook, stirring constantly, until mixture thickens and boils. Boil and stir 1 minute.

Pour cranberry mixture into chafing dish to keep warm. In small long-handled pan, heat brandy just until warm; ignite and pour flaming over cranberry mixture.

SHERBET TORTE

6 egg whites
½ teaspoon cream of tartar
1½ cups granulated sugar
1 pint lime sherbet, slightly softened
1 pint raspberry sherbet, slightly softened
1 cup chilled whipping cream
¼ cup granulated or confectioners' sugar
3 or 4 drops yellow food color

Heat oven to 275°. Cover 2 baking sheets with brown paper. Beat egg whites and cream of tartar until foamy. Beat in 1½ cups sugar, 2 tablespoons at a time; continue beating until stiff and glossy. Do not underbeat.

Divide meringue in half; shape each half into a smooth, even 9-inch circle on brown paper. Bake 1 hour. Turn off oven; leave meringues in oven with door closed 1 hour. Remove from oven and cool.

Place one meringue on serving plate; quickly spread lime sherbet over entire top. Place second meringue on top and spread with raspberry sherbet. Freeze until firm, 6 to 8 hours.

In chilled bowl, beat whipping cream and ¼ cup sugar until stiff. Fold in food color. Spread over raspberry sherbet. Freeze 12 hours. Remove torte from freezer about 15 minutes before serving to make cutting easier. Cut into wedges to serve.

12 to 16 servings.

INDIVIDUAL MERINGUE SHELLS

Heat oven to 275°. Cover baking sheet with brown paper. Beat 3 egg whites (⅓ to ½ cup) and ¼ teaspoon cream of tartar in small mixer bowl until foamy. Beat in ¾ cup sugar, 1 tablespoon at a time; continue beating until stiff and glossy. Do not underbeat. Drop meringue by ⅓ cupfuls onto brown paper. Shape mounds into circles with back of spoon, building up sides.

Bake 1 hour. Turn off oven; leave meringues in oven with door closed 1½ hours. Remove from oven and cool. Fill with ice cream, sherbet or cut-up fruit. If you like, top ice cream with chocolate or butterscotch sauce.

8 to 10 shells.

Variations

CINNAMON-CITRUS MERINGUES: Mix ½ teaspoon cinnamon with the sugar before beating into egg whites. Fill baked meringues with orange sherbet and mandarin orange segments.

CINNAMON-PEACH MERINGUES: Mix ½ teaspoon cinnamon with the sugar before beating into egg whites. Fill baked meringues with vanilla ice cream and top with sliced fresh or thawed frozen peaches.

CREME DE MENTHE MERINGUES: Fold 1 square (1 ounce) unsweetened chocolate, coarsely grated, into meringue after beating. Fill baked meringues with French vanilla ice cream and top with crème de menthe.

HEART MERINGUES: Fold few drops red food color into meringue after beating. Shape mounds into heart shapes with back of spoon, building up sides. Fill baked meringues with strawberry or vanilla ice cream and top with sliced fresh or thawed frozen strawberries.

PEACH-MOCHA MERINGUES: Mix 1 teaspoon instant coffee with the sugar before beating into egg whites. In chilled bowl, beat ½ cup chilled whipping cream, 1 tablespoon sugar and ¼ teaspoon ginger. Fill baked meringues with whipped cream mixture and sliced fresh or thawed frozen peaches.

CHOCOLATE MERINGUE TORTE

6 egg whites
½ teaspoon cream of tartar
2 cups sugar
1 cup chilled whipping cream
2 packages (6 ounces each) semisweet
    chocolate pieces
1 tablespoon instant coffee
¼ cup boiling water
1 teaspoon vanilla

Heat oven to 275°. Cover 2 baking sheets with brown paper. Beat egg whites and cream of tartar until foamy. Beat in sugar, 2 tablespoons at a time; continue beating until stiff and glossy. Do not underbeat. Shape meringue into four 7-inch circles on brown paper. Bake 1 hour. Turn off oven; leave meringues in oven with door closed 1 hour. Remove from oven and cool.

In chilled bowl, beat whipping cream until stiff. Melt chocolate pieces in top of double boiler over hot water. Stir in coffee and boiling water. Beat until creamy and slightly cool. Fold in whipped cream and vanilla. Stack meringues, spreading chocolate mixture between layers and on top. Refrigerate at least 6 hours. Cut into wedges to serve.

10 to 12 servings.

NESSELRODE MERINGUE DESSERT

Meringue Shell (page 41)
1½ quarts vanilla ice cream, slightly
    softened
½ cup chopped toasted almonds
½ cup flaked coconut
¼ cup Nesselrode

Bake Meringue Shell. Mix remaining ingredients. Fill shell with Nesselrode mixture. Freeze 6 to 8 hours. Remove from freezer about 15 minutes before serving to make cutting easier.

12 servings.

VIENNESE WALNUT TORTE

1 package (18.5 ounces) devils food cake
    mix
2 egg whites (¼ cup)
1 cup brown sugar (packed)
2 teaspoons lemon juice
½ cup chopped nuts
1 teaspoon granulated sugar
½ teaspoon cinnamon
1 package (about 3½ ounces) vanilla regular
    pudding and pie filling

Bake cake mix in 2 square pans, 8×8×2 inches, or 2 round layer pans, 9×1½ inches, as directed on package. Cool. Remove from pans; place one layer upside down on baking sheet and one layer top side up on sheet.

Heat oven to 400°. Beat egg whites until foamy. Gradually beat in brown sugar and lemon juice; continue beating until stiff and glossy. Do not underbeat. Spread meringue over tops of layers on baking sheet. Stir together nuts, granulated sugar and cinnamon; sprinkle over meringue. Bake until delicate brown, 6 to 8 minutes. Cool.

Prepare pudding and pie filling as directed on package for pie filling. Cool. Split each layer in half to make 4 layers. Stack layers, spreading ⅓ of the filling between each layer and placing one meringue-topped layer on top. Refrigerate.

Substitutions

Substitute any of the following combinations for the devils food cake mix and vanilla pudding and pie filling:
- ☐ Lemon cake mix and lemon pudding and pie filling.
- ☐ White cake mix and chocolate pudding and pie filling.
- ☐ Yellow or spice cake mix and butterscotch pudding and pie filling.

LEMON SCHAUM TORTE

Meringue Shell (below)
¾ cup sugar
3 tablespoons cornstarch
¼ teaspoon salt
¾ cup water
3 egg yolks, slightly beaten
1 tablespoon butter or margarine
1 teaspoon grated lemon peel
⅓ cup lemon juice
1 cup chilled whipping cream

Bake Meringue Shell. Mix sugar, cornstarch and salt in medium saucepan. Gradually stir in water. Cook over medium heat, stirring constantly, until mixture thickens and boils. Boil and stir 1 minute. Gradually stir at least half of the hot mixture into egg yolks. Blend into hot mixture in pan. Boil and stir 1 minute.

Remove from heat; stir in butter, lemon peel and lemon juice. Cool to room temperature. Spoon into shell. Refrigerate at least 12 hours. In chilled bowl, beat whipping cream until stiff. Spread over filling.

8 to 10 servings.

Meringue Shell

Heat oven to 275°. Cover baking sheet with brown paper. Beat 3 egg whites and ¼ teaspoon cream of tartar until foamy. Beat in ¾ cup sugar, 1 tablespoon at a time; continue beating until stiff and glossy. Do not underbeat. Shape meringue into 9-inch circle on brown paper, building up side. Bake 1 hour. Turn off oven; leave meringue in oven with door closed 1 hour. Remove from oven and cool.

Variations

LEMON ANGEL MERINGUES: Substitute 6 to 8 Individual Meringue Shells (page 40) for the Meringue Shell.

LIME SCHAUM TORTE: Substitute grated lime peel and lime juice for the lemon peel and juice. Stir in 1 or 2 drops green food color.

CLOUD SEVEN TORTE

4 eggs, separated
½ cup granulated sugar
½ cup confectioners' sugar
½ cup shortening
¾ cup confectioners' sugar
3 tablespoons milk
1 cup all-purpose flour*
1 teaspoon baking powder
¼ teaspoon salt
½ cup chopped pecans
2 tablespoons granulated sugar
1 cup chilled whipping cream
1 can (8¾ ounces) crushed pineapple, well
   drained

Heat oven to 325°. Grease and flour 2 round layer pans, 8 or 9 × 1½ inches, or 2 square pans, 8 × 8 × 2 inches. Beat egg whites until foamy. Beat in ½ cup each granulated sugar and confectioners' sugar, 1 tablespoon at a time; continue beating until stiff and glossy. Do not underbeat.

Measure shortening, ¾ cup confectioners' sugar, the egg yolks and milk into large mixer bowl. Blend ½ minute on low speed, scraping bowl constantly. Add flour, baking powder and salt; beat 1 minute on medium speed, scraping bowl occasionally. Spread batter in pans. Spread half of the meringue on batter in each pan. Sprinkle each with half of the pecans, then with 1 tablespoon granulated sugar. Bake until meringue is set, 35 to 40 minutes. Cool in pans.

In chilled bowl, beat whipping cream until stiff. Fold in pineapple. With spatulas, carefully remove layers from pans. Place 1 layer meringue side up on serving plate. Spread with whipped cream mixture. Top with other layer, meringue side up. Refrigerate at least 1 hour.

9 to 12 servings.

* If using self-rising flour, omit baking powder and salt.

CHOCOLATE PASTRY TORTE

1 can (16 ounces) chocolate syrup (1½ cups)
2 teaspoons instant coffee
1 teaspoon cinnamon
1 package (11 ounces) pie crust mix or sticks
2 teaspoons vanilla
2 cups chilled whipping cream*

Heat oven to 425°. Blend syrup, coffee and cinnamon. Add ½ cup syrup mixture to pie crust mix; mix thoroughly. Divide into 6 equal parts.

Roll each part into a 7-inch circle on well-floured cloth-covered board. Trim edges to make even. Place circles on ungreased baking sheets (two on each sheet). Prick with fork. Bake until almost firm, 6 to 8 minutes. Cool pastry circles slightly; loosen while warm with 2 wide spatulas. Cool on wire racks.

In chilled bowl, beat remaining syrup mixture, the vanilla and whipping cream until mixture forms soft peaks. Stack pastry circles, spreading chocolate cream between layers and over top. Refrigerate at least 8 hours.

9 to 12 servings.

* Do not substitute dessert topping mix for the whipping cream.

BOSTON CREAM TORTE

Refrigerate 1 cup whipping cream and the Chocolate Icing Mix from 1 package (15.5 ounces) Boston cream pie mix in small mixer bowl at least 1 hour. Prepare Cream Filling Mix and Yellow Cake Mix as directed on package. Beat whipping cream-icing mixture until stiff. Split cake; fill layers with whipped cream mixture to within ¼ inch of edge. Frost side and top with cream filling. Sprinkle top and side of cake with toasted coconut. Refrigerate.

Cool Classics

Reflect cool calm by being ahead of
the dessert game with these assets-in-reserve.
Here's a batch of desserts that you can
make ahead; they'll remain cool
in your refrigerator or freezer. Bring them out
on cue to entrance a partyful of guests
or ease the hurry-worry of a busy day.

Refrigerated Desserts

Bank on it—suave coffee gelatin, cherries and strawberries on a cloud of meringue, a Bavarian fragranced with fresh orange are all considerate of you. Make them at your own convenience; they're refrigerator-lovers, and most can be safely kept a day or so before you present them. Our gelatin-gems are adaptable, too. Serve them in individual dessert dishes for family dinners. To serve party-style, choose a mold that's interesting or unusual in shape, then garnish gloriously. Try a wreath of mint, clusters of grapes, heapings of berries—whatever your fancy dictates. One practical note for our creamy concoctions: Cool gelatin mixture until it mounds slightly when dropped from a spoon, then fold in the whipped cream.

ALMOND ANGEL TRIFLE

1 package (about 3 ounces) vanilla regular pudding and pie filling
1 cup chilled whipping cream or 1 envelope (about 2 ounces) dessert topping mix
1 teaspoon almond extract
1 can (13¼ ounces) pineapple chunks, drained and cut up
1 white angel food cake, torn into 1-inch pieces (8 to 10 cups)
Toasted slivered almonds
Chopped maraschino cherries

Prepare pudding and pie filling as directed on package for pudding. Cool. In chilled bowl, beat whipping cream until stiff. (If using dessert topping mix, prepare as directed on package.) Fold extract, whipped cream and pineapple into pudding. Spread cake pieces in oblong pan, 13×9×2 inches. Spread pudding mixture over cake pieces. Sprinkle with almonds and cherries. Refrigerate at least 8 hours. To serve, cut into squares or spoon into dessert dishes.

12 to 15 servings.

Pictured on page 43: Three-Fruit Ice Cream (page 55)

STRAWBERRY TRIFLE

1 package (18.5 ounces) yellow cake mix
1 package (about 3 ounces) vanilla regular pudding and pie filling
4 teaspoons sherry (optional)
1 package (16 ounces) frozen strawberry halves, thawed
1 cup chilled whipping cream or 1 envelope (about 2 ounces) dessert topping mix
¼ cup sugar
2 tablespoons toasted slivered almonds

Bake cake mix in oblong pan, 13×9×2 inches, as directed on package. Cool. Prepare pudding and pie filling as directed on package for pudding. Cool.

Cut cake crosswise in half. Use one half as desired. Cut remaining cake into 8 pieces; split each piece horizontally.

Arrange half of the pieces in 2-quart glass serving bowl, cutting pieces to fit shape of bowl. Sprinkle with 2 teaspoons sherry. Pour half of the strawberries (with syrup) over cake; spread with 1 cup of the pudding. Repeat with remaining cake pieces, sherry, strawberries and pudding.

In chilled bowl, beat whipping cream and sugar until stiff. (If using dessert topping mix, prepare as directed on package; omit sugar.) Spread over trifle. Sprinkle with almonds. Refrigerate at least 1 hour. To serve, spoon into dessert dishes.

8 to 10 servings.

Variations
CHOCOLATE-BANANA TRIFLE: Substitute devils food cake mix for the yellow cake mix and 2 large bananas, sliced, for the strawberries. Blend ¾ cup milk into pudding. Garnish trifle with halved maraschino cherries.

PEACH MELBA TRIFLE: Substitute white cake mix for the yellow cake mix and 1 package (10 ounces) frozen raspberries, thawed, plus 1 package (10 ounces) frozen sliced peaches, thawed and drained, for the strawberries.

DATE DREAM DESSERT

2 tablespoons butter or margarine, softened
1 package (14 ounces) date bar mix
¼ cup chopped nuts
½ cup hot water
1 cup chilled whipping cream
2 tablespoons confectioners' sugar
1 teaspoon instant coffee or
  1 teaspoon vanilla

Heat oven to 400°. Mix butter and crumbly mix from date bar mix with fork. Stir in nuts. Spread in oblong pan, 13×9×2 inches. Bake 10 minutes. Crumble with fork and cool.

Stir hot water into Date Filling in small bowl; cool. In chilled bowl, beat whipping cream, sugar and coffee until stiff. Line loaf pan, 9×5×3 inches, with aluminum foil. Spread 1 cup crumbled mixture in pan. Spread half of the whipped cream over crumbled mixture. Layer ½ cup crumbled mixture, the date filling, ½ cup crumbled mixture, remaining whipped cream and crumbled mixture; press lightly. Refrigerate 4 to 5 hours or freeze just until firm.

6 to 8 servings.

NOTE

Meringue-type desserts call for egg whites; what do you do with those leftover yolks? Put them in a tightly lidded jar, cover with water and refrigerate. They'll keep for 2 or 3 days this way. Check the recipes below—they all call for yolks.
Eggnog Sauce (page 7)
Old-fashioned Rice Pudding (page 19)
Whipped Cream Sauce (page 34)
Fresh Strawberry Ice Cream (page 54)
French Vanilla Ice Cream (page 54)
Maple Frango (page 56)
Dark Chocolate Filling (page 79)
Pecan-Fruit Filling (page 88)
Brandy Sauce (page 127)
Peach-Custard Kuchen (page 132)
Zabaglione (page 152)

CHERRY BERRIES ON A CLOUD

6 egg whites
½ teaspoon cream of tartar
¼ teaspoon salt
1¾ cups sugar
2 packages (3 ounces each) cream cheese, softened
1 cup sugar
1 teaspoon vanilla
2 cups chilled whipping cream
2 cups miniature marshmallows
Cherry Berry Topping (below)

Heat oven to 275°. Grease oblong pan, 13×9×2 inches. Beat egg whites, cream of tartar and salt until foamy. Beat in 1¾ cups sugar, 1 tablespoon at a time; continue beating until stiff and glossy. Do not underbeat. Spread in pan. Bake 1 hour. Turn off oven; leave meringue in oven with door closed about 12 hours.

Blend cream cheese, 1 cup sugar and the vanilla. In chilled bowl, beat whipping cream until stiff. Gently fold whipped cream and marshmallows into cream cheese mixture. Spread over meringue. Refrigerate 12 to 24 hours. Serve topped with Cherry Berry Topping.

10 to 12 servings.

Cherry Berry Topping
Stir together 1 can (21 ounces) cherry pie filling, 1 teaspoon lemon juice and 2 cups sliced fresh strawberries or 1 package (16 ounces) frozen strawberries, thawed.

BLUEBERRY MALLOW DESSERT

1¼ cups graham cracker crumbs (about 16
  squares)
¼ cup butter or margarine, melted
1 cup chilled whipping cream or 1 envelope
  (about 2 ounces) dessert topping mix
1 package (3 ounces) cream cheese, softened
½ cup sugar
1 teaspoon vanilla
1 cup miniature marshmallows
1 can (21 ounces) blueberry pie filling,
  chilled

Mix cracker crumbs and butter. Reserve about
1 tablespoon crumb mixture; press remaining
mixture firmly and evenly in bottom of ungreased
square pan, 8×8×2 inches.

In chilled bowl, beat whipping cream until stiff.
(If using dessert topping mix, prepare as directed
on package.) Beat cream cheese, sugar and vanilla
until fluffy. Fold whipped cream and marshmallows
into cream cheese mixture. Spread in pan; sprinkle reserved crumb mixture over top. Refrigerate
at least 4 hours. Serve topped with pie filling.

9 servings.

Substitution

Cherry or peach pie filling can be substituted for
the blueberry pie filling.

NOTE

Whipped cream is a key ingredient in many of
our recipes. As a topping, it also does wonders in
jazzing up just about any dessert you could name.
To insure success, follow these tips. The cream
you use should have at least 35% butterfat content; it should be thoroughly chilled, along with
the bowl and beaters. Don't overbeat, or the
whipped cream will separate. And remember that
whipping causes cream to double in quantity.
Final tip, for do-ahead "instant" toppings: Freeze
whipped cream in small mounds, then package.
Plop an individual mound on each serving of
dessert for a last-minute "special."

BANANA REFRIGERATOR DESSERT

1¼ cups graham cracker crumbs (about 16
  squares)
2 tablespoons granulated sugar
¼ cup butter or margarine, melted
½ cup butter or margarine, softened
1 cup confectioners' sugar
1 egg
½ cup chopped nuts
1 banana, mashed
¼ cup chopped maraschino cherries, drained
1 cup chilled whipping cream or 1 envelope
  (about 2 ounces) dessert topping mix

Mix cracker crumbs, granulated sugar and melted
butter thoroughly. Press half of the mixture firmly
and evenly in bottom of ungreased square pan,
8×8×2 inches.

Beat ½ cup butter, the confectioners' sugar and
egg in small mixer bowl until light and fluffy.
Spread carefully over crumb mixture in pan. Mix
nuts, mashed banana and chopped cherries. Spread
over butter mixture.

In chilled bowl, beat whipping cream until stiff.
(If using dessert topping mix, prepare as directed
on package.) Spread over banana layer. Sprinkle
with remaining crumbs. Cover and refrigerate at
least 12 hours. Serve with sweetened whipped
cream and maraschino cherries if desired.

9 servings.

Variation

PINEAPPLE REFRIGERATOR DESSERT: Omit nuts,
mashed banana and chopped cherries. Fold 1 can
(20 ounces) crushed pineapple, drained, into
whipped cream.

PINK PEPPERMINT LAYER DESSERT

1 cup vanilla wafer or graham cracker
   crumbs (about 16 wafers or 14 squares)
½ cup butter or margarine, softened
1 cup confectioners' sugar
2 ounces melted unsweetened chocolate (cool)
3 eggs
½ cup chopped nuts
1 cup chilled whipping cream or 1 envelope
   (about 2 ounces) dessert topping mix
½ cup crushed peppermint candies
1 cup miniature marshmallows

Sprinkle ½ cup of the crumbs evenly in ungreased square pan, 8×8×2 or 9×9×2 inches. Beat butter, sugar, chocolate and eggs in small mixer bowl until light and fluffy. Stir in nuts. Spread evenly over crumbs in pan. Sprinkle remaining crumbs over chocolate layer.

In chilled bowl, beat whipping cream until stiff. (If using dessert topping mix, prepare as directed on package.) Fold peppermint candies and marshmallows into whipped cream.

Spoon whipped cream mixture over crumbs; spread evenly to sides of pan. Refrigerate at least 12 hours before serving.

Serve garnished with sweetened whipped cream and shaved chocolate if desired.

9 to 12 servings.

BLUEBERRY-LEMON LIGHT PARFAITS

1 package (3 ounces) lemon-flavored gelatin
1 cup chilled whipping cream or 1 envelope
    (about 2 ounces) dessert topping mix
¼ cup confectioners' sugar
½ teaspoon vanilla
1½ cups vanilla ice cream, softened
2 cups fresh blueberries or 1 package (10
    ounces) frozen blueberries, thawed

Prepare gelatin as directed on package except—refrigerate, stirring occasionally, until mixture mounds slightly when dropped from a spoon. In chilled bowl, beat whipping cream and sugar until stiff. (If using dessert topping mix, prepare as directed on package; omit sugar.) Stir in vanilla.

Beat gelatin in small mixer bowl ½ minute. Beat in ice cream on low speed until smooth. Beat ½ minute on high speed. Alternate layers of gelatin mixture, whipped cream and blueberries in parfait glasses or in 1½-quart glass serving bowl. Serve immediately or refrigerate until serving time.

6 to 8 servings.

Variation
STRAWBERRY-LEMON LIGHT PARFAITS: Substitute 2 cups fresh strawberries, sliced, for the blueberries.

NOTE

To unmold a gelatin mixture, dip container, just up to the edge, into warm (not hot) water. Loosen edge of gelatin with tip of paring knife. Put a plate on top of the mold and—holding both tightly —invert the plate and mold. Shake container gently; carefully lift it up and off the gelatin mold. Repeat the process if necessary.

Alternate method: Place a plate on top of the mold and invert plate and mold. Use a kitchen towel wrung out in hot water to press around the mold, making sure you press it into any indentations. Shake mold gently, then remove as described above. If gelatin mold does not slide out easily, reapply hot towel.

RICE CHANTILLY WITH LINGONBERRY SAUCE

½ cup sugar
1 envelope unflavored gelatin
¼ teaspoon salt
2 cups milk
4 egg yolks, slightly beaten
1 cup chilled whipping cream
1 cup cooked rice
1 can (8½ ounces) crushed pineapple,
    drained, or ⅓ cup finely cut-up mixed
    candied fruit
1 teaspoon vanilla
Lingonberry Sauce (below)

Stir together sugar, gelatin and salt in saucepan. Gradually stir in milk and egg yolks. Cook over medium heat, stirring constantly, just until mixture boils. (Do not boil or mixture will curdle.) Refrigerate, stirring occasionally, until mixture mounds slightly when dropped from a spoon.

In chilled bowl, beat whipping cream until stiff. Fold whipped cream, rice, pineapple and vanilla into gelatin mixture. Pour into 1½-quart mold or 8 dessert dishes or molds. Refrigerate until firm, about 4 hours. Unmold on serving plate and serve with Lingonberry Sauce.

8 servings.

Lingonberry Sauce
Heat 1 carton (16 ounces) water-packed lingonberries and 1 cup sugar to boiling, stirring until sugar is dissolved. Cook 5 minutes, stirring occasionally. Cool.

NOTE

Give gelatin mixtures a quick chill. Set the pan in a bowl of ice and water, then stir frequently until mixture mounds slightly. Experiment—try mixing bowls, custard cups, small baking pans, plastic containers as molds. But do make sure you know just how much your substitute mold holds. To measure, fill mold with water, then measure by cupfuls.

Fresh Orange Bavarian

FRESH ORANGE BAVARIAN

1 cup boiling water
1 package (3 ounces) orange-flavored gelatin
½ cup sugar
1 tablespoon grated orange peel
1 cup orange juice
1 cup chilled whipping cream or 1 envelope
  (about 2 ounces) dessert topping mix

Pour boiling water over gelatin in bowl; stir until gelatin is dissolved. Stir in sugar, orange peel and juice. Refrigerate, stirring occasionally, until mixture mounds slightly when dropped from a spoon.

In chilled bowl, beat whipping cream until stiff. (If using dessert topping mix, prepare as directed on package.) Beat gelatin mixture until foamy. Fold in whipped cream. Pour into 4-cup mold or 6 to 8 dessert dishes or molds. Refrigerate until firm, about 4 hours. Unmold on serving plate.

6 to 8 servings.

COFFEE JELLY

¼ cup sugar
2 tablespoons instant coffee
1 envelope unflavored gelatin
⅛ teaspoon salt
2 cups boiling water
1½ teaspoons vanilla
Light cream or sweetened whipped cream

Stir together sugar, coffee, gelatin and salt in small bowl. Pour boiling water over gelatin mixture; stir until gelatin is dissolved. Stir in vanilla. If desired, pour into mold. Refrigerate until firm, about 3 hours. Spoon into dessert dishes or unmold on serving plate. Serve with cream.

4 servings.

STRAWBERRY BAVARIAN CREAM

1 package (10 ounces) frozen sliced strawberries, thawed
1 cup boiling water
1 package (3 ounces) strawberry-flavored
  gelatin
1 cup chilled whipping cream

Drain strawberries, reserving syrup. Pour boiling
water over gelatin in bowl; stir until gelatin is
dissolved. Add enough cold water to reserved
syrup to measure 1 cup; stir into dissolved gelatin. Refrigerate, stirring occasionally, until mixture
mounds slightly when dropped from a spoon.

In chilled bowl, beat whipping cream until stiff.
Beat gelatin mixture until foamy. Fold gelatin and
strawberries into whipped cream. Pour into 4-cup
mold or 6 to 8 individual molds. Refrigerate until
firm, about 4 hours. Unmold on serving plate. If
desired, serve with sweetened whipped cream and
garnish with strawberries or other fruits.

6 to 8 servings.

CHOCOLATE MOUSSE

4 ounces sweet cooking chocolate
1 tablespoon sugar
½ cup light cream
2 eggs, separated
½ teaspoon vanilla
¼ cup sugar

Heat chocolate, 1 tablespoon sugar and the cream
in medium saucepan over medium heat, stirring
constantly, until chocolate melts and mixture is
smooth. Remove from heat. Beat egg yolks slightly; slowly stir in chocolate mixture. Blend in
vanilla. Beat egg whites until foamy. Gradually
beat in ¼ cup sugar just until stiff peaks form.
Fold in chocolate mixture. Pour into soufflé cups
or other small serving dishes. Refrigerate.

6 to 8 servings.

CHEESECAKES

Meet the tycoons of the cheesecake world! Chocolate,
cherry, apricot—all of these are lavish in flavor and
topping, rich with velvety cream cheese bases. Our
Cherries on Cheesecake, for instance, may become
your specialty—its unusual ground almond crust is a
perfect complement to the smooth filling and luscious
almond-flavored dark cherry topping.

CHERRIES ON CHEESECAKE

1½ cups ground unblanched almonds
3 tablespoons sugar
2 tablespoons butter or margarine, softened
1 package (8 ounces) cream cheese, softened
1 can (14 ounces) sweetened condensed milk
⅓ cup lemon juice
1 teaspoon vanilla
Dark Sweet Cherry Topping (below)

Heat oven to 400°. Stir together almonds, sugar
and butter. Press mixture firmly and evenly in
bottom and against side of ungreased 9-inch pie
pan. Bake until light golden brown, 6 to 8 minutes. Cool.

Beat cream cheese in small mixer bowl until
fluffy. Gradually add condensed milk, beating
constantly. Mix in lemon juice and vanilla. Pour
into baked crust. Refrigerate until set, 2 to 3
hours. Spoon Dark Sweet Cherry Topping over
each serving.

8 servings.

Dark Sweet Cherry Topping
1 can (16 ounces) dark sweet cherries,
  drained
½ cup port
1 tablespoon kirsch
2 teaspoons cornstarch
¼ teaspoon almond extract

Mix all ingredients in saucepan; heat to boiling.
Boil and stir 1 minute. Cool.

FROZEN APRICOT CHEESECAKE

1¼ cups vanilla wafer or gingersnap
  crumbs (about 20 cookies)
3 eggs, separated
¼ cup sugar
1 cup chilled whipping cream or 1 envelope
  (about 2 ounces) dessert topping mix
1 package (8 ounces) cream cheese, softened
¾ cup sugar
⅛ teaspoon salt
1 tablespoon apricot brandy, orange-flavored
  liqueur or vanilla
Apricot Sauce (below)

Spread 1 cup of the crumbs in ungreased square pan, 9×9×2 inches. Beat egg whites until foamy. Beat in ¼ cup sugar, 1 tablespoon at a time; continue beating until stiff and glossy.

In chilled bowl, beat whipping cream until stiff. (If using dessert topping mix, prepare as directed on package.) In large mixer bowl, beat egg yolks, cream cheese, ¾ cup sugar, the salt and brandy until smooth and creamy. Fold in whipped cream and meringue.

Pour over crumbs in pan; sprinkle with remaining crumbs. Freeze until firm, 6 to 8 hours. Cut into squares; spoon warm Apricot Sauce over each serving.

12 to 16 servings.

Apricot Sauce
1 cup apricot jam
¼ cup orange juice
2 tablespoons apricot brandy or orange-
  flavored liqueur (optional)

Heat jam and orange juice over low heat until mixture is hot. Remove from heat; stir in brandy. Cool slightly.

About 1¼ cups.

BLUEBERRY CHEESECAKE

1¼ cups graham cracker crumbs (about
  16 squares)
2 tablespoons sugar
3 tablespoons butter or margarine, melted
2 packages (8 ounces each) plus 1 package
  (3 ounces) cream cheese, softened
1 cup sugar
2 teaspoons grated lemon peel
¼ teaspoon vanilla
3 eggs
Blueberry Glaze (below)

Heat oven to 350°. Stir together cracker crumbs and 2 tablespoons sugar. Mix in butter thoroughly. Press mixture evenly in bottom of ungreased 9-inch springform pan. Bake 10 minutes. Cool.

Reduce oven temperature to 300°. Beat cream cheese in large mixer bowl. Gradually add 1 cup sugar, beating until fluffy. Add lemon peel and vanilla. Beat in eggs, one at a time. Pour over crumb mixture.

Bake until center is firm, about 1 hour. Cool to room temperature. Spread with Blueberry Glaze. Refrigerate at least 3 hours. Loosen edge of cheesecake with knife before removing side of pan.

12 servings.

Blueberry Glaze
Drain 1 can (16 ounces) blueberries, reserving liquid. Add enough water to blueberry liquid to measure 1 cup. Mix ½ cup sugar and 2 tablespoons cornstarch in small saucepan. Stir in the 1 cup liquid. Cook, stirring constantly, until mixture thickens and boils. Boil and stir 1 minute. Remove from heat; stir in blueberries. Cool.

Variation
CHERRY CHEESECAKE: Substitute 1 can (16 ounces) pitted red tart cherries for the blueberries. Stir in 4 drops red food color.

CRANBERRY CHEESECAKE

1¼ cups graham cracker crumbs (about 16
    squares)
2 tablespoons sugar
¼ cup butter or margarine, melted
2 packages (8 ounces each) cream cheese,
    softened
2 eggs
¾ cup sugar
2 teaspoons vanilla
1 cup dairy sour cream
2 tablespoons sugar
2 teaspoons vanilla
Cranberry Topping (below), Dark Sweet
    Cherry Topping (page 50) or sweetened sliced
    strawberries

Heat oven to 350°. Stir together cracker crumbs
and 2 tablespoons sugar. Mix in butter thoroughly.
Press mixture firmly and evenly in bottom of ungreased square pan, 9×9×2 inches, or in bottom
and side of 9-inch pie pan. Beat cream cheese
slightly. Add eggs, ¾ cup sugar and 2 teaspoons
vanilla; beat until light and fluffy. Pour over crumb
mixture.

Bake until firm, 25 minutes. Blend sour cream,
2 tablespoons sugar and 2 teaspoons vanilla; spread
carefully over warm cheesecake. Cool. Refrigerate
at least 3 hours. Spoon Cranberry Topping over
each serving.

9 to 12 servings.

Cranberry Topping
Mix ¾ cup sugar and ½ cup corn syrup in saucepan; heat to boiling. Add 2 cups fresh or thawed
frozen cranberries; heat to boiling. Simmer 1 minute; remove from heat. Cool.

CHOCOLATE CHEESECAKE

1¼ cups chocolate wafer or graham cracker
    crumbs (about 18 wafers or 16 squares)
2 tablespoons sugar
3 tablespoons butter or margarine, melted
2 packages (8 ounces each) plus 1 package
    (3 ounces) cream cheese, softened
1 cup sugar
¼ cup cocoa
2 teaspoons vanilla
3 eggs
Coconut-Pecan Topping (below)

Heat oven to 350°. Stir together crumbs and 2
tablespoons sugar; mix in butter thoroughly. Press
mixture evenly in bottom of ungreased 9-inch
springform pan. Bake 10 minutes. Cool.

Reduce oven temperature to 300°. Beat cream
cheese in large mixer bowl. Gradually add 1 cup
sugar and the cocoa, beating until fluffy. Add
vanilla. Beat in eggs, one at a time. Pour over
crumb mixture.

Bake until center is firm, about 1 hour. Cool to
room temperature. Spread with topping. Refrigerate at least 3 hours. Loosen edge of cheesecake
with knife before removing side of pan.

12 servings.

Coconut-Pecan Topping
2 tablespoons butter or margarine
⅓ cup light cream or evaporated milk
2 tablespoons brown sugar
2 egg yolks or 1 egg
½ teaspoon vanilla
½ cup chopped pecans
½ cup flaked coconut

Cook butter, cream, sugar and egg yolks in small
saucepan over low heat, stirring constantly, until
thickened. Remove from heat. Stir in vanilla,
pecans and coconut. Cool.

Chocolate Cheesecake (page 52)

FROZEN DESSERTS

Melt-in-the-mouth delights every one, these all take to long-range planning. Consider these goodies: Avocado-Lime Sherbet, Watermelon Ice, Frosty Pumpkin Squares, Brownie Alaska, ice creams for every taste. And there are a dozen ideas to turn commercial vanilla ice cream into your own house brand!

FRESH STRAWBERRY ICE CREAM

1 cup sugar
¼ teaspoon salt
1 cup milk
3 egg yolks, beaten
1 teaspoon vanilla
2 cups chilled whipping cream
1 pint fresh strawberries (2 cups)
Few drops red food color

Prepare as directed for French Vanilla Ice Cream (right) except—mix only ½ cup of the sugar with the egg yolk mixture. Crush strawberries with remaining ½ cup sugar. After adding cream to cooked mixture, stir in sweetened crushed berries and food color.

1 quart.

Variations

CHOCOLATE ICE CREAM: Mix 1 cup sugar with the egg yolk mixture. Omit strawberries. Stir 2 ounces melted unsweetened chocolate (do not use premelted) into hot mixture in saucepan; omit food color.

FRESH PEACH ICE CREAM: Substitute 4 or 5 peeled ripe peaches for the strawberries. Crush peaches with remaining ½ cup sugar. After adding cream, stir in sweetened crushed peaches; omit food color.

FROZEN STRAWBERRY ICE CREAM: Substitute 1 package (16 ounces) frozen strawberry halves, thawed, for the fresh strawberries; omit ½ cup sugar. After adding cream, stir in strawberries and food color.

FRENCH VANILLA ICE CREAM

½ cup sugar
¼ teaspoon salt
1 cup milk
3 egg yolks, beaten
1 tablespoon vanilla
2 cups chilled whipping cream

For crank-type freezer: Mix sugar, salt, milk and egg yolks in saucepan. Cook over medium heat, stirring constantly, just until bubbles appear around edge. Cool to room temperature. Stir in vanilla and whipping cream.

Pour into freezer can; put dasher in place. Cover can and adjust crank. Place can in freezer tub. Fill freezer tub ⅓ full of ice; add remaining ice alternately with layers of rock salt (6 parts ice to 1 part rock salt). Turn crank until it turns with difficulty. Drain water from freezer tub. Remove lid; take out dasher. Pack mixture down. Replace lid. Repack in ice and rock salt. Let stand to ripen several hours.

For refrigerator: Mix sugar, salt, milk and egg yolks in saucepan. Cook over medium heat, stirring constantly, just until bubbles appear around edge. Cool to room temperature. Stir in vanilla.

Pour into refrigerator tray. Freeze until partially frozen, ½ to 1 hour. In chilled bowl, beat whipping cream until soft peaks form. Spoon partially frozen mixture into another chilled bowl; beat until smooth. Fold in whipped cream. Pour into 2 refrigerator trays; freeze until firm, about 3 hours, stirring often during first hour. Cover to prevent crystals from forming.

1 quart.

Variation

VANILLA BEAN ICE CREAM: Omit vanilla. Add one 3-inch piece of vanilla bean to milk-egg yolk mixture before cooking. Before cooling, remove bean and split lengthwise in half. With tip of small knife, scrape the tiny seeds into the cooked mixture; discard bean.

THREE-FRUIT ICE CREAM

2 cups chilled whipping cream
2 cups sugar
2 cups milk
2 bananas
1 cup orange juice
⅓ cup lemon juice

For crank-type freezer: Pour whipping cream, sugar and milk into freezer can; put dasher in place. Cover can and adjust crank. Place can in freezer tub. Fill freezer tub ⅓ full of ice; add remaining ice alternately with layers of rock salt (6 parts ice to 1 part rock salt). Turn crank until mixture is a slushy consistency, about 10 minutes. Mash bananas; mix with orange juice and lemon juice. Add to can and continue turning until crank turns with difficulty. Drain water from freezer tub. Remove lid; take out dasher. Pack mixture down. Replace lid. Repack in ice and rock salt. Let stand to ripen several hours.

For refrigerator: In chilled bowl, beat whipping cream until soft peaks form; fold in sugar and milk. Pour into square pan, 9×9×2 inches, or freezer container. Freeze until partially frozen, ½ to 1 hour. Mash bananas; mix with orange juice and lemon juice. Blend in partially frozen mixture; beat until light and fluffy but not melted. Pour into pan or freezer container; cover to prevent crystals from forming. Freeze until firm, at least 4 hours, stirring several times.

About 2 quarts.

RASPBERRY ICE CREAM

1 package (10 ounces) frozen raspberries, thawed
½ cup sugar
2 cups light cream (20%)

Blend raspberries in blender on high speed until raspberries are liquefied, about 10 seconds. Add sugar and cream. Blend on high speed until well mixed, 10 to 15 seconds.

Pour into refrigerator tray. Freeze until mushy, about 1 hour. Pour into blender; blend on medium speed until smooth, about 1 minute. Return to refrigerator tray. Freeze until firm, about 8 hours.

1 quart.

Note: If you don't have a blender, press raspberries through sieve. Beat all ingredients in small mixer bowl until blended. Freeze until mushy; beat until smooth. Freeze until firm.

BLACK CHERRY YOGURT FREEZE

Line 12 medium muffin cups with paper baking cups. Prepare 1 package (7.2 ounces) fluffy white frosting mix as directed. Mix in 2 cartons (8 ounces each) black cherry-flavored yogurt (2 cups). Divide mixture among paper-lined muffin cups. Freeze until firm, about 4 hours. Remove from freezer just before serving and garnish with mint leaves or fresh fruit.

12 servings.

Variations
APRICOT YOGURT FREEZE: Substitute apricot-flavored yogurt for the black cherry-flavored yogurt.

RED RASPBERRY YOGURT FREEZE: Substitute red raspberry-flavored yogurt for the black cherry-flavored yogurt.

MAPLE FRANGO

4 egg yolks
½ cup maple-flavored syrup
1 cup chilled whipping cream
½ teaspoon vanilla

Beat egg yolks in small mixer bowl until thick and lemon colored. Heat syrup just to boiling. Pour about half of the hot syrup very slowly in a thin stream into egg yolks, beating constantly on medium speed. Stir egg yolk mixture into syrup in pan. Cook over low heat, stirring constantly, until slightly thickened. Cool.

In chilled bowl, beat whipping cream until stiff. Fold in vanilla and egg yolk mixture. Pour into refrigerator tray. Freeze until firm, at least 4 hours. If desired, garnish each serving with Chocolate Curls (page 79).

6 servings.

Note: For a low-calorie dessert, substitute ½ cup evaporated skim milk for the whipping cream. Freeze milk in small bowl until crystals form around edge, about 30 minutes. Beat until stiff; fold in vanilla and egg yolk mixture.

BISCUIT TORTONI

⅔ cup vanilla wafer or macaroon cookie crumbs
   (about 12 cookies)
¼ cup cut-up red candied cherries
½ cup chopped salted almonds
1 quart vanilla ice cream, slightly softened
Red and green candied cherries

Line 8 medium muffin cups with paper baking cups. Mix cookie crumbs, cut-up cherries and almonds. Fold into ice cream. Divide ice-cream mixture among paper-lined muffin cups. Arrange red cherry half and slices of green cherry on each to resemble a flower. Freeze until firm, about 4 hours.

8 servings.

ORANGE MALLOW

32 large marshmallows
1 teaspoon grated orange peel
⅔ cup orange juice
1 cup chilled whipping cream or 1 envelope
   (about 2 ounces) dessert topping mix

Heat marshmallows, orange peel and juice in saucepan over medium heat, stirring constantly, until marshmallows are melted. Cool at room temperature until thickened, about 15 minutes.

In chilled bowl, beat whipping cream until stiff. (If using dessert topping mix, prepare as directed on package.) Stir marshmallow mixture to blend. Fold into whipped cream. Pour into square pan, 8×8×2 inches. Freeze until firm, about 4 hours.

9 servings.

Variation
MOCHA MALLOW: Omit orange peel and juice and heat ½ cup water, 1 tablespoon cocoa and 1 teaspoon instant coffee with the marshmallows.

CHOCOLATE MALLOW CUPS

1 package (6 ounces) semisweet chocolate
   pieces
1 tablespoon plus 1 teaspoon shortening
Orange Mallow or Mocha Mallow (above)

Melt chocolate pieces and shortening over medium heat, stirring frequently, until smooth, 3 to 4 minutes.

Line 10 to 12 medium muffin cups with paper baking cups. Coat bottom and side of each cup with thin layer of chocolate mixture by swirling 1 tablespoon chocolate mixture in each cup with back of spoon. Refrigerate cups while making mallow. Divide mallow among chocolate cups and freeze until firm, 6 to 8 hours. Remove paper baking cups before serving.

10 to 12 servings.

FROZEN STRAWBERRY DESSERT

Butter Crunch (below)
1 package (10 ounces) frozen sliced straw-
  berries, partially thawed
1 cup sugar
1 egg white
2 tablespoons lemon juice
1 cup chilled whipping cream

Prepare Butter Crunch. Spread ⅔ of the mixture (about 1⅔ cups) in bottom of ungreased oblong pan, 13×9×2 inches. Beat strawberries (with syrup), sugar, egg white and lemon juice in large mixer bowl on high speed until slightly thickened, about 5 minutes. In chilled small mixer bowl, beat whipping cream until stiff.

Fold whipped cream into strawberry mixture. Pour evenly over Butter Crunch in pan. Sprinkle remaining Butter Crunch evenly over top. Cover and freeze until firm, at least 6 hours. Serve garnished with sweetened whipped cream and fresh or frozen strawberries if desired.

15 servings.

Butter Crunch

½ cup butter or margarine, softened
¼ cup brown sugar (packed)
1 cup all-purpose flour
½ cup chopped pecans, walnuts or flaked
  coconut

Heat oven to 400°. With hands, mix butter, sugar, flour and pecans. Press mixture evenly in ungreased square pan, 9×9×2 inches. Bake until light brown, about 12 minutes, stirring occasionally. Crumble baked crust with spoon; cool.

Note: Butter Crunch is delicious as a topping for ice cream, pudding or applesauce. Store in tightly covered container in refrigerator or freeze for future use.

LEMON CRUNCH

1 can (13 ounces) evaporated milk
Butter Crunch (left)
1 can (6 ounces) frozen lemonade
  concentrate, partially thawed
5 drops yellow food color

Pour milk into small mixer bowl; place in freezer until crystals form around edge, about 1 hour. Prepare Butter Crunch. Reserve ¼ cup crumb mixture; press remaining mixture in ungreased square pan, 9×9×2 inches.

Beat chilled milk until stiff. Stir in lemonade concentrate and food color. Pour into pan; sprinkle reserved crumb mixture over top. Freeze until firm. Remove from freezer 10 minutes before serving.

9 to 12 servings.

Variation

CHERRIES SUPREME: Omit evaporated milk, lemonade concentrate and food color. Pack ½ gallon vanilla ice cream, softened, over crumbs in pan. Just before serving, heat 1 can (21 ounces) cherry pie filling, stirring occasionally. If you wish, stir in 2 tablespoons brandy, kirsch or rum. Spoon over each serving.

SUNFLOWER NUT SUNDAES

Slightly soften 1 quart vanilla ice cream. Stir in ⅓ cup toasted salted sunflower nuts. Spread in refrigerator tray or loaf pan, 9×5×3 inches. Freeze until firm, about 4 hours. Top each serving with 1 tablespoon honey, maple-flavored syrup or butterscotch ice-cream topping.

8 servings.

VANILLA ICE-CREAM STIR-INS

Slightly soften 1 quart vanilla ice cream. Stir in any of the following for a new flavor. Turn into 2 refrigerator trays or 1 loaf pan, 9×5×3 inches. Cover to prevent crystals from forming. Freeze until firm, about 4 hours.

Apricot-Almond Ice Cream: ¼ cup light rum, ½ cup roasted diced almonds and ½ cup apricot preserves. Serve with lemon, fudge or coconut cake, or on brownies.

Banana Ice Cream: 2 bananas, mashed, and if desired, ¼ cup thawed frozen orange juice concentrate. Serve plain or topped with chocolate sauce. Great over orange or applesauce cake.

Cinnamon Ice Cream: 2 teaspoons cinnamon. Good on apple, peach or blueberry pie.

Coffee Ice Cream: 1 tablespoon instant coffee. Delicious on chocolate cake.

Daiquiri Ice Cream: 1 envelope (about ⅝ ounce) daiquiri mix and ¼ cup light rum. Delicious on wedges of angel food or lemon chiffon cake.

Ginger-Rum Ice Cream: 2 tablespoons chopped crystallized ginger, ¼ cup light rum and 2 teaspoons instant coffee. Try on chocolate cake or on slices of banana nut bread.

Marshmallow-Almond Ice Cream: Blend 1 cup marshmallow crème and 1 tablespoon hot water; stir in ¼ cup orange juice and ½ cup diced roasted almonds.

Mincemeat Ice Cream: ¾ cup prepared mincemeat. Try on gingerbread or pumpkin pie.

Mixed Fruit Ice Cream: 1 can (6 ounces) frozen Hawaiian punch concentrate, partially thawed.

Peanut Butter Ice Cream: ½ cup chunky peanut butter. Serve plain or topped with chocolate sauce.

Pistachio Ice Cream: ½ cup chopped pistachio nuts, 1 teaspoon almond extract and 6 to 8 drops green food color.

Raisin-Rum Ice Cream: Pour ¼ cup rum over ½ cup golden raisins. Cover and refrigerate 2 to 3 hours before stirring into ice cream.

FRESH LEMON SHERBET

2 cups light cream (20%)
1¼ cups sugar
1 to 2 tablespoons grated lemon peel
⅓ cup lemon juice (about 1½ lemons)
1 or 2 drops yellow food color

Mix all ingredients. Pour into refrigerator tray or square pan, 8×8×2 inches. Freeze until firm, about 4 hours.

About 1 quart.

Variation

FRESH LEMON MOUSSE: Substitute 2 cups chilled whipping cream for the light cream; use 2 tablespoons grated lemon peel and beat all ingredients in chilled large mixer bowl until stiff. Freeze until firm, about 2 hours.

AVOCADO-LIME SHERBET

1 ripe avocado, mashed (about ¾ cup)
½ cup sugar
1 can (6 ounces) frozen concentrate for limeade, thawed
1 cup chilled whipping cream
1 or 2 drops green food color

Stir together avocado, sugar and concentrate until sugar is dissolved. Pour into refrigerator tray or square pan, 8×8×2 or 9×9×2 inches. Freeze until mushy, about 45 minutes.

In chilled bowl, beat whipping cream until stiff. In another chilled bowl, beat avocado mixture until smooth. Fold avocado mixture and food color into whipped cream. Turn into refrigerator tray. Freeze until firm, about 4 hours.

About 1 quart.

Pictured from top, clockwise: Raspberry Ice Cream (page 55), Fresh Lemon Sherbet (page 58), Avocado-Lime Sherbet (page 58), Watermelon Ice (page 62)

Place sherbet balls in pan that has been chilled in the freezer.

Layer the sherbet balls, alternating colors; fill in spaces with whipped ice cream.

Sherbet Polka-dot Dessert

SHERBET POLKA-DOT DESSERT

2 pints lime sherbet
2 pints raspberry sherbet
2 pints orange sherbet
2 quarts chocolate chip ice cream
1½ cups chilled whipping cream
½ teaspoon almond extract

Working quickly, make balls of sherbet with small ice-cream scoop (#40) or teaspoon; place in chilled jelly roll pan. Freeze until balls are firm, about 4 hours.

Slightly soften ice cream; beat until fluffy. Layer sherbet balls in chilled tube pan, 10×4 inches, alternating colors and filling in spaces between balls in each layer with whipped ice cream. Freeze until firm, at least 12 hours. (Dessert can be covered and frozen for several days.) In chilled bowl, beat whipping cream and almond extract until stiff. Unmold dessert and frost with whipped cream.

20 servings.

SPUMONI ICE-CREAM LOAF

1 pint chocolate ice cream
1 pint vanilla ice cream
¼ cup cut-up mixed candied fruit
1 teaspoon rum flavoring
1 pint pistachio ice cream

Line loaf pan, 9×5×3 inches, with aluminum foil. Slightly soften chocolate ice cream; spread in pan. Freeze until firm, at least 1 hour. Slightly soften vanilla ice cream; stir in fruit and flavoring. Spread over chocolate ice cream in pan. Freeze until firm. Slightly soften pistachio ice cream; spread over top. Cover; freeze until firm.

Invert pan to remove loaf; remove foil from ice cream. Dip knife into hot water and cut ice cream into slices.

6 to 8 servings.

PISTACHIO ICE-CREAM BOMBE

2 pints pistachio ice cream
1 pint dark cherry ice cream
1 pint coffee ice cream

Cut pistachio ice cream into 1-inch slices. Line bottom and side of chilled 1½- to 2-quart metal mold or bowl with slices; press firmly with spoon to form even layer. Freeze until firm, at least 1 hour. Repeat with dark cherry ice cream. Freeze until firm, at least 1 hour. Slightly soften coffee ice cream. Press in center of mold. Cover; freeze until firm, about 24 hours.

Invert mold on chilled serving plate. Dip a cloth into hot water; wring out cloth and place over top of mold for just a few minutes. Lift off mold. Return to freezer until serving time. Remove from freezer 10 to 15 minutes before serving to make cutting easier. Garnish as desired with pressurized whipped cream, maraschino cherries, preserved kumquats or mint leaves.

8 to 10 servings.

Variations
Try any of the following ice-cream combinations:
☐ *Chocolate Ice Cream (page 54), butter pecan ice cream, orange sherbet.*
☐ *Chocolate ice cream, French vanilla ice cream, Coffee Ice Cream (page 58).*
☐ *Pistachio Ice Cream (page 58), orange sherbet, Apricot-Almond Ice Cream (page 58).*
☐ *Peppermint ice cream, Marshmallow-Almond Ice Cream (page 58), chocolate ice cream.*
☐ *Strawberry ice cream, Pistachio Ice Cream (page 58), chocolate ice cream.*
☐ *Chocolate ice cream, Ginger-Rum Ice Cream (page 58), Pistachio Ice Cream (page 58).*

CRUNCHY ICE-CREAM SQUARES

2 cups coarsely crushed corn flake or whole wheat flake cereal
1 can (3½ ounces) flaked coconut (1⅓ cups)
½ cup chopped nuts
½ cup brown sugar (packed)
⅓ cup butter or margarine, melted
½ gallon vanilla, butter pecan, butterscotch revel or chocolate ice cream, softened

Mix cereal, coconut, nuts, sugar and butter. Press ⅔ of the cereal mixture evenly in ungreased oblong pan, 13×9×2 inches. Pack ice cream over cereal layer; press to make even. Sprinkle remaining cereal mixture on top. Freeze until firm, at least 12 hours.

15 servings.

FROSTY PUMPKIN SQUARES

1¼ cups graham cracker crumbs (about 16 squares)
¼ cup butter or margarine, melted
1 cup mashed cooked pumpkin
½ cup brown sugar (packed)
½ teaspoon salt
½ teaspoon cinnamon
½ teaspoon ginger
¼ teaspoon nutmeg
1 quart vanilla ice cream, softened

Mix cracker crumbs and butter. Reserve 2 to 3 tablespoons crumb mixture; press remaining mixture firmly and evenly in bottom of ungreased square pan, 8×8×2 or 9×9×2 inches.

Beat pumpkin, sugar, salt and spices until well blended. Stir in ice cream. Pour into pan; sprinkle reserved crumb mixture over top. Freeze until firm, about 4 hours. Remove from freezer 10 to 15 minutes before serving to make cutting easier.

9 servings.

STRAWBERRY ICE

1 package (3 ounces) strawberry-flavored
    gelatin
½ cup sugar
1½ cups boiling water
1 package (16 ounces) frozen sliced straw-
    berries, partially thawed
¼ cup orange juice
¼ cup lemon juice

Stir together gelatin and sugar. Pour boiling water over gelatin mixture in large bowl; stir until gelatin is dissolved. Stir in remaining ingredients.

Pour into 2 refrigerator trays. Freeze until mushy, about 1 hour. Remove from trays; beat until smooth. Return to trays; freeze until firm, about 1 hour.

About 1 quart.

CRANBERRY ICE

1 pound fresh cranberries
2 cups water
2 cups sugar
¼ cup lemon juice
1 teaspoon grated orange peel
2 cups cold water

Cook cranberries in 2 cups water until skins are broken, about 10 minutes. Press through sieve to make a smooth pulp. Stir in sugar, lemon juice, orange peel and 2 cups cold water. Pour into square pan, 8 × 8 × 2 inches. Freeze until firm, stirring 2 or 3 times to keep mixture smooth. Remove from freezer about 10 minutes before serving.

About 1 quart.

CIDER ICE

Stir together 2 cups apple cider and ½ cup light corn syrup. Pour into refrigerator tray. Freeze until edges are firm and center is mushy, about 2 hours. Turn into chilled small mixer bowl; beat on low speed until smooth. Beat on high speed until white and foamy (do not overbeat). Pour into refrigerator tray. Freeze until firm.

About 2½ cups.

Variation

TRIPLE FRUIT ICE: Add ½ cup orange juice and ¼ cup lemon juice.

WATERMELON ICE

8 cups 1-inch pieces watermelon (½ medium
    watermelon)
1 cup sugar
¼ cup lemon juice

Remove seeds from watermelon. Measure half of the watermelon pieces, sugar and lemon juice into blender. Blend on high speed until mixture is smooth and sugar is dissolved. Repeat. Pour into 2 refrigerator trays. Freeze until firm, about 2 hours.

About 1 quart.

Note: If you don't have a blender, press watermelon pieces through sieve. Blend thoroughly with sugar and lemon juice.

ORANGE BAKED ALASKAS

1 *quart vanilla ice cream or lemon, lime*
  or orange sherbet
3 *large seedless oranges*
4 *egg whites*
½ *teaspoon cream of tartar*
½ *cup granulated sugar or brown sugar*
  (packed)

Scoop ice cream into 6 balls. Freeze until firm, at least 6 hours. Cut oranges crosswise in half; if necessary, cut very thin slice from bottom of each half so oranges will stand upright. Cut around edges and membranes to loosen; remove fruit and membrane from shells. Line bottom of each shell with cut-up fruit. Refrigerate.

Move oven rack to lowest position. Heat oven to 500°. Beat egg whites and cream of tartar until foamy. Beat in sugar, 1 tablespoon at a time; continue beating until stiff and glossy. Do not underbeat. Place orange shells on ungreased baking sheet; fill each shell with an ice-cream ball. Completely cover ice cream with meringue, sealing it to edge of shells.

Bake until meringue is light brown, 2 to 3 minutes. Serve immediately.

6 servings.

Variation
GRAPEFRUIT BAKED ALASKAS: Substitute 3 medium grapefruit for the oranges.

NOTE

These spectacular little beauties are sure to reap a large number of compliments. They're really a less-fuss version of the traditional baked Alaska —with a couple of further bonus-points. First, they're lighter (especially when made with sherbet); second, they have a surprise layer of refreshing orange to add zest—and to delight the fresh-fruit aficionado. Here's a thought—why not try them for an extra-special birthday celebration for a person who looks forward to the unusual?

STRAWBERRY ALASKA JUBILEE

2 quarts strawberry ice cream, softened
1 package (18.5 ounces) yellow cake mix
6 egg whites
½ teaspoon cream of tartar
1 cup sugar
Strawberries Jubilee (page 29)

Line 1½-quart bowl with aluminum foil. Pack ice cream in bowl. Freeze until firm. Bake cake mix in 2 round layer pans, 9×1½ inches, as directed on package. Cool completely. (Reserve 1 layer for another dessert.)

Cover baking sheet with aluminum foil. Place cake layer on baking sheet. Invert bowl with ice cream on cake; remove bowl and foil. Place cake and ice cream in freezer while preparing meringue. (Ice cream must be very hard before it is covered with meringue.)

Move oven rack to lowest position. Heat oven to 500°. Beat egg whites and cream of tartar until foamy. Beat in sugar, 1 tablespoon at a time; continue beating until stiff and glossy. Do not underbeat. Completely cover cake and ice cream with meringue, sealing it to foil.

Bake until meringue is light brown, 3 to 5 minutes. Trim foil to edge of meringue; transfer cake to serving plate. Let stand 10 to 15 minutes before serving to make cutting easier. Serve with Strawberries Jubilee.

12 to 16 servings.

Variation
LEMON ALASKA: Substitute lemon sherbet for the ice cream and lemon cake mix for the yellow cake mix. If desired, serve with Raspberry-Currant Sauce (page 141) or Tangy Mincemeat Sauce (page 140).

Note: Dessert can be frozen up to 24 hours before or after baking meringue.

GINGERBREAD ALASKA

1 package (14.5 ounces) gingerbread mix
1-quart brick chocolate chip ice cream
4 egg whites
½ teaspoon cream of tartar
⅔ cup brown sugar (packed)

Bake gingerbread mix as directed on package. Cool 10 minutes; remove from pan and cool completely.

Cover baking sheet with aluminum foil. Place gingerbread on baking sheet; place ice cream on top. Trim gingerbread around ice cream, leaving a 1-inch edge. Place in freezer while preparing meringue. (Ice cream must be very hard before it is covered with meringue.)

Move oven rack to lowest position. Heat oven to 500°. Beat egg whites and cream of tartar until foamy. Beat in sugar, 1 tablespoon at a time; continue beating until stiff and glossy. Do not underbeat. Completely cover gingerbread and ice cream with meringue, sealing it to foil.

Bake until meringue is light brown, 3 to 5 minutes. Trim foil to edge of meringue; transfer dessert to serving plate. Let stand 10 to 15 minutes before serving to make cutting easier. Cut dessert lengthwise in half; cut each half into 6 slices.

12 servings.

Variations
BROWNIE ALASKA: Substitute 1 package (15.5 ounces) fudge brownie mix for the gingerbread mix; bake as directed on package. Substitute peppermint, cherry, coffee or Neapolitan ice cream for the chocolate chip ice cream and granulated sugar for the brown sugar. If desired, top with chocolate sauce.

GINGER ALASKA JUBILEE: Substitute vanilla ice cream for the chocolate chip ice cream. Serve slices topped with Flaming Oranges (page 29).

Note: Dessert can be frozen up to 24 hours before or after baking meringue.

Cake Creations

Baking a cake is so satisfying! Whether it's
a candle-lit birthday beauty, an ethereal angel
or a lush chocolate torte—doesn't every cake
you bake get a warm reception?
Well, here are some real collector's items
to help you bask in
that special cake-baker's glory.

Special Flavor Cakes

Whatever happened to hearty and oh-so-satisfying cakes like pumpkin, prune and applesauce? Look no further—you'll find lots of fruits, lots of spices, and best of all, lots of old-time flavor in the cakes in this section. The texture is rich and moist; these cakes will be applauded served as is, straight from the pan. Or you can frost or glaze them. At those limited-time times, be sure to check the special collection of mix-quick versions we've included!

JEWELED FRUITCAKE

1 package (8 ounces) dried apricots (about 2 cups)
1 package (8 ounces) pitted dates (about 1½ cups)
¾ pound whole Brazil nuts (about 1½ cups)
1 cup drained red and green maraschino cherries
⅓ pound red and green candied pineapple, cut up (about 1 cup)
¾ cup all-purpose flour*
¾ cup sugar
½ teaspoon baking powder
½ teaspoon salt
3 eggs (½ to ⅔ cup)
1½ teaspoons vanilla

Heat oven to 300°. Line loaf pan, 9×5×3 or 8½×4½×2½ inches, with aluminum foil; grease. Leave apricots, dates, nuts and cherries whole; mix all ingredients thoroughly. Spread mixture evenly in pan.

Bake until wooden pick inserted in center comes out clean, 1 hour 45 minutes. If necessary, cover with aluminum foil the last 30 minutes of baking to prevent excessive browning. Remove from pan; cool. Wrap; refrigerate or freeze.

* If using self-rising flour, omit baking powder and salt.

Pictured on page 65: Bonnie Butter Cake (page 77)

GRAHAM CRACKER CAKE

3 eggs, separated
1 cup brown sugar (packed)
⅔ cup all-purpose flour*
3 teaspoons baking powder
¼ teaspoon salt
2 cups graham cracker crumbs (about 24 squares)
1 cup milk
⅓ cup butter or margarine, softened
1 teaspoon vanilla
½ cup finely chopped nuts
Sweetened Whipped Cream (below) or Satiny Beige Frosting (page 68)

Heat oven to 350°. Grease and flour 2 round layer pans, 9×1½ inches. Beat egg whites in small mixer bowl until foamy. Beat in ½ cup of the sugar, 1 tablespoon at a time; continue beating until stiff and glossy. Do not underbeat.

Blend remaining sugar, the flour, baking powder, salt, cracker crumbs, ½ cup of the milk, the butter and vanilla in large mixer bowl on medium speed 1 minute, scraping bowl constantly. Add remaining milk and the egg yolks; beat 1 minute, scraping bowl frequently. Fold in nuts and meringue. Pour into pans.

Bake until wooden pick inserted in center comes out clean and cake begins to leave side of pan, 30 to 40 minutes. Cool 10 minutes; remove from pans and cool. (Cake is delicate—handle carefully.) Fill layers and frost cake with Sweetened Whipped Cream.

* Do not use self-rising flour in this recipe.

Sweetened Whipped Cream
In chilled bowl, beat 2 cups chilled whipping cream, ⅓ cup sugar and 2 teaspoons vanilla until stiff.

LEMON GOURMET CAKE

⅔ cup dairy sour cream
1 package (14.3 ounces) creamy lemon
  frosting mix
1 package (18.5 ounces) lemon cake mix
¼ cup butter or margarine, softened

Refrigerate sour cream and frosting mix in small mixer bowl at least 2 hours. Bake cake mix in 2 square layer pans as directed on package. Cool. Blend butter and sour cream mixture; beat on low speed 1 minute. Do not overbeat or mixture may become thin. Fill layers and frost top of cake. Refrigerate.

Variation

CHOCOLATE GOURMET CAKE: Substitute creamy white frosting mix and devils food cake mix for the lemon frosting mix and lemon cake mix. Garnish with Chocolate Curls (page 79).

SOUR CREAM SPICE CAKE

2 cups all-purpose flour*
1½ cups brown sugar (packed)
1¼ teaspoons baking soda
1 teaspoon baking powder
½ teaspoon salt
2 teaspoons cinnamon
¾ teaspoon cloves
½ teaspoon nutmeg
¼ cup butter or margarine, softened
¼ cup shortening
2 eggs (⅓ to ½ cup)
1 cup dairy sour cream
½ cup water
1 cup raisins, chopped
½ cup chopped walnuts
Penuche Frosting (right)

Heat oven to 350°. Grease and flour oblong pan, 13×9×2 inches, or 2 round layer pans, 8 or 9× 1½ inches. Measure all ingredients except frosting into large mixer bowl. Blend ½ minute on low speed, scraping bowl constantly. Beat 3 minutes on high speed, scraping bowl occasionally. Pour batter into pan(s).

Bake until wooden pick inserted in center comes out clean, oblong 40 to 45 minutes, layers 30 to 35 minutes. Cool. Frost with Penuche Frosting.

* If using self-rising flour, decrease soda to ¾ teaspoon and omit baking powder and salt.

High Altitude (5000 feet): Heat oven to 375°. If using 8×1½-inch layer pans, grease and flour 3 pans. Increase flour to 2¼ cups and decrease baking powder to ½ teaspoon.

Penuche Frosting
½ cup butter or margarine
1 cup brown sugar (packed)
¼ cup milk
2 cups confectioners' sugar

Melt butter in saucepan. Stir in brown sugar. Heat to boiling, stirring constantly. Boil and stir over low heat 2 minutes. Stir in milk; heat to boiling. Remove from heat and cool to lukewarm.

Gradually stir in confectioners' sugar. Place pan of frosting in bowl of ice and water; beat until spreading consistency. If frosting becomes too stiff, heat slightly, stirring constantly.

PEANUT BUTTER CAKE

Prepare 1 package (18.5 ounces) yellow cake mix as directed except—before blending, add 1 cup crunchy or creamy peanut butter. Frost cake with Peanut Butter Frosting (below) or Fudge Frosting (page 72).

Peanut Butter Frosting
3 cups confectioners' sugar
¼ cup crunchy peanut butter
¼ to ⅓ cup milk

Mix sugar and peanut butter; stir in milk. Beat until spreading consistency.

SPICY PRUNE CAKE

1 cup boiling water
1 cup cut-up pitted uncooked prunes
2 cups all-purpose flour*
1½ cups sugar
1¼ teaspoons baking soda
1 teaspoon salt
1 teaspoon cinnamon
1 teaspoon nutmeg
1 teaspoon cloves
½ cup salad oil
3 eggs (½ to ⅔ cup)
1 teaspoon vanilla
1 cup chopped nuts
Satiny Beige Frosting (below)

Pour boiling water over prunes in large mixer bowl; let stand 2 hours.

Heat oven to 350°. Grease and flour oblong pan, 13×9×2 inches, or 2 round layer pans, 9×1½ inches. Measure remaining ingredients except frosting into mixer bowl with prunes. Blend 1 minute on low speed, scraping bowl constantly. Beat 2 minutes on medium speed, scraping bowl occasionally. Pour batter into pan(s).

Bake until wooden pick inserted in center comes out clean, oblong 45 to 50 minutes, layers 35 to 40 minutes. Cool. Frost cake with Satiny Beige Frosting.

* If using self-rising flour, decrease soda to ½ teaspoon and omit salt.

Note: This recipe is not recommended for use at high altitude.

Satiny Beige Frosting
½ cup brown sugar (packed)
¼ cup light corn syrup
2 tablespoons water
2 egg whites (¼ cup)
½ teaspoon vanilla

Mix sugar, corn syrup and water in small saucepan. Cover; heat to rolling boil over medium heat. Remove cover and boil rapidly, without stirring, to 242° on candy thermometer (or until small amount of mixture dropped into very cold water forms a firm ball which holds its shape until pressed).

As mixture boils, beat egg whites until stiff peaks form. Pour hot syrup very slowly in a thin stream into the beaten egg whites, beating constantly on medium speed. Beat on high speed until stiff peaks form; add vanilla during last minute of beating.

Variation
WHITE MOUNTAIN FROSTING: Substitute granulated sugar for the brown sugar and increase vanilla to 1 teaspoon.

PRUNE RING CAKE

Prepare Spicy Prune Cake (left), as directed except —pour batter into greased and floured 9- or 12-cup bundt pan or tube pan, 10×4 inches. Bake 50 to 55 minutes. Cool 10 minutes. Remove from pan. If desired, spread cake with Lemon Glaze (page 84), Browned Butter Glaze (page 84) or serve wedges of cake with whipped cream cheese and warm Lemon Sauce (page 12).

MAPLE SYRUP CAKE

1 package (18.5 ounces) yellow cake mix
⅓ cup sugar
1 teaspoon cinnamon
1 cup maple-flavored syrup
½ cup chopped nuts

Bake cake mix in oblong pan, 13×9×2 inches, as directed on package. Cool 5 minutes; score into large diamond shapes. Mix sugar and cinnamon; sprinkle on top of cake. Heat syrup slightly; pour over cake. Sprinkle nuts over top. Let stand a few minutes; serve from pan. Delicious served warm or cool.

Prune Ring Cake (page 68)

BANANA NUT CAKE

2 cups all-purpose flour*
1⅔ cups sugar
1¼ teaspoons baking soda
1 teaspoon salt
¾ teaspoon baking powder
⅔ cup shortening
⅔ cup buttermilk
3 eggs (½ to ⅔ cup)
1¼ cups mashed ripe banana (about 3 medium)
⅔ cup finely chopped nuts
Vanilla Butter Frosting (below)

Heat oven to 350°. Grease and flour oblong pan, 13×9×2 inches, or three 8-inch or two 9-inch round layer pans. Measure all ingredients except frosting into large mixer bowl. Blend ½ minute on low speed, scraping bowl constantly. Beat 3 minutes on high speed, scraping bowl occasionally. Pour batter into pan(s).

Bake until wooden pick inserted in center comes out clean, oblong 45 to 50 minutes, layers 35 to 40 minutes. Cool. Frost cake with Vanilla Butter Frosting.

* Do not use self-rising flour in this recipe.

High Altitude (5000 feet): Heat oven to 375°. Increase flour to 2¼ cups; decrease sugar to 1 cup plus 3 tablespoons.

Vanilla Butter Frosting
⅓ cup butter or margarine, softened
3 cups confectioners' sugar
1½ teaspoons vanilla
About 2 tablespoons milk

Blend butter and sugar. Stir in vanilla and milk; beat until smooth and spreading consistency.

Note: For three 8-inch layers, use ½ cup butter or margarine, softened, 4½ cups confectioners' sugar, 2 teaspoons vanilla and about 3 tablespoons milk.

APPLESAUCE CAKE

2½ cups all-purpose flour*
2 cups sugar
1½ teaspoons baking soda
1½ teaspoons salt
¼ teaspoon baking powder
¾ teaspoon cinnamon
½ teaspoon cloves
½ teaspoon allspice
1½ cups canned applesauce
½ cup water
½ cup shortening
2 eggs (⅓ to ½ cup)
1 cup raisins
½ cup chopped walnuts
Browned Butter Frosting (below) or Satiny Beige Frosting (page 68)

Heat oven to 350°. Grease and flour oblong pan, 13×9×2 inches, or 2 round layer pans, 8 or 9× 1½ inches. Measure all ingredients except frosting into large mixer bowl. Blend ½ minute on low speed, scraping bowl constantly. Beat 3 minutes on high speed, scraping bowl occasionally. Pour batter into pan(s).

Bake until wooden pick inserted in center comes out clean, oblong 60 to 65 minutes, layers 50 to 55 minutes. Cool. Frost cake with Browned Butter Frosting.

* Do not use self-rising flour in this recipe.

High Altitude (5000 feet): Heat oven to 375°. If using 8×1½-inch layer pans, grease and flour 3 pans. Increase flour to 2⅔ cups and decrease soda to 1 teaspoon. Bake the 8-inch layers 40 to 50 minutes.

Browned Butter Frosting
Heat ⅓ cup butter or margarine in saucepan over medium heat until delicate brown. Cool slightly. Blend in 3 cups confectioners' sugar. Stir in 1½ teaspoons vanilla and 2 tablespoons milk; beat until smooth and spreading consistency.

QUICK APPLESAUCE CAKE

1 package (18.5 ounces) yellow cake mix
3 eggs (½ to ⅔ cup)
¼ cup water
1 jar (15 ounces) applesauce (about 1¾
  cups)
1 teaspoon cinnamon
½ teaspoon allspice
¼ teaspoon cloves
¼ teaspoon nutmeg

Heat oven to 350°. Grease and flour oblong pan, 13×9×2 inches. Blend all ingredients on low speed in large mixer bowl. Beat 4 minutes on medium speed, scraping bowl occasionally. Pour batter into pan.

Bake until wooden pick inserted in center comes out clean, 40 to 45 minutes. Cool slightly. If desired, serve with sweetened whipped cream or frost cake with Browned Butter Frosting (page 70).

High Altitude (5000 feet): Heat oven to 375°. Stir 2 tablespoons flour into cake mix; continue as directed above.

QUICK BANANA CAKE

1 package (18.5 ounces) yellow cake mix
⅛ teaspoon baking soda
1 cup mashed banana (2 to 3 medium)
½ cup finely chopped nuts (optional)

Heat oven to 350°. Grease and flour oblong pan, 13×9×2 inches. Prepare cake mix as directed on package except—stir soda into dry mix; use 1 cup plus 4 teaspoons water and add banana. Fold in nuts. Pour batter into pan.

Bake until wooden pick inserted in center comes out clean, 35 to 40 minutes.

High Altitude (5000 feet): Heat oven to 375°. Increase water to 1¼ cups.

QUICK PUMPKIN CAKE

1 package (18.5 ounces) yellow cake mix
2 eggs (⅓ to ½ cup)
¼ cup water
2 teaspoons baking soda
1 can (16 ounces) pumpkin
2 teaspoons pumpkin pie spice
Caramel Fluff Topping or Honey-Ginger
  Topping (below)

Heat oven to 350°. Grease and flour 12-cup bundt pan or oblong pan, 13×9×2 inches. Blend all ingredients except Caramel Fluff Topping on low speed in large mixer bowl. Beat 4 minutes on medium speed. Pour batter into pan.

Bake until wooden pick inserted in center comes out clean, 40 to 45 minutes. Cool. Serve with one of the toppings.

High Altitude (5000 feet): Heat oven to 375°. Stir 2 tablespoons flour into cake mix. Increase water to ⅓ cup and decrease soda to ½ teaspoon.

Caramel Fluff Topping
In chilled bowl, beat 1 cup chilled whipping cream, ⅓ cup brown sugar (packed) and ½ teaspoon vanilla.

2 cups.

Honey-Ginger Topping
In chilled bowl, beat 1 cup chilled whipping cream; gradually add 2 tablespoons honey and ¼ teaspoon ginger.

2 cups.

Variations
PUMPKIN NUT CAKE: Fold ½ cup chopped walnuts or pecans into batter.

PUMPKIN RAISIN CAKE: Fold ½ cup raisins into batter.

Chocolate Cakes

Such good cakes grow on the chocolate tree! A velvet cream, a chocolate-cherry, a buttermallow, a brandy-dandy. The choices are many, because such a lot of other flavors marry happily with chocolate. Why, there's almost unlimited variety in our Best Chocolate Cake recipe alone. Frost "as you like it" or use it in any of these recipes that call for a chocolate cake mix.

CHOCOLATE-CHERRY CAKE

Prepare Best Chocolate Cake (right) as directed except—beat in 20 maraschino cherries, finely cut up and drained, and ½ teaspoon almond extract. Frost cake with Chocolate-Cherry Frosting (below).

Chocolate-Cherry Frosting
¼ cup butter or margarine, softened
2 ounces melted unsweetened chocolate (cool)
2 cups confectioners' sugar
¼ teaspoon almond extract
3 to 4 tablespoons maraschino cherry syrup

Mix butter, chocolate and sugar. Stir in extract and cherry syrup; beat until smooth and spreading consistency.

CHOCOLATE NESSELRODE CAKE

Bake Best Chocolate Cake (right) in 2 round layer pans, 9 × 1½ inches, as directed. Cool. Split cake to make 4 layers. Fill layers and frost top of cake with Nesselrode Filling (below). Frost side of cake with Cocoa Fluff Topping (page 87) or sweetened whipped cream. Refrigerate.

Nesselrode Filling
In chilled bowl, beat 1 cup chilled whipping cream and ¼ cup confectioners' sugar until stiff. Fold in ¼ cup Nesselrode and about 6 drops red food color.

BEST CHOCOLATE CAKE

2 cups all-purpose flour*
2 cups sugar
1 teaspoon baking soda
1 teaspoon salt
½ teaspoon baking powder
¾ cup water
¾ cup buttermilk
½ cup shortening
2 eggs (⅓ to ½ cup)
1 teaspoon vanilla
4 ounces melted unsweetened chocolate (cool)
Fudge Frosting (below) or Penuche Frosting
   (page 67)

Heat oven to 350°. Grease and flour oblong pan, 13 × 9 × 2 inches, or three 8-inch or two 9-inch round layer pans. Measure all ingredients except frosting into large mixer bowl. Blend ½ minute on low speed, scraping bowl constantly. Beat 3 minutes on high speed, scraping bowl occasionally. Pour batter into pan(s).

Bake until wooden pick inserted in center comes out clean, oblong 40 to 45 minutes, layers 30 to 35 minutes. Cool. Frost cake with Fudge Frosting.

* If using self-rising flour, omit soda, salt and baking powder.

High Altitude (5000 feet): Heat oven to 375°. Decrease sugar to 1¾ cups, soda to ¾ teaspoon and baking powder to ¼ teaspoon.

Fudge Frosting
2 cups sugar
½ cup shortening
3 ounces unsweetened chocolate
⅔ cup milk
½ teaspoon salt
2 teaspoons vanilla

Mix all ingredients except vanilla in 2½-quart saucepan. Heat to rolling boil, stirring occasionally. Boil 1 minute without stirring. Place pan in bowl of ice and water. Beat until frosting is smooth and spreading consistency; stir in vanilla.

CHOCOLATE VELVET CREAM CAKE

1 package (15.4 ounces) chocolate fudge
  frosting mix
1½ cups whipping cream
1 teaspoon vanilla
1 package (18.5 ounces) devils food cake
  mix
Thin Icing (below)

Refrigerate 2 cups of the frosting mix, the whipping cream and vanilla in small mixer bowl at least 1 hour. Bake cake mix in 2 round layer pans, 9 × 1½ inches, as directed on package. Cool. Split cake to make 4 layers. Beat frosting mixture until stiff; fill layers. Spread top of cake with Thin Icing, allowing some to drizzle down side. If desired, sprinkle top with nuts. Refrigerate.

Thin Icing
Blend remaining frosting mix, 2 to 3 tablespoons hot water and 1 tablespoon light corn syrup; beat until smooth. Stir in 1 to 2 teaspoons water if necessary.

Variations
LEMON PISTACHIO CREAM CAKE: Use 1 package (14.3 ounces) creamy lemon frosting mix and 1 package (18.5 ounces) lemon cake mix. Garnish cake with chopped pistachio nuts.

MOCHA ALMOND CREAM CAKE: Add 2 teaspoons instant coffee to the frosting mix-whipping cream mixture. Garnish cake with diced roasted almonds.

NOTE

Are you stumped when a recipe calls for split cake layers? No need to be—the technique is fairly simple. First, be sure the layers are completely cool. Use wooden picks to indicate several points halfway up the side of each layer. Using this "equator" as a guide, carefully slice through each layer with a long, thin (and very sharp) knife. Perfect!

Here's another method: Split the layers by using a heavy piece of sewing thread. Pull it back and forth across the side of each layer, like a saw.

ICE-CREAM SUNDAE CAKE

1 package (18.5 ounces) devils food cake
  mix
3 pints ice cream (coffee, cherry or
  peppermint)
1 package (7.2 ounces) fluffy white frosting
  mix
½ cup chocolate ice-cream topping
Chopped nuts

Bake cake mix in 2 round layer pans, 9 × 1½ inches, as directed on package. Cool. Split cake to make 4 layers. Soften ice cream slightly. Working quickly, fill layers, spreading 1 pint ice cream between each. Wrap side of cake in double thickness of aluminum foil. Freeze until firm, about 8 hours.

Just before serving, prepare frosting mix as directed on package. Frost side and top of cake. Spoon topping over cake, allowing some to drizzle down side. Sprinkle nuts over top.

QUICK PUDDING TORTE

1 package (about 19 ounces) any flavor
  layer cake mix
1 package (about 4½ ounces) instant
  pudding and pie filling (vanilla, chocolate,
  butterscotch or lemon)
⅓ cup milk
2 cups chilled whipping cream
½ teaspoon vanilla
Chopped nuts or flaked coconut (optional)

Bake cake mix in 2 round layer pans, 9 × 1½ inches, as directed on package. Cool. Split cake to make 4 layers.

Blend pudding and pie filling and milk in large mixer bowl; stir until mix is dissolved. Add whipping cream and vanilla; beat until mixture is just stiff enough to spread. (Do not overbeat or mixture may appear curdled.) Fill and frost cake with pudding mixture. Garnish with nuts. Refrigerate.

CHOCOLATE BRANDY CAKE

1 package (18.5 ounces) devils food cake mix
1⅓ cups buttermilk
2 eggs (⅓ to ½ cup)
⅓ cup honey
⅓ cup brandy
Brandy Whipped Cream (below)
Grated chocolate, chocolate curls or chopped
  pistachio nuts

Heat oven to 350°. Grease and flour 2 round layer pans, 9 × 1½ inches. Blend cake mix (dry), buttermilk and eggs in large mixer bowl on low speed until moistened, scraping bowl constantly. Beat 3 minutes on medium speed, scraping bowl frequently. Pour batter into pans.

Bake until cake springs back when touched lightly in center, 25 to 30 minutes. Cool in pans about 10 minutes; remove from pans.

Warm honey in small saucepan over low heat. Remove from heat; stir in brandy. Spoon over bottoms of warm cake layers. Cool completely. Fill layers and frost cake with Brandy Whipped Cream. Refrigerate at least 1 hour. At serving time, garnish with grated chocolate.

Note: This recipe is not recommended for use at high altitude.

Brandy Whipped Cream
In chilled bowl, beat 2 cups chilled whipping cream and ¼ cup confectioners' sugar until soft peaks form. Gradually beat in 3 tablespoons brandy.

NOTE

Helpful hints on how to frost a two-layer cake: Brush loose crumbs from cooled layers. Place bottom layer upside down on serving plate. Use a small flexible spatula to spread about ⅓ cup of frosting to within ¼ inch of layer edge; top with second layer, right side up. Coat side of cake with a thin layer of frosting to seal in crumbs. Swirl more frosting up side to form ¼-inch ridge above rim of cake. Top with remaining frosting.

CHOCOLATE-COCONUT-PECAN CAKE

Refrigerate 1 cup dairy sour cream and 1 package (9.9 ounces) coconut-pecan frosting mix in small mixer bowl at least 1 hour. Bake 1 package (18.5 ounces) German chocolate cake mix in round layer pans as directed. Cool. Beat sour cream mixture on low speed until blended; fill layers and frost top of cake. Refrigerate.

CHOCOLATE SOUR CREAM RAISIN CAKE

1 package (18.5 ounces) devils food cake mix
¾ cup brown sugar (packed)
¾ cup granulated sugar
3 tablespoons cornstarch
1½ cups dairy sour cream
2 eggs or 4 egg yolks, beaten
1 cup raisins
½ cup chopped nuts
1 teaspoon vanilla
Chocolate Glaze (page 87)

Heat oven to 350°. Grease and flour oblong pan, 13 × 9 × 2 inches. Bake cake mix as directed on package. Cool cake in pan.

In medium saucepan, mix sugars and cornstarch; blend in sour cream and eggs. Cook over medium heat, stirring constantly, until mixture thickens and boils. Boil and stir 1 minute. Remove from heat; stir in raisins, nuts and vanilla. Cool. Spread over cake. Pour Chocolate Glaze over topping; spread carefully until topping is evenly covered. Serve immediately or refrigerate.

CHOCOLATE BUTTERMALLOW CAKE

1 package (18.5 ounces) devils food cake mix
1 cup brown sugar (packed)
3 tablespoons flour
¾ cup light cream (20%)
2 tablespoons butter or margarine
1 teaspoon vanilla
½ cup chopped nuts
Marshmallow Frosting (right)
½ ounce melted unsweetened chocolate

Heat oven to 350°. Grease and flour oblong pan, 13×9×2 inches. Bake cake mix as directed on package. Cool cake in pan.

Stir together sugar and flour in small saucepan. Stir in cream gradually. Cook over medium heat, stirring constantly, until mixture thickens and boils. Boil and stir 1 minute. Remove from heat; blend in butter and vanilla. Cool.

Spread filling over top of cake. Sprinkle nuts over filling. Frost top with Marshmallow Frosting. Using teaspoon, drizzle melted chocolate in lengthwise lines on frosting; immediately draw a spatula or knife across lines to form a pattern.

Marshmallow Frosting

2 egg whites (¼ cup)
1½ cups sugar
¼ teaspoon cream of tartar
1 tablespoon light corn syrup
⅓ cup water
1½ cups miniature marshmallows

Combine egg whites, sugar, cream of tartar, corn syrup and water in top of double boiler. Blend 1 minute on low speed with electric mixer. Place over boiling water; beat on high speed until stiff peaks form, about 7 minutes. Remove from heat. Add marshmallows; beat until frosting is spreading consistency.

QUICK COCOA CAKE

1½ cups all-purpose flour*
1 cup sugar
3 tablespoons cocoa
1 teaspoon baking soda
½ teaspoon salt
⅓ cup salad oil
1 tablespoon vinegar
1 tablespoon vanilla
1 cup water
Cocoa Fluff Topping or Chocolate Crunch
   Topping (page 87)

Heat oven to 350°. Grease square pan, 9×9×2 inches. Measure all ingredients except topping into large mixer bowl. Blend ½ minute on low speed, scraping bowl constantly. Beat 1 minute on high speed, scraping bowl occasionally. Pour batter into pan.

Bake until wooden pick inserted in center comes out clean, 25 to 30 minutes. Serve warm, with Cocoa Fluff Topping.

* Do not use self-rising flour in this recipe.

High Altitude (5000 feet): Heat oven to 375°. Continue as directed above.

Note: Ingredients can be mixed in the pan: Measure dry ingredients into ungreased pan; stir with fork. Add remaining ingredients; mix until smooth.

NOTE

When you don't want the world to know how hurried you are, Quick Cocoa Cake is the dessert for you! It's delicious served warm. And what's the quickest topping you can think of? Well, a dusting of confectioners' sugar takes only a minute, and looks and tastes great. Scoops of ice cream take very little longer. Get a jazzy effect by combining different colors and flavors. Or try a quickie that comes out looking like honest-to-goodness frosting. Break milk chocolate candy bars into small pieces; arrange on hot cake. When they melt, spread them over the top.

Yellow and White Cakes

Colors that make you think of sun, outdoors and lots of fun. And so they should. These cakes may seem standard, but each adapts in a practical manner to a range of splendid variations. Bonnie Butter becomes Broiled Coconut Praline, Silver White turns into Festive Cranberry—with just a few alterations. And we offer two choice versions of that perennial favorite, Pound Cake.

SOUR CREAM STREUSEL CAKE

1 package (18.5 ounces) yellow cake mix
1 cup brown sugar (packed)
¾ cup chopped walnuts
¼ cup firm butter or margarine
3 eggs (½ to ⅔ cup)
1½ cups dairy sour cream

Heat oven to 350°. Grease and flour oblong pan, 13×9×2 inches. Mix ⅔ cup of the cake mix (dry), the sugar, walnuts and butter until crumbly; set aside.

Beat eggs slightly with fork; blend in sour cream. Mix in remaining cake mix. (Batter will be thick and slightly lumpy.) Spread half of the batter in pan; sprinkle half of the sugar mixture over batter. Spoon and gently spread remaining batter in pan; sprinkle with remaining sugar mixture.

Bake until wooden pick inserted in center comes out clean, 40 to 45 minutes. Serve warm.

High Altitude (5000 feet): Heat oven to 375°. Prepare sugar mixture; stir 2 tablespoons flour into remaining cake mix. Continue as directed above.

Variations
Blend one of the following into batter:
- ☐ 2 tablespoons grated orange peel
- ☐ 2 tablespoons grated lemon peel
- ☐ 1 cup chopped cranberries
- ☐ 1 cup raisins
- ☐ 1 to 2 tablespoons powdered instant coffee

BONNIE BUTTER CAKE

⅔ cup butter or margarine, softened
1¾ cups sugar
2 eggs (⅓ to ½ cup)
1½ teaspoons vanilla
3 cups cake flour or 2¾ cups all-purpose
  flour*
2½ teaspoons baking powder
1 teaspoon salt
1¼ cups milk
Chocolate French Silk Frosting (below)

Heat oven to 350°. Grease and flour oblong pan, 13×9×2 inches, or two 9-inch or three 8-inch round layer pans. Blend butter, sugar, eggs and vanilla in large mixer bowl ½ minute on low speed, scraping bowl constantly. Beat 5 minutes on high speed, scraping bowl occasionally. On low speed, mix in flour, baking powder and salt alternately with milk. Pour batter into pan(s).

Bake until wooden pick inserted in center comes out clean, oblong 45 to 50 minutes, layers 30 to 35 minutes. Cool. Frost cake with Chocolate French Silk Frosting.

* If using self-rising flour, omit baking powder and salt.

High Altitude (5000 feet) for all-purpose flour: Heat oven to 375°. Decrease sugar to 1¼ cups plus 2 tablespoons. Increase flour to 3 cups. Decrease baking powder to 2¼ teaspoons. Increase milk to 1⅓ cups. Do not use 13×9×2-inch pan.

Chocolate French Silk Frosting
2⅔ cups confectioners' sugar
⅔ cup butter or margarine, softened
2 ounces melted unsweetened chocolate (cool)
¾ teaspoon vanilla
2 tablespoons milk

Blend sugar, butter, chocolate and vanilla in small mixer bowl on low speed. Gradually add milk; beat until smooth and fluffy.

BROILED COCONUT PRALINE CAKE

Heat oven to 350°. Grease and flour oblong pan, 13×9×2 inches. Bake Bonnie Butter Cake (left) or 1 package (18.5 ounces) yellow cake mix as directed. Cool slightly.

Set oven control at broil and/or 550°. Spread Broiled Coconut Topping (below) over warm cake. Place cake with top 5 inches from heat. Broil until topping is golden brown and bubbly, about 3 minutes. (Watch carefully—mixture burns easily.) Serve warm.

Broiled Coconut Topping
¼ cup butter or margarine, softened
⅔ cup brown sugar (packed)
1 cup flaked coconut
½ cup chopped nuts
3 tablespoons milk

Mix butter, sugar, coconut and nuts. Stir in milk.

QUICK POUND CAKE

Heat oven to 325°. Generously grease and flour tube pan, 10×4 inches. Blend 2 packages (16 ounces each) golden pound cake mix, 1⅓ cups water and 4 eggs in large mixer bowl on low speed until moistened, scraping bowl constantly. Beat 3 minutes on medium speed, scraping bowl occasionally. Pour batter into pan.

Bake until wooden pick inserted in center comes out clean, 1 hour 10 minutes. (Crack on top of cake is characteristic.) Cool 10 minutes in pan; remove from pan and cool completely. Glaze cake or serve with fruit sauce or ice-cream topping.

High Altitude (5000 feet): Heat oven to 350°. Follow directions above except—stir 6 tablespoons flour into dry mix. Use 1½ cups water and 4 eggs. Bake about 60 minutes.

GOLDEN POUND CAKE

1¼ cups butter or margarine, softened
2¾ cups sugar
5 eggs (about 1 cup)
1 teaspoon vanilla
3 cups all-purpose flour*
1 teaspoon baking powder
¼ teaspoon salt
1 cup evaporated milk

Heat oven to 350°. Grease and flour tube pan, 10×4 inches, or 12-cup bundt pan. Measure butter, sugar, eggs and vanilla into large mixer bowl. Blend ½ minute on low speed, scraping bowl constantly. Beat 5 minutes on high speed, scraping bowl occasionally. On low speed, mix in flour, baking powder and salt alternately with milk. Pour batter into pan.

Bake until wooden pick inserted in center comes out clean, 70 to 80 minutes. Cool in pan about 20 minutes; remove from pan.

* Do not use self-rising flour in this recipe.

SILVER WHITE CAKE

2¼ cups cake flour or 2 cups all-purpose
    flour*
1½ cups sugar
3½ teaspoons baking powder
1 teaspoon salt
½ cup shortening
1 cup milk
1 teaspoon vanilla
4 egg whites (½ cup)
White Mountain Frosting (page 68)
Flaked or shredded coconut

Heat oven to 350°. Grease and flour oblong pan, 13×9×2 inches, or 2 round layer pans, 8 or 9×1½ inches. Measure flour, sugar, baking powder, salt, shortening, milk and vanilla into large mixer bowl. Blend ½ minute on low speed, scraping bowl constantly. Beat 2 minutes on high speed,

scraping bowl occasionally. Add egg whites; beat 2 minutes on high speed, scraping bowl occasionally. Pour batter into pan(s).

Bake until wooden pick inserted in center comes out clean, oblong 35 to 40 minutes, layers 30 to 35 minutes. Frost cake with White Mountain Frosting and sprinkle with coconut. If desired, fill layers with Clear Lemon Filling (below).

* Do not use self-rising flour in this recipe.

High Altitude (5000 feet) for all-purpose flour: Heat oven to 375°. Increase flour to 2¼ cups; decrease sugar to 1¼ cups and baking powder to 2¼ teaspoons. Increase milk to 1 cup plus 2 tablespoons. Bake as directed except—if using 8×1½-inch layer pans, use 3 pans.

Clear Lemon Filling
¾ cup sugar
3 tablespoons cornstarch
¼ teaspoon salt
¾ cup water
1 teaspoon grated lemon peel
1 tablespoon butter or margarine
⅓ cup lemon juice
4 drops yellow food color (optional)

Mix sugar, cornstarch and salt in saucepan. Gradually stir in water. Cook over medium heat, stirring constantly, until mixture thickens and boils. Boil and stir 1 minute.

Remove from heat; add lemon peel and butter. Gradually stir in lemon juice and food color. Cool. If filling is too soft, refrigerate until set.

CHOCOLATE CURL CAKE

Prepare Silver White Cake (page 78) or 1 package (18.5 ounces) white cake mix in 2 round layer pans as directed except—fold 2 squares (1 ounce each) unsweetened chocolate, coarsely grated, into batter. Bake as directed; cool.

Fill layers with Dark Chocolate Filling (below). Frost cake with White Mountain Frosting (page 68) or 1 package (7.2 ounces) fluffy white frosting mix prepared as directed. Garnish top with Chocolate Curls (below) or grated chocolate.

Dark Chocolate Filling
¾ cup sugar
¼ cup light cream (20%)
1 tablespoon butter or margarine
1 square (1 ounce) unsweetened chocolate,
  cut up
2 egg yolks, beaten

Mix sugar, cream, butter and chocolate in saucepan. Cook over medium heat, stirring constantly, until butter and chocolate are melted. Gradually stir at least half of the hot mixture into egg yolks. Stir into remaining hot mixture in saucepan. Heat to boiling, stirring constantly. Boil and stir 1 minute. Remove from heat; cool without stirring.

Chocolate Curls
With a vegetable parer or thin, sharp knife, slice across block of sweet milk chocolate with long, thin strokes. Large-size milk chocolate candy bars can also be used.

NOTE

For cakes in reserve: Put unfrosted cakes into the freezer without wrapping; when they're frozen firm, freezer-wrap and store them. They'll keep up to 6 months. If you're freezing a frosted cake, put cake in box (to prevent crushing), wrap the box and freeze. Frozen cakes slice easily. Or cut your cake into family-size portions or into single slices before freezing. You can keep frosted cakes up to 3 months.

STRAWBERRY CHANTILLY TORTE

1 package (15.4 ounces) creamy white
  frosting mix
1½ cups whipping cream
1 package (18.5 ounces) white cake mix
1 pint fresh strawberries

Refrigerate frosting mix and whipping cream in small mixer bowl at least 1 hour. Bake cake mix in 2 round layer pans as directed on package. Cool. Slice strawberries lengthwise; reserve ½ cup for garnish. Split cake to make 4 layers. Beat frosting mixture until soft peaks form. Fill layers with ⅔ cup frosting mixture and about ½ cup strawberries. Frost top of cake with remaining frosting mixture; garnish with reserved berries. Refrigerate.

GRAHAM CRACKER CAKE DESSERT

2 cups graham cracker crumbs (about 30
  squares)
¾ cup chopped nuts
¾ cup brown sugar (packed)
2 teaspoons cinnamon
¾ cup butter or margarine, melted
1 package (18.5 ounces) white or
  devils food cake mix
Cocoa Fluff Topping (page 87)

Heat oven to 350°. Mix cracker crumbs, nuts, sugar, cinnamon and butter. Press half of the crumb mixture evenly in bottom of ungreased oblong pan, 13 × 9 × 2 inches. Prepare cake mix as directed on package. Pour half of the batter over crumb mixture in pan; sprinkle with half of the remaining crumb mixture. Repeat with remaining batter and remaining crumb mixture.

Bake 50 to 55 minutes. Cool, and if desired, refrigerate. Cut into squares. Top each serving with Cocoa Fluff Topping.

12 servings.

GREAT CHERRY CAKE

*Silver White Cake (page 78) or 1 package
(18.5 ounces) white cake mix*
*1 package (7 ounces) fluffy cherry frosting
mix*
1 cup chilled whipping cream
*1 can (16 ounces) dark sweet or pitted red
tart cherries, well drained, or 1 cup
maraschino cherries, well drained*
*1 can (8 ounces) crushed pineapple, well
drained*
½ cup chopped almonds
Whole, sliced or slivered almonds

Bake Silver White Cake or white cake mix in 2
round layer pans, 9 × 1½ inches, as directed. Cool.
Split cake to make 4 layers. Prepare frosting mix
as directed on package; set aside. In chilled bowl,
beat whipping cream until stiff; fold into frosting.
Reserve 1 cup of the mixture for top. Quarter
cherries, reserving 6 to 8 whole cherries for top.

Fold quartered cherries, pineapple and chopped
almonds into frosting-whipped cream mixture;
fill layers. Spread top of cake with reserved 1 cup
mixture. Decorate with reserved whole cherries
and whole, sliced or slivered almonds. Refrigerate.

FESTIVE CRANBERRY CAKE

Bake Silver White Cake (page 78) or 1 package
(18.5 ounces) white cake mix in 2 round layer
pans, 9 × 1½ inches, as directed. Cool. Split cake
to make 4 layers. In chilled bowl, beat 1½ cups
chilled whipping cream and ⅓ cup confectioners'
sugar until stiff. Spread each layer with ¼ of the
whipped cream. Spoon ¼ of 1 jar (14-ounce size)
cranberry-orange relish over each layer; swirl
relish into the whipped cream. Stack layers. Refrigerate 1 to 2 hours before serving.

Variation
SCANDINAVIAN LINGONBERRY CAKE: Substitute 1 jar
(14 ounces) lingonberries for the cranberry-orange
relish.

Angels, Chiffons and Cake Rolls

Introducing the lighthearted members of the cake
family—our high, wide and handsome angels, tender
chiffons and cake rolls. Try our basic made-from-
scratch Angel Food Deluxe or ring easy changes on
a mix with Mocha Almond Angel or Rainbow Delight
Cake. The chiffon trio pictured on page 86 will give
you an idea of the variety available with these cakes.
Or maybe you'd prefer a cake roll—Chocolate
Cream Roll, anyone?

RIO-REVEL CAKE

*1 package (15 or 16 ounces) white angel
food cake mix*
*1 package (4 ounces) chocolate flavor
whipped dessert mix*
¼ cup light rum
1 ounce unsweetened chocolate
¼ teaspoon shortening
1½ cups chilled whipping cream
⅓ cup confectioners' sugar
Brazil Nut Curls (below)

Bake cake mix as directed on package. Cool. Split
cake to make 3 layers. Prepare dessert mix as
directed on package except—substitute rum for
¼ cup of the water. Refrigerate 15 to 20 minutes;
spread two of the cake layers with dessert mix.
Refrigerate layers separately until dessert mix is
firm, about 1 hour.

Melt chocolate and shortening over low heat; cool.
Reassemble cake. In chilled bowl, beat whipping
cream and sugar until stiff. Frost cake. Drizzle
chocolate around top edge of cake, allowing some
to run down side. Garnish with Brazil Nut Curls.
Refrigerate.

Brazil Nut Curls
Place 10 to 15 shelled Brazil nuts in boiling water
4 or 5 minutes to soften. Cut into very thin slices
with vegetable parer. Nuts will slice easily if dipped
into hot water frequently.

ANGEL FOOD DELUXE

1 cup cake flour
1½ cups confectioners' sugar
12 egg whites (1½ cups)
1½ teaspoons cream of tartar
¼ teaspoon salt
1 cup granulated sugar
1½ teaspoons vanilla
½ teaspoon almond extract
Creamy Glaze (right) or sweetened
    whipped cream and sweetened
    sliced strawberries

Heat oven to 375°. Stir together flour and confectioners' sugar; set aside. Beat egg whites, cream of tartar and salt in large mixer bowl on medium speed until foamy. Add granulated sugar, 2 tablespoons at a time, beating on high speed until meringue holds stiff peaks. Gently fold in flavorings. Sprinkle flour-sugar mixture, ¼ cup at a time, over meringue, folding in gently just until flour-sugar mixture disappears. Push batter into ungreased tube pan, 10 × 4 inches. Gently cut through batter with spatula to remove air bubbles.

Bake until top springs back when touched lightly with finger, 30 to 35 minutes. Invert pan on funnel; let hang until cake is completely cool. Spread cake with Creamy Glaze or serve with whipped cream and berries.

Note: This recipe is not recommended for use at high altitude.

Creamy Glaze
⅓ cup butter or margarine
2 cups confectioners' sugar
1½ teaspoons vanilla
2 to 4 tablespoons hot water

Melt butter in saucepan. Blend in sugar and vanilla. Stir in water, 1 tablespoon at a time, until glaze is desired consistency.

Variations
BUTTER-RUM GLAZE: Substitute 2 tablespoons white rum or 1½ teaspoons rum flavoring for the vanilla; stir in hot water, 1 teaspoon at a time, until glaze is desired consistency.

DELUXE ORANGE GLAZE: Substitute 2 tablespoons orange-flavored liqueur for the vanilla; stir in hot water, 1 teaspoon at a time, until glaze is desired consistency.

GATEAU PARISIENNE

1 package (15 or 16 ounces) white angel
    food cake mix
1 teaspoon pumpkin pie spice
1½ cups chilled whipping cream
⅓ cup confectioners' sugar
¼ cup dark crème de cacao
Frosted Grapes (below)

Prepare cake mix as directed on package except
—during last ½ minute of beating, add pumpkin
pie spice. Bake as directed; cool.

In chilled bowl, beat whipping cream and sugar
until stiff. Fold in crème de cacao. Frost cake. Garnish with Frosted Grapes. Refrigerate.

Frosted Grapes
Dip small bunches of grapes in water; roll in
granulated sugar.

RAINBOW DELIGHT CAKE

1 package (15 or 16 ounces) white angel
    food cake mix
2 cups chilled whipping cream
½ cup confectioners' sugar
Few drops green food color
¼ teaspoon almond extract
Few drops yellow food color
½ teaspoon rum flavoring
Few drops red food color
¼ teaspoon peppermint extract

Bake cake mix as directed on package. Cool. Split
cake to make 3 layers. In chilled bowl, beat whipping cream and sugar until stiff.

To 1 cup of the whipped cream, stir in green food
color and almond extract. Spread between first
and second cake layers. To 1 cup of the whipped
cream, stir in yellow food color and rum flavoring. Spread between second and third layers. To
remaining 2 cups whipped cream, stir in red food
color and peppermint extract. Frost cake.

ANGEL ALEXANDER

1 package (15 or 16 ounces) white angel
    food cake mix
2 tablespoons light cream
½ cup white crème de cacao
1½ cups chilled whipping cream
¼ cup confectioners' sugar
Chocolate Curls (page 79)

Bake cake mix as directed on package. Cool. Place
cake on serving plate. Stir together light cream
and crème de cacao. With narrow 5-inch skewer,
punch several holes of various depths in cake;
pour cream mixture into holes.

In chilled bowl, beat whipping cream and sugar
until stiff. Frost cake; garnish with chocolate curls.
Refrigerate.

Variation
MINTED ANGEL CAKE: Substitute ½ cup green crème
de menthe for the white crème de cacao. Garnish
with maraschino cherries and mint leaves.

LEMON-COCONUT CAKE

1 package (15 or 16 ounces) white angel
    food cake mix
1 can (14 ounces) sweetened condensed milk
2 teaspoons grated lemon peel
¼ cup lemon juice
½ cup shredded coconut, toasted

Bake cake mix as directed on package. Cool. Stir
together milk, lemon peel and juice until thickened. Refrigerate 30 minutes.

Split cake to make 3 layers; fill each with about
⅓ cup lemon mixture. Spread remaining mixture
over side and top of cake. Sprinkle top with coconut. Refrigerate.

LINGONBERRY ANGEL TORTE

1 package (15 or 16 ounces) white angel
  food cake mix
1 package (7.2 ounces) fluffy white frosting
  mix
1½ cups whipping cream
¾ cup sugar
1 tablespoon cornstarch
¼ cup water
1½ cups lingonberries

Bake cake mix as directed on package. Cool. Refrigerate frosting mix and whipping cream in small mixer bowl at least 1 hour. Stir together sugar and cornstarch in small saucepan; mix in water and lingonberries. Heat to boiling; simmer 10 minutes. Cool.

Split cake to make 3 layers. Fill layers with lingonberry mixture. Beat frosting-cream mixture until soft peaks form. Frost cake. Refrigerate.

Note: If fresh lingonberries are not available, substitute 1 jar (14¾ ounces) lingonberries, drained, or 1 jar (14 ounces) cranberry-orange relish.

CHERRY FLUFF ANGEL FOOD

1 package (15 or 16 ounces) white angel
  food cake mix
1½ cups chilled whipping cream
⅓ cup confectioners' sugar
12 well-drained maraschino cherries, cut up
2 tablespoons maraschino cherry syrup
⅓ cup chopped walnuts

Bake cake mix as directed on package. Cool. In chilled bowl, beat whipping cream and sugar until stiff. Fold in cherries, cherry syrup and walnuts. Frost cake. Refrigerate.

STRAWBERRY-FILLED ANGEL FOOD

1 package (15 or 16 ounces) white angel
  food cake mix
3 cups chilled whipping cream
⅓ cup confectioners' sugar
2 drops red food color
1 package (10 ounces) frozen sliced strawberries, thawed and drained
½ cup miniature marshmallows or 6 large
  marshmallows, quartered
⅔ cup toasted slivered almonds

Bake cake mix as directed on package. Cool. Place cake upside down; slice off entire top of cake about 1 inch down and set aside. Make cuts down into cake 1 inch from outer edge and 1 inch from edge of hole, leaving substantial "walls" on each side. With curved knife or spoon, remove cake within cuts, being careful to leave a base of cake 1 inch thick. Place cake on serving plate.

In chilled bowl, beat whipping cream and sugar until stiff. Stir in food color. Fold strawberries, marshmallows and ⅓ cup of the almonds into half of the whipped cream. Spoon into cake cavity. Press mixture firmly into cavity to avoid holes in cut slices. Replace top of cake and press gently.

Frost cake with remaining whipped cream. Sprinkle with ⅓ cup almonds. Refrigerate until set, at least 4 hours.

MOCHA ALMOND ANGEL

Prepare 1 package (15 or 16 ounces) white angel food cake mix as directed except—substitute cold strong coffee for the water. Bake as directed; cool.

Prepare 1 package (7.2 ounces) fluffy white frosting mix as directed. Fold in ½ cup dairy sour cream. Frost cake. Garnish top with sliced almonds. Refrigerate.

LEMON CHIFFON CAKE

2¼ cups cake flour or 2 cups all-purpose
  flour*
1½ cups sugar
3 teaspoons baking powder
1 teaspoon salt
½ cup salad oil
5 egg yolks (with cake flour) or 7 egg yolks
  (with all-purpose flour)
¾ cup cold water
2 teaspoons grated lemon peel
2 teaspoons vanilla
1 cup egg whites (7 or 8)
½ teaspoon cream of tartar
Lemon Glaze (below)

Heat oven to 325°. Stir together flour, sugar, baking powder and salt. Make a "well" and add in order: oil, egg yolks, water, lemon peel and vanilla. Beat until smooth.

Beat egg whites and cream of tartar in large mixer bowl until whites form very stiff peaks. Gradually pour egg yolk mixture over beaten whites, gently folding just until blended. Pour into ungreased tube pan, 10 × 4 inches.

Bake until top springs back when touched lightly, about 75 minutes. Invert pan on funnel; let hang until cake is completely cool. Spread with glaze.

* If using self-rising flour, omit baking powder and salt.

High Altitude (5000 feet) for all-purpose flour: Heat oven to 350°. Increase flour to 2¼ cups and decrease baking powder to 1½ teaspoons. Beat egg whites just until stiff. Bake 60 to 65 minutes.

Lemon Glaze
⅓ cup butter or margarine, softened
2 cups confectioners' sugar
½ teaspoon grated lemon peel
2 to 4 tablespoons lemon juice

Blend butter, sugar and lemon peel. Stir in lemon juice, 1 tablespoon at a time, until glaze is desired consistency.

COCONUT-LEMON DELIGHT

Prepare 1 package (18.5 ounces) lemon chiffon cake mix as directed except—after folding batter into egg whites, gently fold in 1 cup toasted flaked coconut. Bake as directed; cool. Remove from pan and spread Browned Butter Glaze (below) over top of cake, allowing some to drizzle down side.

Browned Butter Glaze
⅓ cup butter or margarine
2 cups confectioners' sugar
1½ teaspoons vanilla
2 to 4 tablespoons hot water

Heat butter in saucepan over medium heat until delicate brown. Cool slightly. Blend in sugar and vanilla. Stir in water, 1 tablespoon at a time, until glaze is desired consistency.

MINCEMEAT CHIFFON CAKE

Prepare 1 package (18.5 ounces) lemon chiffon cake mix as directed except—after folding batter into egg whites, gently fold in ½ cup prepared mincemeat. Bake as directed; cool. Serve with Hard Sauce (page 36).

LEMON-PINEAPPLE CHIFFON CAKE

Prepare 1 package (18.5 ounces) lemon chiffon cake mix as directed except—fold ½ cup pineapple preserves into cake batter before folding batter into egg whites. Bake as directed; cool. Serve with sweetened whipped cream.

CITRUS CHIFFON CAKE

*1 package (18.5 ounces) lemon chiffon
  cake mix
1½ cups chilled whipping cream
3 tablespoons confectioners' sugar
2 teaspoons orange extract
¼ teaspoon almond extract
1 cup flaked coconut*

Bake cake mix as directed on package, adding the grated peel. Cool.

In chilled bowl, beat whipping cream, sugar and extracts until soft peaks form. Fold in coconut. Frost cake. If desired, sprinkle top with coconut and garnish with orange sections. Refrigerate.

TOASTED LEMON MERINGUE CAKE

*1 package (18.5 ounces) lemon chiffon
  cake mix
Clear Lemon Filling (page 78)
1 package (7.2 ounces) fluffy white frosting
  mix*

Bake cake mix as directed on package. Cool. Split cake to make 3 layers. Reserve small amount of Clear Lemon Filling; fill layers with remaining filling.

Heat oven to 400°. Cover baking sheet with aluminum foil. Place cake on baking sheet. Prepare frosting mix as directed on package. Frost cake. Bake until delicate brown, 8 to 10 minutes. Mix reserved filling and small amount hot water. Drizzle around top edge of cake, allowing some to run down side. Serve immediately.

LEMON-RASPBERRY TORTE

*1 package (18.5 ounces) lemon chiffon cake
  mix
1½ cups chilled whipping cream
⅓ cup confectioners' sugar
2 packages (10 ounces each) frozen raspberries, thawed and drained (reserve
  ½ cup syrup)
1 package (7.2 ounces) fluffy white frosting
  mix
1½ teaspoons cornstarch*

Bake cake mix as directed on package. Cool. Split cake to make 3 layers. In chilled bowl, beat whipping cream and sugar until stiff. Fold in raspberries. Fill layers with raspberry-cream mixture. Prepare frosting mix as directed on package. Frost cake.

Stir cornstarch into reserved raspberry syrup. Cook over medium heat, stirring constantly, until mixture thickens and boils. Boil and stir 1 minute. Cool. Drizzle raspberry sauce around top edge of cake, allowing some to run down side. Refrigerate.

LEMON MIST TORTE

*1 package (14.3 ounces) creamy lemon
  frosting mix
1½ cups whipping cream
1 package (18.5 ounces) lemon chiffon cake
  mix
Chopped pistachio nuts*

Refrigerate frosting mix and whipping cream in small mixer bowl at least 1 hour. Bake cake mix as directed on package. Cool. Split cake to make 3 layers. Beat frosting-cream mixture until stiff. Fill layers and frost top of cake. Decorate top with nuts. Refrigerate.

Pictured from bottom, clockwise: Lemon Two-Egg Chiffon Cake (page 88), Mahogany Chiffon Cake (page 87), Toasted Lemon Meringue Cake (page 85)

MAHOGANY CHIFFON CAKE

¾ cup boiling water
½ cup cocoa
1¾ cups cake flour or 1½ cups all-purpose
  flour
1¾ cups sugar
1½ teaspoons baking soda
1 teaspoon salt
½ cup salad oil
7 egg yolks
2 teaspoons vanilla
1 cup egg whites (7 or 8)
½ teaspoon cream of tartar
Chocolate Glaze (below) or Cake Toppings (right)

Blend boiling water and cocoa; set aside to cool. Heat oven to 325°. Stir together flour, sugar, soda and salt. Make a "well" and add in order: oil, egg yolks, cooled cocoa mixture and the vanilla. Beat until smooth.

Beat egg whites and cream of tartar in large mixer bowl until whites form very stiff peaks. Gradually pour egg yolk mixture over beaten whites, gently folding *just* until blended. Pour into ungreased tube pan, 10 × 4 inches.

Bake until top springs back when touched lightly, 65 to 70 minutes. Invert pan on funnel; let hang until cake is completely cool. Spread with glaze or serve with one of the toppings.

High Altitude (5000 feet) for all-purpose flour: Heat oven to 350°. Increase flour to 1¾ cups and decrease soda to ¾ teaspoon. Beat egg whites *just* until stiff.

Chocolate Glaze

⅓ cup butter or margarine
2 ounces unsweetened chocolate
2 cups confectioners' sugar
1½ teaspoons vanilla
2 to 4 tablespoons hot water

Melt butter and chocolate in saucepan over low heat. Remove from heat; stir in sugar and vanilla. Stir in water, 1 tablespoon at a time, until glaze is desired consistency.

CAKE TOPPINGS

Cocoa Fluff Topping
In chilled bowl, beat 1 cup chilled whipping cream, ½ cup confectioners' sugar and ¼ cup cocoa. Also good on chocolate or angel food cake.

2 cups.

Crème de Cacao Topping
In chilled bowl, beat 1 cup chilled whipping cream. Fold in ¼ cup crème de cacao. Delicious on any cake.

2 cups.

Mint Fluff Topping
In chilled bowl, beat 1 cup chilled whipping cream. Fold in 3 tablespoons green crème de menthe. Try on angel food cake, too.

2 cups.

Pink Peppermint Fluff Topping
In chilled bowl, beat 1 cup chilled whipping cream. Fold in ½ cup crushed peppermint stick candy. Good served on chocolate or angel food cake.

2½ cups.

Chocolate Crunch Topping
In chilled bowl, beat 1 cup chilled whipping cream. Crush 3 chilled bars (¾ ounce each) chocolate-covered toffee candy. Fold crushed candy into whipped cream. Also good on gingerbread, chocolate or angel food cake.

3 cups.

NOTE

When you bake angel or chiffon cakes in a tube pan, always place oven rack in the lowest position. To test the baked cake, touch top lightly. When cracks in top feel dry and no imprint remains, cake is done. To remove cake from pan: Let cool, inverted, then loosen cake by sliding metal spatula or table knife between cake and side of pan. Use short up and down strokes.

LEMON TWO-EGG CHIFFON CAKE

2 eggs, separated
1½ cups granulated sugar
2¼ cups cake flour
3 teaspoons baking powder
1 teaspoon salt
⅓ cup salad oil
1 cup milk
1 teaspoon vanilla
1 teaspoon grated lemon peel
Pecan-Fruit Filling (right)
1 cup chilled whipping cream
¼ cup confectioners' sugar

Heat oven to 350°. Grease and flour 2 round layer pans, 8 or 9×1½ inches. Beat egg whites until foamy in small mixer bowl. Beat in ½ cup of the granulated sugar, 1 tablespoon at a time; continue beating until very stiff and glossy. Set aside.

Measure remaining granulated sugar, the flour, baking powder and salt into large mixer bowl. Add oil, half of the milk, the vanilla and lemon peel. Blend on low speed until moistened, scraping bowl constantly. Beat 1 minute on high speed, scraping bowl constantly. Add remaining milk and the egg yolks. Blend on low speed. Beat 1 minute on high speed, scraping bowl frequently. Fold in meringue. Pour batter into pans.

Bake until wooden pick inserted in center comes out clean, 30 to 35 minutes. Cool. Fill layers and frost top to within 1 inch of edge with Pecan-Fruit Filling. In chilled bowl, beat whipping cream and confectioners' sugar until stiff. Spread on side and top edge of cake. Refrigerate.

High Altitude (5000 feet): Heat oven to 375°. If using 8×1½-inch layer pans, grease and flour 3 pans. Increase flour to 2½ cups; decrease baking powder to 1½ teaspoons and increase milk to 1 cup plus 2 tablespoons. Bake 25 to 30 minutes.

Pecan-Fruit Filling

2 egg yolks
⅔ cup dairy sour cream
⅔ cup sugar
1 cup finely chopped pecans
⅔ cup flaked coconut
½ cup finely chopped raisins
½ cup finely cut-up candied cherries

Blend egg yolks and sour cream; stir in sugar. Cook over low heat, stirring constantly, until mixture thickens. Remove from heat; stir in remaining ingredients. Cool.

QUICK JELLY ROLL

Heat oven to 350°. Prepare 1 package (18.5 ounces) lemon chiffon cake mix as directed except—pour half of the batter into ungreased jelly roll pan, 15½×10½×1 inch, spreading batter to corners. Pour remaining batter into ungreased loaf pan, 9×5×3 inches. Bake roll 20 to 25 minutes, loaf 45 to 55 minutes.

Cool roll 10 minutes. Loosen cake from edges of pan; invert on towel generously sprinkled with confectioners' sugar. Trim stiff edges of cake if necessary. While hot, roll cake and towel from narrow end. Cool on wire rack. Invert loaf to cool. (Use loaf as desired.)

Unroll cake; remove towel. Spread about ⅔ cup jelly or jam over cake. Roll up; sprinkle with confectioners' sugar.

10 to 12 servings.

High Altitude (5000 feet): Heat oven to 375°. Stir 3 tablespoons flour into Cake Batter Mix (packet 2). Continue as directed above except—bake roll 15 to 20 minutes, loaf 35 to 40 minutes.

OLD-FASHIONED JELLY ROLL

3 eggs (½ to ⅔ cup)
1 cup granulated sugar
⅓ cup water
1 teaspoon vanilla
1 cup cake flour or ¾ cup all-purpose flour*
1 teaspoon baking powder
¼ teaspoon salt
About ⅔ cup jelly or jam
Confectioners' sugar

Heat oven to 375°. Line jelly roll pan, 15½ × 10½ × 1 inch, with aluminum foil or waxed paper; grease. Beat eggs in small mixer bowl on high speed until very thick and lemon colored, 3 to 5 minutes. Pour eggs into large mixer bowl; gradually beat in granulated sugar. On low speed, blend in water and vanilla. Gradually add flour, baking powder and salt, beating just until batter is smooth. Pour into pan, spreading batter to corners.

Bake until wooden pick inserted in center comes out clean, 12 to 15 minutes. Loosen cake from edges of pan; immediately invert on towel generously sprinkled with confectioners' sugar. Carefully remove foil; trim stiff edges of cake if necessary. While hot, roll cake and towel from narrow end. Cool on wire rack at least 30 minutes.

Unroll cake; remove towel. Beat jelly with fork just enough to soften; spread over cake. Roll up; sprinkle with confectioners' sugar.

10 to 12 servings.

* If using self-rising flour, omit baking powder and salt.

High Altitude (5000 feet) for all-purpose flour: Heat oven to 400°. Grease foil *generously.* Beat eggs on high speed just until soft peaks form, about 3 minutes. Decrease sugar to ¾ cup plus 2 tablespoons and baking powder to ¾ teaspoon. Continue as directed above.

Variations

Prepare Old-fashioned Jelly Roll or Quick Jelly Roll (page 88) except—omit jelly and try one of the following:

CRANBERRY ROLL: Beat 1 cup chilled whipping cream and ¼ cup confectioners' sugar in chilled bowl until stiff. Spread ¾ cup cranberry-orange relish over unrolled cake. Cover relish with whipped cream; roll up cake. Refrigerate.

ICE-CREAM ROLL: Slightly soften 1 pint strawberry, cherry or peppermint ice cream. Spread over unrolled cake. Roll up carefully. Place seam side down on piece of aluminum foil, 18 × 12 inches. Wrap; freeze until firm, about 4 hours. Remove from freezer about 15 minutes before serving.

LEMON CAKE ROLL: Spread Clear Lemon Filling (page 78) over unrolled cake; roll up. Refrigerate at least 1 hour. Serve with sweetened whipped cream if desired.

PEACH CREAM ROLL: Beat 1 cup chilled whipping cream, ¼ cup confectioners' sugar and ½ teaspoon cinnamon in chilled bowl until stiff. Fold in 1 package (10 ounces) frozen sliced peaches, thawed and drained, or 1 cup sliced fresh peaches or nectarines. Spread mixture over unrolled cake; roll up. Refrigerate.

RAINBOW SHERBET ROLL: Beginning at narrow end, spread 1½ cups raspberry sherbet on ⅓ of unrolled cake. Spread 1½ cups orange sherbet on next ⅓ of cake and 1½ cups lime sherbet on remaining cake. Roll up carefully. Place seam side down on piece of aluminum foil, 18 × 12 inches. Wrap; freeze until firm, about 4 hours. Remove from freezer about 15 minutes before serving.

STRAWBERRY CREAM ROLL: Beat ½ cup chilled whipping cream and 2 tablespoons confectioners' sugar in chilled bowl until stiff. Spread over unrolled cake. Sprinkle 2 cups sliced fresh strawberries over whipped cream; roll up cake. Refrigerate. If desired, garnish with sliced strawberries and serve with additional sweetened whipped cream.

CHOCOLATE CREAM ROLL

1 cup cake flour or ¾ cup all-purpose flour*
¼ cup cocoa
1 teaspoon baking powder
¼ teaspoon salt
3 eggs (½ to ⅔ cup)
1 cup granulated sugar
⅓ cup water
1 teaspoon vanilla
1 cup chilled whipping cream
¼ cup confectioners' sugar

Heat oven to 375°. Line jelly roll pan, 15½ × 10½ × 1 inch, with aluminum foil or waxed paper; grease. Stir together flour, cocoa, baking powder and salt; set aside.

Beat eggs in small mixer bowl on high speed until very thick and lemon colored, 3 to 5 minutes. Pour eggs into large mixer bowl; gradually beat in granulated sugar. On low speed, blend in water and vanilla. Gradually add flour mixture, beating just until batter is smooth. Pour into pan, spreading batter to corners.

Bake until wooden pick inserted in center comes out clean, 12 to 15 minutes. Loosen cake from edges of pan; invert on towel sprinkled with confectioners' sugar. Carefully remove foil; trim stiff edges of cake if necessary. While hot, roll cake and towel from narrow end. Cool on wire rack.

One to three hours before serving, unroll cake; remove towel. In chilled bowl, beat whipping cream and ¼ cup confectioners' sugar until stiff. Spread whipped cream over cake. Roll up; sprinkle with confectioners' sugar, or if desired, spread with Chocolate Glaze (page 26).

10 to 12 servings.

* If using self-rising flour, omit baking powder and salt.

High Altitude (5000 feet) for all-purpose flour: Heat oven to 400°. Grease foil *generously.* Beat eggs on high speed *just* until soft peaks form, about 3 minutes. Decrease granulated sugar to ¾ cup plus 2 tablespoons and baking powder to ¾ teaspoon. Continue as directed at left.

Variations
Prepare Chocolate Cream Roll except—try one of the following:

CHERRY ALMOND ROLL: Fold ¼ cup chopped maraschino cherries and ¼ cup diced roasted almonds into the whipped cream.

CHOCOLATE GINGER ROLL: Fold 2 tablespoons finely chopped crystallized ginger or ¼ cup ginger marmalade into the whipped cream.

CHOCOLATE ICE-CREAM ROLL: Omit the whipping cream and ¼ cup confectioners' sugar; slightly soften 1 pint peppermint, coffee or butter pecan ice cream. Spread over cake. Roll up carefully. Place seam side down on piece of aluminum foil, 18 × 12 inches. Wrap; freeze until firm, about 4 hours. Remove from freezer about 15 minutes before serving.

COCONUT-PECAN ROLL: Omit ¼ cup confectioners' sugar; in chilled bowl, beat the whipping cream until stiff. Fold in 1 package (9.9 ounces) coconut-pecan frosting mix.

CHOCOLATE-PISTACHIO ROLL: Add ½ teaspoon cinnamon to flour mixture. Blend in ½ teaspoon almond extract with the water and vanilla. Beat 2 tablespoons cocoa with the whipping cream and confectioners' sugar; fold in 2 tablespoons chopped pistachio nuts. If desired, garnish roll with additional chopped pistachio nuts.

Perfect Pies

Americans can't seem to get enough of pie.
And here are pies for every taste.
The people-pleaser pictured is an unusual
Lemon Slice Pie. And there's
Deep Dish Apple in the oven, Frozen Chocolate
in the freezer, Sweet Potato on the table—
and a smile on every face!

Fruit Pies

It's the inside story that counts with a fruit pie! Some of these put together winning combinations—like cherry-pineapple, blueberry-rhubarb or cranberry-apple. Others star the deservedly popular traditional fillings—apple, peach, berry. Serve them warm, with ice cream, sherbet, yogurt. For fun, vary the pastry (see page 111). One suggestion: pastry-with-nuts for Strawberry Glacé Pie.

DEEP DISH APPLE PIE

Pastry for 9-inch One-crust Pie (page 111)
1½ cups sugar
½ cup all-purpose flour*
1 teaspoon nutmeg
1 teaspoon cinnamon
¼ teaspoon salt
12 cups thinly sliced pared tart apples
   (about 12 medium)
2 tablespoons butter or margarine

Heat oven to 425°. Prepare pastry as directed except—roll into 10-inch square. Fold in half; cut slits near center. Stir together sugar, flour, nutmeg, cinnamon and salt. Mix lightly with apples. Turn into ungreased square pan, 9×9×2 inches. Dot with butter. Cover with pastry; fold edges under just inside edges of pan.

Bake until crust is golden brown and juice begins to bubble through slits in crust, 50 to 60 minutes. Serve warm, and if desired, with cream or ice cream.

* If using self-rising flour, omit salt.

Substitutions

Two packages (20 ounces each) frozen sliced apples, partially thawed, can be substituted for the fresh apples.

Three cans (20 ounces each) pie-sliced apples, drained, can be substituted for the fresh apples; use half the amounts of sugar, flour, nutmeg, cinnamon and salt. Bake 45 minutes.

Pictured on page 91: Ingredients for Lemon Slice Pie (page 96)

CHERRY-PINEAPPLE PIE

Pastry for 9-inch Two-crust Pie (page 111)
1 can (20 ounces) cherry pie filling
1 can (13½ ounces) pineapple tidbits,
   drained
1 tablespoon butter or margarine

Heat oven to 425°. Prepare pastry. Mix cherry pie filling and pineapple tidbits. Turn into pastry-lined pie pan. Dot with butter. Cover with top crust, which has slits cut in it; seal and flute. Cover edge with 2- to 3-inch strip of aluminum foil to prevent excessive browning; remove foil last 15 minutes of baking.

Bake until crust is golden brown and juice begins to bubble through slits in crust, 40 to 45 minutes. Serve warm.

PEACH-APRICOT PIE

Pastry for 9-inch Two-crust Pie (page 111)
5 cups sliced peeled fresh peaches (about
   9 medium)
¼ cup apricot jam or preserves
1 teaspoon lemon juice
¾ cup brown sugar (packed)
¼ cup all-purpose flour
¼ teaspoon cinnamon
2 tablespoons butter or margarine

Heat oven to 425°. Prepare pastry. Toss peaches, apricot jam and lemon juice. Stir together sugar, flour and cinnamon; mix lightly with peach mixture. Turn into pastry-lined pie pan. Dot with butter. Cover with top crust, which has slits cut in it; seal and flute. Cover edge with 2- to 3-inch strip of aluminum foil to prevent excessive browning; remove foil last 15 minutes of baking.

Bake until crust is golden brown and juice begins to bubble through slits in crust, 35 to 45 minutes. Serve warm, and if desired, with ice cream.

PEACH MELBA PIE

Pastry for 9-inch Two-crust Pie (page 111)
½ cup sugar
2 tablespoons cornstarch
*1 can (29 ounces) plus 1 can (17 ounces)
  peach slices, drained (reserve ¼ cup
  syrup)*
*1 package (10 ounces) frozen red rasp-
  berries, thawed and drained (reserve ½
  cup syrup)*
1 tablespoon butter or margarine
Vanilla ice cream
Melba Sauce (below)

Heat oven to 425°. Prepare pastry. Mix sugar, corn-starch and reserved peach syrup in saucepan. Heat to boiling over medium heat, stirring constantly. Boil and stir 1 minute. Pour hot syrup over peach slices. Spread raspberries evenly in pastry-lined pie pan; cover with peach mixture. Dot with butter. Cover with top crust, which has slits cut in it; seal and flute. Cover edge with 2- to 3-inch strip of aluminum foil to prevent excessive browning; remove foil last 15 minutes of baking.

Bake until crust is golden brown and juice begins to bubble through slits in crust, 40 to 45 minutes. Serve warm or cool, with ice cream and Melba Sauce.

Melba Sauce

Combine 2 teaspoons cornstarch, ¼ cup currant jelly and reserved ½ cup raspberry syrup in small saucepan. Heat to boiling over medium heat, stirring constantly. Boil and stir 1 minute. Cool.

NOTE

It's easy to give top crusts a blue-ribbon look. Take your choice—shiny, sugary or glazed. For a shiny top, brush the crust lightly with milk before baking. For a sugary crust, use your fingers or a pastry brush to moisten crust lightly with water, then sprinkle on a little sugar. To glaze a crust, brush lightly with beaten egg (or egg yolk mixed with a little water) before baking.

PEACH BLOSSOM PIE

Pastry for 9-inch Two-crust Pie (page 111)
½ cup sugar
2 tablespoons cornstarch
*1 can (29 ounces) plus 1 can (17 ounces)
  peach slices, drained (reserve ¼ cup
  syrup)*
¼ cup red cinnamon candies
1 tablespoon butter or margarine

Heat oven to 425°. Prepare pastry. Mix sugar, cornstarch and reserved peach syrup in saucepan. Cook over medium heat, stirring constantly, until mixture thickens and boils. Pour hot syrup over peach slices. Add cinnamon candies; mix lightly. Turn into pastry-lined pie pan. Dot with butter. Cover with top crust, which has slits cut in it; seal and flute. Cover edge with 2- to 3-inch strip of aluminum foil to prevent excessive browning; remove foil last 15 minutes of baking.

Bake until crust is golden brown and juice begins to bubble through slits in crust, 40 to 45 minutes. Serve warm, and if desired, with ice cream.

FRESH PURPLE PLUM PIE

Pastry for 9-inch Two-crust Pie (page 111)
¾ cup sugar
2 tablespoons cornstarch
3 cups sliced pitted fresh purple plums
1 tablespoon lemon juice
Vanilla ice cream

Heat oven to 400°. Prepare pastry. Stir together sugar and cornstarch. Mix lightly with plums. Turn into pastry-lined pie pan. Sprinkle with lemon juice. Cover with top crust, which has slits cut in it; seal and flute. Cover edge with 2- to 3-inch strip of aluminum foil to prevent excessive browning; remove foil last 15 minutes of baking.

Bake until crust is golden brown and juice begins to bubble through slits in crust, 50 to 60 minutes. Serve warm, with ice cream.

FRESH PEAR PIE

Pastry for 9-inch Two-crust Pie (page 111)
½ cup sugar
⅓ cup all-purpose flour
½ teaspoon mace (optional)
4 cups sliced pared fresh pears (about 7 medium)
1 tablespoon lemon juice
2 tablespoons butter or margarine

Heat oven to 425°. Prepare pastry. Stir together sugar, flour and mace. Mix lightly with pears. Turn into pastry-lined pie pan. Sprinkle with lemon juice and dot with butter. Cover with top crust, which has slits cut in it; seal and flute. Cover edge with 2- to 3-inch strip of aluminum foil to prevent excessive browning; remove foil last 15 minutes of baking.

Bake until crust is golden brown and juice begins to bubble through slits in crust, 40 to 50 minutes. Serve warm, and if desired, with ice cream or wedges of cheese.

Substitution
Two cans (16 ounces each) sliced pears, drained, can be substituted for the fresh pears; decrease sugar to ⅓ cup.

NOTE

A lattice top on a fruit pie lets all the color and bubbly goodness show through. Here's an easy way to make a lattice top. Start by rolling out a circle of pastry as you would for a standard top crust. Now—cut the pastry into strips, each about ½ inch wide. Place 5 to 7 strips across the filling in the pie pan, then criss-cross these with another 5 to 7 strips arranged diagonally on top of the first ones. You can twist the strips of pastry before you put them down on the pie filling if you want to achieve a fancy spiral design. Trim off the ends of the strips so they're even with the side of the pie pan and fold the edge of the lower crust up over the ends of the strips. Build up a high edge so juices won't overflow. Seal and flute.

FRESH BERRY PIE

Pastry for 9-inch Two-crust Pie (page 111)
1 cup sugar
¼ cup all-purpose flour
4 cups fresh berries (boysenberries, blackberries, loganberries or raspberries)
2 tablespoons butter or margarine
1 to 2 teaspoons sugar

Heat oven to 425°. Prepare pastry. Mix 1 cup sugar and the flour. Toss lightly with berries. Turn into pastry-lined pie pan. Dot with butter. Cover with top crust, which has slits cut in it; seal and flute. Moisten top crust lightly with water; sprinkle evenly with 1 to 2 teaspoons sugar. Cover edge with 2- to 3-inch strip of aluminum foil to prevent excessive browning; remove foil last 15 minutes of baking.

Bake until crust is golden brown and juice begins to bubble through slits in crust, 35 to 45 minutes. Serve warm, and if desired, with ice cream.

FRESH CRANBERRY-APPLE PIE

Pastry for 9-inch Two-crust Pie (page 111)
1¾ to 2 cups sugar
¼ cup all-purpose flour
3 cups sliced pared tart apples (about 3 medium)
2 cups fresh or thawed frozen cranberries
2 tablespoons butter or margarine

Heat oven to 425°. Prepare pastry. Mix sugar and flour. Alternate layers of apples, cranberries and sugar mixture in pastry-lined pie pan, beginning and ending with apples. Dot with butter. Cover with top crust, which has slits cut in it; seal and flute. Cover edge with 2- to 3-inch strip of aluminum foil to prevent excessive browning; remove foil last 15 minutes of baking.

Bake until crust is golden brown and juice begins to bubble through slits in crust, 40 to 50 minutes. Serve warm, and if desired, with ice cream.

Fresh Cranberry-Apple Pie (page 94)

BLUEBERRY-RHUBARB PIE

Pastry for 9-inch Two-crust Pie (page 111)
1⅓ cups sugar
⅓ cup all-purpose flour or 3 tablespoons
  cornstarch
½ teaspoon grated orange peel (optional)
2 cups cut-up fresh rhubarb (about 1
  pound)
2 cups fresh or thawed frozen blueberries
2 tablespoons butter or margarine
Sugar

Heat oven to 425°. Prepare pastry. Stir together 1⅓ cups sugar, the flour and orange peel. Turn rhubarb into pastry-lined pie pan; sprinkle with half of the sugar mixture. Repeat with blueberries and remaining sugar mixture. Dot with butter. Cover with top crust, which has slits cut in it; sprinkle with sugar. Seal and flute. Cover edge with 2- to 3-inch strip of aluminum foil to prevent excessive browning; remove foil last 15 minutes of baking.

Bake until crust is golden brown and juice begins to bubble through slits in crust, 40 to 50 minutes. Serve warm.

Substitution
One package (16 ounces) frozen rhubarb, partially thawed, can be substituted for the fresh rhubarb; decrease sugar to 1 cup.

Variation
STRAWBERRY-RHUBARB PIE: Substitute 2 cups fresh strawberries for the blueberries.

NOTE

Advance-planning tip: Fruit pies freeze well. If you bake pies before freezing them, you'll prevent soggy crusts. To thaw, let wrapped pies stand at room temperature for 30 minutes. Then remove freezer wrap and heat pie in a 350° oven for 30 minutes. Freeze empty pie shells unbaked, then bake without thawing. All pie-makers please note: Custard pies, cream pies and pies with a meringue topping do not freeze well.

STRAWBERRY GLACE PIE

9-inch Baked Pie Shell (page 111)
6 cups fresh strawberries (about 1½ quarts)
1 cup sugar
3 tablespoons cornstarch
½ cup water
1 package (3 ounces) cream cheese, softened

Bake pie shell. Cool. Mash enough berries to measure 1 cup. Mix sugar and cornstarch; stir in water and crushed berries. Cook over medium heat, stirring constantly, until mixture thickens and boils. Boil and stir 1 minute. Cool. Beat cream cheese until smooth; spread on bottom of pie shell. Fill shell with remaining whole berries; pour cooked berry mixture over top. Refrigerate until set, about 3 hours.

Variation
RASPBERRY GLACE PIE: Substitute 6 cups fresh raspberries for the strawberries.

LEMON SLICE PIE

2 large lemons
2 cups sugar
1 teaspoon salt
Pastry for 9-inch Two-crust Pie (page 111)
4 eggs

Grate 2 teaspoons peel from lemons; reserve. Pare lemons, removing all white membrane. Cut lemons into very thin slices. Place slices in bowl; add reserved lemon peel, the sugar and salt and set aside.

Heat oven to 425°. Prepare pastry. Beat eggs thoroughly. Pour over lemon slices and sugar; mix well. Turn into pastry-lined pie pan. Cover with top crust, which has slits cut in it; seal and flute. Cover edge with 2- to 3-inch strip of aluminum foil to prevent excessive browning; remove foil last 15 minutes of baking.

Bake until knife inserted near edge of pie comes out clean, 45 to 50 minutes. Cool.

CREAM, CUSTARD AND MERINGUE PIES

You'll find old favorites and new variations here. What about peanut pie instead of pecan? Or sweet potato instead of pumpkin pie? Cream and custard fillings spoil easily at room temperatures. Always refrigerate them, but do not freeze.

COCONUT CREAM PIE

9-inch Baked Pie Shell (page 111)
⅔ cup sugar
¼ cup cornstarch
½ teaspoon salt
3 cups milk
4 egg yolks, slightly beaten
2 tablespoons butter or margarine, softened
2 teaspoons vanilla
¾ cup flaked coconut
Sweetened whipped cream
¼ cup flaked coconut

Bake pie shell. Cool. Mix sugar, cornstarch and salt in medium saucepan. Gradually stir in milk. Cook over medium heat, stirring constantly, until mixture thickens and boils. Boil and stir 1 minute. Gradually stir at least half of the hot mixture into egg yolks. Blend into hot mixture in pan. Boil and stir 1 minute. Remove from heat; stir in butter and vanilla. Stir in ¾ cup coconut. Pour into pie shell; press plastic wrap onto filling. Refrigerate at least 2 hours. Remove plastic wrap; top pie with whipped cream and sprinkle with ¼ cup coconut.

Variation
BANANA CREAM PIE: Increase vanilla to 1 tablespoon plus 1 teaspoon and omit coconut. Cover filling in saucepan with waxed paper; cool to room temperature. Arrange a layer of sliced bananas (2 large) ½ inch deep in baked pie shell or Graham Cracker Crust (page 99); pour in cooled filling.

IMPERIAL CHERRY CREAM PIE

9-inch Baked Pie Shell (page 111)
1 package (about 3½ ounces) vanilla instant pudding and pie filling
1 envelope (about 2 ounces) dessert topping mix
1½ cups milk
1 can (21 ounces) cherry pie filling, drained (reserve syrup)

Bake pie shell. Cool. Blend pudding, topping mix and milk in large mixer bowl on low speed. Beat on high speed until soft peaks form, about 3 minutes. Fold in pie filling. Pour into pie shell. Refrigerate until firm, about 2 hours. Serve topped with reserved syrup.

PECAN PIE

Pastry for 9-inch One-crust Pie (page 111)
3 eggs
⅔ cup sugar
½ teaspoon salt
⅓ cup butter or margarine, melted
1 cup dark or light corn syrup
1 cup pecan halves or broken pecans

Heat oven to 375°. Prepare pastry. Beat eggs, sugar, salt, butter and syrup thoroughly. Stir in pecans. Pour into pastry-lined pie pan. Bake until filling is set and pastry is golden brown, 40 to 50 minutes. Serve warm or cool.

Variations
HONEY PECAN PIE: Substitute ½ cup honey for ½ cup of the corn syrup.

PEANUT PIE: Substitute 1 cup salted peanuts for the pecans.

TOASTED SUNFLOWER NUT PIE: Substitute 1 cup toasted sunflower nuts for the pecans.

PUMPKIN PIE

Pastry for 9-inch One-crust Pie (page 111)
2 eggs
1 can (16 ounces) pumpkin
¾ cup sugar
½ teaspoon salt
1 teaspoon cinnamon
½ teaspoon ginger
¼ teaspoon cloves
1⅔ cups evaporated milk or light cream

Heat oven to 425°. Prepare pastry. Beat eggs slightly with rotary beater; beat in remaining ingredients. Pour into pastry-lined pie pan. (To prevent spills, place pie pan on oven rack or on open oven door when filling with pumpkin mixture.) Bake 15 minutes.

Reduce oven temperature to 350°. Bake until knife inserted in center comes out clean, 45 minutes. Cool. If desired, serve with sweetened whipped cream.

Variations

CARROT PIE: Cook about 1½ pounds carrots until very tender. Drain thoroughly; mash enough to measure 2 cups. Substitute mashed carrots for the pumpkin.

SQUASH PIE: Substitute 2 cups mashed cooked winter squash for the pumpkin.

SWEET POTATO PIE: Substitute 2 cups mashed cooked sweet potato for the pumpkin.

NOTE

Little additions can create a big effect. For an enjoyable taste complement to pumpkin pie, add a helping of shredded orange peel or chopped nuts to the pastry (see page 111). Or top each serving with a delicious dollop of Caramel Fluff Topping or Honey-Ginger Topping (see page 71). Treat the teen-age crowd by introducing them to the super taste of pumpkin pie with Peanut Crunch Topping: Just fold ¼ cup finely crushed peanut brittle into 1 cup whipped cream. A delectable topping that's easy as pie!

SOUR CREAM-RAISIN PIE

9-inch Baked Pie Shell (page 111)
1 tablespoon plus 1½ teaspoons cornstarch
1 cup plus 2 tablespoons sugar
¼ teaspoon salt
¾ teaspoon nutmeg
1½ cups dairy sour cream
3 egg yolks
1½ cups raisins
1 tablespoon lemon juice
Brown Sugar Meringue (below)

Bake pie shell. Cool. Heat oven to 400°. Mix cornstarch, sugar, salt and nutmeg in medium saucepan. Blend in sour cream. Stir in egg yolks, raisins and lemon juice. Cook over medium heat, stirring constantly, until mixture thickens and boils. Boil and stir 1 minute. Pour into pie shell.

Heap meringue onto hot pie filling; spread over filling, carefully sealing meringue to edge of crust to prevent shrinking or weeping. Swirl or pull up points for a decorative top. Bake until delicate brown, about 10 minutes. Cool away from draft.

Brown Sugar Meringue

3 egg whites
¼ teaspoon cream of tartar
6 tablespoons brown sugar
½ teaspoon vanilla

Beat egg whites and cream of tartar until foamy. Beat in brown sugar, 1 tablespoon at a time; continue beating until stiff and glossy. Do not underbeat. Beat in vanilla.

LEMON MERINGUE PIE

9-inch Baked Pie Shell (page 111)
1½ cups sugar
⅓ cup plus 1 tablespoon cornstarch
1½ cups water
3 egg yolks, slightly beaten
3 tablespoons butter or margarine
2 teaspoons grated lemon peel
½ cup lemon juice
2 drops yellow food color (optional)
Meringue (below)

Bake pie shell. Cool. Heat oven to 400°. Mix sugar and cornstarch in medium saucepan. Gradually stir in water. Cook over medium heat, stirring constantly, until mixture thickens and boils. Boil and stir 1 minute. Gradually stir at least half of the hot mixture into egg yolks. Blend into hot mixture in pan. Boil and stir 1 minute. Remove from heat; stir in butter, lemon peel, lemon juice and food color. Pour into pie shell.

Heap meringue onto hot pie filling; spread over filling, carefully sealing meringue to edge of crust to prevent shrinking or weeping. Bake until delicate brown, about 10 minutes. Cool away from draft.

Meringue
3 egg whites
¼ teaspoon cream of tartar
6 tablespoons sugar
½ teaspoon vanilla

Beat egg whites and cream of tartar until foamy. Beat in sugar, 1 tablespoon at a time; continue beating until stiff and glossy. Do not underbeat. Beat in vanilla.

Refrigerated and Frozen Pies

Here's where you can really get creative with crusts! Try graham cracker or cookie crusts, meringue shells, butter crunch, even a toasted coconut crust. Mix and match them to different fillings. Your choice includes such scrumptious flavors as mandarin orange, pineapple mallow, ginger ice cream. These cool customers have all the virtues of other refrigerated desserts—plus the universal appeal of pie. You can make them ahead of time; they'll keep their composure in refrigerator or freezer.

MANDARIN ORANGE FLUFF PIE

Graham Cracker Crust (below) or Butter
   Crunch Crust (page 104)
1 can (11 ounces) mandarin orange
   segments, drained (reserve syrup)
1 package (3 ounces) orange-flavored gelatin
1 teaspoon grated lemon peel
3 tablespoons lemon juice
1 cup chilled whipping cream

Bake pie crust. Cool. Add enough water to reserved syrup to measure 1¼ cups. Heat to boiling in small saucepan. Remove from heat; stir in gelatin until dissolved. Stir in lemon peel and juice. Refrigerate, stirring occasionally, until mixture mounds slightly when dropped from a spoon.

In chilled bowl, beat whipping cream until stiff. Fold gelatin mixture and mandarin orange segments into whipped cream. Pour into crust. Refrigerate until set, about 2 hours. Garnish with sweetened whipped cream and maraschino cherries if desired.

Graham Cracker Crust
Heat oven to 350°. Mix 1½ cups graham cracker crumbs (about 20 squares), 3 tablespoons sugar and ⅓ cup butter or margarine, melted. Press mixture firmly and evenly against bottom and side of ungreased 9-inch pie pan. Bake 10 minutes. Cool.

LIME CHIFFON PIE

9-inch Baked Pie Shell (page 111), Toasted
   Coconut Crust (page 106) or Butter Crunch
   Crust (page 104)
½ cup sugar
1 envelope unflavored gelatin
4 eggs, separated
⅔ cup water
⅓ cup lime juice
1 tablespoon grated lime peel
Few drops green food color
½ teaspoon cream of tartar
½ cup sugar

Bake pie shell. Cool. Stir together ½ cup sugar
and the gelatin in small saucepan. Blend egg yolks,
water and lime juice; stir into sugar mixture. Cook
over medium heat, stirring constantly, just until
mixture boils. Stir in lime peel and food color.
Refrigerate, stirring occasionally, until mixture
mounds slightly when dropped from a spoon.

Beat egg whites and cream of tartar until foamy.
Beat in ½ cup sugar, 1 tablespoon at a time; continue beating until stiff and glossy. Do not underbeat. Fold lime mixture into meringue; pile into
pie shell. Refrigerate until set, at least 3 hours. If
desired, serve with sweetened whipped cream.

Variations

LEMON CHIFFON PIE: Substitute lemon juice and
lemon peel for the lime juice and lime peel. Omit
food color.

ORANGE CHIFFON PIE: Substitute 1 cup orange juice
for the water and lime juice, orange peel for the
lime peel. Omit food color.

PUMPKIN CHIFFON PIE

9-inch Baked Pie Shell (page 111)
⅔ cup brown sugar (packed)
1 tablespoon unflavored gelatin
½ teaspoon each salt, ginger, cinnamon and
   nutmeg
1¼ cups canned or mashed cooked pumpkin
3 eggs, separated
½ cup milk
¼ teaspoon cream of tartar
½ cup granulated sugar
Sweetened whipped cream
Caramelized Almonds (below)

Bake pie shell. Cool. Mix brown sugar, gelatin,
salt and spices in saucepan. Blend pumpkin, egg
yolks and milk; stir into sugar mixture. Cook over
medium heat, stirring constantly, just until mixture
boils. Refrigerate, stirring occasionally, until mixture mounds slightly when dropped from a spoon.

Beat egg whites and cream of tartar until foamy.
Beat in granulated sugar, 1 tablespoon at a time;
continue beating until stiff and glossy. Do not
underbeat. Fold pumpkin mixture into meringue;
pile into pie shell. Refrigerate until set, at least
3 hours. Garnish with whipped cream and sprinkle with Caramelized Almonds.

Caramelized Almonds

Cook 2 tablespoons sugar in skillet over low heat,
stirring constantly, until sugar melts and turns light
brown. Stir in ½ cup sliced almonds. Pour into
buttered shallow pan; let set. Break into pieces.

NOTE

Chiffon pies, light and airy delights, freeze beau-
tifully. Freeze them unwrapped, then wrap and
store. Don't keep them for more than 1 month,
please! To thaw, remove from freezer and let
stand in refrigerator for 1½ to 2 hours. A few of
these stored away add up to real frozen assets in
the dessert department.

Pictured from top: Mandarin Orange Fluff Pie (page 99), Pink Peppermint Pie (page 103), Pumpkin Chiffon Pie (page 100)

DIVINE LIME PIE

Meringue Pie Shell (right)
4 egg yolks
½ cup sugar
¼ teaspoon salt
⅓ cup fresh lime juice (2 to 3 limes)
2 or 3 drops green food color
1 cup chilled whipping cream
1 tablespoon grated lime peel

Bake meringue shell. Cool. Beat egg yolks in small mixer bowl until light and lemon colored. Mix sugar, salt, lime juice and egg yolks in saucepan. Cook over medium heat, stirring constantly, until mixture thickens, about 5 minutes. Cool; stir in food color.

In chilled bowl, beat whipping cream until stiff. Fold in lime mixture and grated lime peel. Pile into meringue shell. Refrigerate at least 4 hours. If desired, garnish with sweetened whipped cream and grated lime peel or lime twists.

Meringue Pie Shell
Heat oven to 275°. Beat 4 egg whites and ¼ teaspoon cream of tartar until foamy. Beat in 1 cup sugar, 1 tablespoon at a time; continue beating until stiff and glossy, about 10 minutes. Do not underbeat. Pile into lightly greased 9-inch pie pan, pressing meringue up against side of pan. Bake 1 hour. Turn off oven; leave meringue in oven with door closed 1 hour. Remove from oven; cool away from draft.

PERFECT PIES 103

CHERRY JUBILEE CHIFFON PIE

9-inch Baked Pie Shell (page 111)
1 can (16 ounces) pitted dark sweet cherries, drained (reserve syrup)
1 package (3 ounces) cherry-flavored gelatin
1 envelope (about 2 ounces) dessert topping mix

Bake pie shell. Cool. Combine reserved syrup and enough water to measure 1½ cups in saucepan; stir in gelatin. Cook over medium heat, stirring constantly, just until mixture boils. Refrigerate, stirring occasionally, until mixture mounds slightly when dropped from a spoon. Cut cherries in half. Prepare topping mix as directed on package. Fold in gelatin mixture and cherries. Pile into pie shell. Refrigerate until set, at least 3 hours.

PINK PEPPERMINT PIE

Chocolate Cookie Crust (right)
24 large marshmallows
½ cup milk
1 teaspoon vanilla
⅛ teaspoon salt
6 drops peppermint extract
6 drops red food color
1 cup chilled whipping cream or 1 envelope (about 2 ounces) dessert topping mix
2 tablespoons crushed peppermint candy

Bake pie crust. Cool. Heat marshmallows and milk in saucepan over low heat, stirring constantly, just until marshmallows are melted. Remove from heat; stir in vanilla, salt, extract and food color. Refrigerate, stirring occasionally, until mixture mounds slightly when dropped from a spoon.

In chilled bowl, beat whipping cream until stiff. (If using dessert topping mix, prepare as directed on package.) Stir marshmallow mixture until blended; fold into whipped cream. Pour into crust. Refrigerate about 12 hours. Just before serving, sprinkle with crushed candy.

GRASSHOPPER PIE

Chocolate Cookie Crust (below)
3 cups miniature marshmallows or 32 large marshmallows
½ cup milk
1½ cups chilled whipping cream
¼ cup green crème de menthe
3 tablespoons white crème de cacao
Few drops green food color (optional)

Bake pie crust. Cool. Heat marshmallows and milk in saucepan over low heat, stirring constantly, just until marshmallows are melted. Refrigerate, stirring occasionally, until mixture mounds slightly when dropped from a spoon.

In chilled bowl, beat whipping cream until stiff. Stir marshmallow mixture until blended; stir in crème de menthe and crème de cacao. Fold into whipped cream. Fold in food color. Pour into pie crust. If desired, sprinkle grated semisweet chocolate over top. Refrigerate at least 4 hours.

Chocolate Cookie Crust
Heat oven to 350°. Mix 1½ cups chocolate wafer crumbs and ¼ cup butter or margarine, melted, in ungreased 9-inch pie pan. Press evenly against bottom and side of pan. Bake 10 minutes. Cool.

Variation
BRANDY ALEXANDER PIE: Substitute ¼ cup dark crème de cacao for the crème de menthe and 3 tablespoons brandy for the white crème de cacao. Omit green food color.

PINEAPPLE MALLOW PIE

Butter Crunch Crust (below)
32 large marshmallows or 3 cups miniature
    marshmallows
1 can (20 ounces) crushed pineapple,
    drained (reserve ½ cup syrup)
1 cup chilled whipping cream or 1 envelope
    (about 2 ounces) dessert topping mix
1 teaspoon vanilla
¼ teaspoon salt

Bake pie crust. Cool. Heat marshmallows and reserved syrup in saucepan over low heat, stirring constantly, just until marshmallows are melted. Refrigerate, stirring occasionally, until mixture mounds slightly when dropped from a spoon.

In chilled bowl, beat whipping cream until stiff. (If using dessert topping mix, prepare as directed on package.) Stir marshmallow mixture until blended; fold into whipped cream. Reserve ½ cup crushed pineapple for garnish; fold remaining pineapple, the vanilla and salt into marshmallow-cream mixture. Pour into crust; garnish with reserved pineapple. Refrigerate until set, 2 to 3 hours.

Butter Crunch Crust
¾ cup all-purpose flour*
¼ cup plus 2 tablespoons butter or
    margarine, softened
3 tablespoons brown sugar
¼ cup finely chopped nuts

Heat oven to 400°. Mix all ingredients with hands until crumbly. Press firmly and evenly against bottom and side of ungreased 9-inch pie pan. Bake until light brown, 10 to 15 minutes. Cool.

* Do not use self-rising flour in this recipe. If using quick-mixing flour, add 1 tablespoon milk.

CHOCOLATE ALMOND CRUNCH PIE

Almond Crunch Crust (below)
1½ cups miniature marshmallows or
    16 large marshmallows
½ cup milk
1 bar (8 ounces) milk chocolate
1 cup chilled whipping cream

Bake pie crust. Cool. Heat marshmallows, milk and chocolate in saucepan over low heat, stirring constantly, just until chocolate and marshmallows are melted and mixture is smooth. Refrigerate, stirring occasionally, until mixture mounds slightly when dropped from a spoon.

In chilled bowl, beat whipping cream until stiff. Fold chocolate mixture into whipped cream. Pour into pie crust. Refrigerate until set, about 8 hours.

8 to 10 servings.

Almond Crunch Crust
Heat oven to 400°. Mix 1½ cups ground blanched almonds, 3 tablespoons sugar and 2 tablespoons butter or margarine, softened. Press mixture firmly and evenly against bottom and side of ungreased 9-inch pie pan. Bake 6 to 8 minutes. Cool.

MERINGUE PARFAIT PIES

For each pie, bake Meringue Pie Shell (page 102). Cool. Spoon or scoop 1 quart ice cream into meringue shell. Top with sauce and serve immediately. Or place in freezer; top with sauce just before serving.

☐ Fill meringue shell with chocolate revel ice cream and top with Butter Praline Sauce (page 140).

☐ Fill meringue shell with pink peppermint ice cream and top with Fudge Sauce (page 140).

☐ Fill meringue shell with vanilla ice cream and top with Dark Sweet Cherry Topping (page 50).

BUTTER CRUNCH ALASKA PIE

Butter Crunch Crust (page 104)
3. pints any flavor ice cream, slightly
    softened
3 egg whites
¼ teaspoon cream of tartar
6 tablespoons sugar
½ teaspoon vanilla

Bake pie crust. Cool. Pack ice cream in crust. Freeze until firm, about 8 hours.

Move oven rack to lowest position. Heat oven to 500°. Beat egg whites and cream of tartar until foamy. Beat in sugar, 1 tablespoon at a time; continue beating until stiff and glossy. Do not underbeat. Beat in vanilla. Heap meringue over ice cream; spread over ice cream, carefully sealing to edge of crust.

Bake until meringue is light brown, 3 to 5 minutes. Let stand 10 to 15 minutes before serving to make cutting easier.

GINGER ICE-CREAM PIE

1½ cups gingersnap crumbs
¼ cup butter or margarine, melted
1 quart vanilla ice cream
¼ cup chopped crystallized ginger

Heat oven to 350°. Mix gingersnap crumbs and butter. Reserve 1 to 2 tablespoons crumb mixture for garnish. Press remaining crumb mixture firmly and evenly against bottom and side of ungreased 9-inch pie pan. Bake 10 minutes. Cool.

Soften ice cream slightly; stir in ginger. Spoon into pie crust; sprinkle reserved crumb mixture over top. Freeze until firm, about 4 hours. Remove from freezer 10 to 15 minutes before serving.

PUMPKIN ICE-CREAM PIE

9-inch Baked Pie Shell (page 111) or Graham
    Cracker Crust (page 99)
1 pint vanilla ice cream
2 to 3 tablespoons chopped crystallized
    ginger
1 cup canned or mashed cooked pumpkin
1 cup sugar
1 teaspoon pumpkin pie spice
½ teaspoon ground ginger
½ teaspoon salt
½ cup chopped walnuts
1 cup chilled whipping cream

Bake pie shell. Cool. Soften ice cream slightly; quickly fold in crystallized ginger. Spread in pie shell. Freeze until ice cream is solid.

Stir together pumpkin, sugar, pumpkin pie spice, ground ginger, salt and walnuts. In chilled bowl, beat whipping cream until stiff; fold into pumpkin mixture. Pour over ice cream in pie shell. Freeze several hours. Remove from freezer 10 to 15 minutes before serving.

CRUNCHY NUT ICE-CREAM PIE

1½ cups ground pecans, walnuts or almonds
3 tablespoons sugar
2 tablespoons butter or margarine, softened
1 quart vanilla ice cream
Strawberry Sauce (page 141) or Rich
    Chocolate Sauce (page 140)

Heat oven to 400°. Mix nuts, sugar and butter. Press firmly and evenly against bottom and side of ungreased 9-inch pie pan. Bake 6 to 8 minutes. Cool.

Spoon or scoop ice cream into pie shell. Freeze until firm, about 4 hours. Remove from freezer 10 to 15 minutes before serving. Cut into wedges; spoon Strawberry Sauce over each serving.

TOASTED COCONUT ICE-CREAM PIE

Toasted Coconut Crust (below)
1 quart vanilla ice cream
1 package (10 ounces) frozen strawberries
  or raspberries, thawed

Bake pie crust. Cool. Spoon or scoop ice cream into pie crust. Freeze until firm, about 4 hours. Remove from freezer 10 to 15 minutes before serving. Cut into wedges; spoon berries over each serving.

Toasted Coconut Crust

Heat oven to 300°. Mix 3 tablespoons butter or margarine, melted, and 1 can (3½ ounces) flaked coconut (1½ cups). Press firmly and evenly against bottom and side of ungreased 9-inch pie pan. Bake until golden brown, 20 to 25 minutes.

FROZEN LEMON PIE

Graham Cracker Crust (page 99)
3 eggs, separated
½ cup sugar
1 cup chilled whipping cream or 1 envelope
  (about 2 ounces) dessert topping mix
2 teaspoons grated lemon peel
¼ cup lemon juice

Bake pie crust as directed except—reserve 2 tablespoons crumbs for garnish. Beat egg whites until foamy. Beat in sugar, 1 tablespoon at a time; continue beating until stiff and glossy. Do not underbeat. Beat egg yolks until thick and lemon colored; fold into meringue. In chilled bowl, beat whipping cream until stiff. (If using dessert topping mix, prepare as directed on package.) Fold whipped cream, lemon peel and juice into egg yolk-meringue mixture. Pour into crust; sprinkle reserved crumbs over top. Freeze until firm, about 4 hours. Remove from freezer 10 to 15 minutes before serving.

FROZEN CHOCOLATE PIE

9-inch Baked Pie Shell (page 111)
1 cup confectioners' sugar
½ cup butter or margarine, softened
6 ounces semisweet chocolate, melted and
  cooled
1 teaspoon vanilla
4 eggs
1 cup chilled whipping cream
2 tablespoons confectioners' sugar

Bake pie shell. Cool. Blend 1 cup confectioners' sugar and the butter in small mixer bowl on low speed until fluffy. Blend in chocolate and vanilla. On high speed, beat in eggs, one at a time, beating thoroughly after each addition. Pour into pie shell. Freeze several hours. Remove from freezer 10 to 15 minutes before serving, then serve pie immediately.

In chilled bowl, beat whipping cream and 2 tablespoons confectioners' sugar until stiff. Pile onto pie, and if desired, garnish with chocolate curls.

8 to 10 servings.

NOTE

Here are two simple but successful ways to melt chocolate squares or pieces. You can melt them in a heavy saucepan over low heat—just make sure the pan is heavy and the heat low. This one's a little more trouble but there's no danger of scorching: Melt chocolate in small heatproof bowl or top of double boiler over hot—not boiling—water.

Equivalent Quantities:

1 package (6 ounces) semisweet chocolate pieces	= 1 cup
1 square (1 ounce) unsweetened chocolate	= 1 envelope (1 ounce) premelted chocolate
1 package (8 ounces) unsweetened chocolate	= 8 squares (1 ounce each)

Turnovers and Tarts

What a varied cast of characters this is! Some are casual enough to pop into lunchboxes; others appear as formal desserts. What could be more sophisticated, for instance, than French Pear Tart? Our flaky puff pastries rival what you might find in French restaurants—but they're very easy to make.

APPLE SQUARES WITH CARDAMOM SAUCE

Pastry for 9-inch Two-crust Pie (page 111)
2 or 3 medium apples, pared and sliced
8 teaspoons sugar
1 tablespoon butter or margarine
Cardamom Sauce (below)

Heat oven to 425°. Prepare pastry as directed except—roll each round on floured cloth-covered board into rectangle, 16×8 inches. Cut each rectangle crosswise into 4 strips, 8×4 inches. Place 6 or 7 apple slices on half of each strip; sprinkle with 1 teaspoon sugar and dot with butter. Moisten edges of strips with water; fold pastry over apple slices and press edges together with floured fork to seal. Cut slits or apple shape on top of each pastry square. Place on ungreased baking sheet. Bake until golden brown, 15 to 20 minutes. Serve warm with Cardamom Sauce.

8 squares.

Cardamom Sauce
⅔ cup brown sugar (packed)
1 tablespoon cornstarch
⅔ cup water
1 tablespoon lemon juice
2 teaspoons butter or margarine
⅛ teaspoon cardamom or cinnamon

Mix sugar and cornstarch in small saucepan; stir in remaining ingredients. Heat to boiling, stirring constantly. Boil and stir 1 minute. Serve warm.

About 1 cup.

FRENCH PEAR TART

Pastry for 9-inch One-crust Pie (page 111)
½ cup currant jelly, melted
2 or 3 fresh pears, pared and thinly sliced
1 to 2 tablespoons brown sugar
Dairy sour cream or sweetened whipped
* cream*

Heat oven to 425°. Prepare pastry as directed except—roll on floured cloth-covered board into rectangle, 12×10 inches. Trim edges to make even. Place rectangle on ungreased baking sheet. Brush ½-inch edge around rectangle with water; fold moistened edges onto rectangle and press lightly with floured fork.

Brush half of the currant jelly on rectangle up to folded edges. Arrange pear slices in rows, overlapping slices, on jelly-covered pastry. Sprinkle sugar over slices.

Bake until pastry is golden brown, 20 to 25 minutes. Brush remaining currant jelly on slices and pastry edges. Cut into 6 squares; serve warm or cool, topped with sour cream.

6 servings.

Variation

FRENCH BANANA TART: Substitute apricot jam, sieved, for the currant jelly and 3 or 4 bananas, sliced, for the pears. Dip slices into lemon juice before arranging on pastry.

NOTE

Tips on buying pears: The bell-shaped Bartlett is the most common variety of summer pear. It's clear yellow when ripe, available from July through November. The oval-shaped Anjou is the most popular winter pear. It can be yellow, yellow-green or green when ripe. To test, press gently at stem end; it should yield to pressure. Other winter varieties: Bosc, Comice and Seckel. If pears are too firm, let them stand at room temperature for a few days. Pears are best for cooking and baking when slightly underripe and firm.

Summer Jewel Tarts (page 109), Caramel Butter Tarts (page 110), Apple Squares (page 107), Lemon Curd Tarts (page 109), Strawberry-Cheese Tartlets (page 112), Tart Shells (page 111)

SUMMER JEWEL TARTS

Tart Shells (page 111)
2 cups fresh seedless green grapes
1 cup fresh raspberries or sliced strawberries
1 cup fresh blueberries
1½ cups sliced peeled fresh peaches (about 2 medium)
½ cup sliced banana
Orange Glacé (below)
Whole strawberries

Bake tart shells. Cool. Toss grapes, raspberries, blueberries, peaches and banana with Orange Glacé. Fill tart shells with fruit mixture. Garnish each with strawberries. Refrigerate.

8 tarts.

Orange Glacé
Stir together ½ cup sugar, 2 tablespoons cornstarch and ⅛ teaspoon salt in saucepan. Stir in ⅔ cup orange juice and ⅓ cup water. Cook over medium heat, stirring constantly, until mixture thickens and boils. Boil and stir 1 minute. Cool.

LEMON CURD TARTS

Tart Shells (page 111)
3 eggs
1 cup sugar
¾ cup butter or margarine, softened
1 tablespoon grated lemon peel
½ cup lemon juice

Bake tart shells. Cool. Beat eggs slightly in small saucepan; stir in remaining ingredients. Cook over low heat, stirring constantly, until mixture coats a metal spoon, 8 to 10 minutes. Cool. Divide mixture among tart shells. Refrigerate. If desired, garnish tarts with sweetened whipped cream.

8 tarts.

SWEDISH ALMOND TARTS

Foil Tart Shells (below)
2 egg whites
¼ cup sugar
½ cup ground blanched almonds
6 tablespoons raspberry jam

Heat oven to 375°. Prepare tart shells; reserve pastry scraps.

Beat egg whites until foamy. Gradually add sugar; beat until stiff peaks form. Fold in almonds. Spread 1 tablespoon jam over bottom of each tart shell; spoon in ⅓ cup almond filling and spread evenly.

Roll pastry scraps; cut into ¼-inch strips. Crisscross 2 strips on each almond-filled tart. Place on baking sheet. Bake until filling is delicate golden brown, 20 to 25 minutes. Cool; remove foil.

6 tarts.

Foil Tart Shells
Prepare pastry as directed for 9-inch One-crust Pie (page 111) except—divide into 6 equal parts. Place each part on 5-inch square of heavy-duty aluminum foil; roll each into circle, about 5 inches in diameter. Trim edges of foil and pastry to make neat circle. Shape foil and pastry together into tart by turning up 1½-inch edge; flute.

NOTE

Some "nuts and bolts" information about nuts. They're all high in energy value and contain some vegetable protein. So you're really adding extra nutrition when you sprinkle them as toppings or add them to pie crusts. Unshelled nuts can become rancid, so after you've opened a can, package or jar, store the remaining nuts in the refrigerator. To store them for longer periods of time, put them in the freezer in tightly covered containers or plastic bags.

To chop nuts by hand, use a French knife. Hold down the point with one hand; with the other hand, rock the knife up and down, swiveling from side to side as you do so.

CARAMEL BUTTER TARTS

1 cup all-purpose flour
½ cup butter or margarine, softened
¼ cup confectioners' sugar
3 tablespoons butter or margarine, softened
1 cup brown sugar (packed)
1 egg, beaten
½ teaspoon salt
¼ cup currants or cut-up raisins

Heat oven to 350°. With hands, mix flour, ½ cup butter and the confectioners' sugar thoroughly. Divide into 24 parts. Press each part against bottom and side of ungreased small muffin cup (1¾ inches in diameter). Do not allow pastry to extend above tops of cups.

Mix 3 tablespoons butter and the brown sugar. Stir in egg, salt and currants. Spoon scant tablespoonful mixture into each cup. Bake until light brown, about 20 minutes. Invert muffin pan to remove tarts. After 15 minutes, turn tarts right sides up on wire rack; cool.

24 tarts.

Note: Tarts can be wrapped and frozen up to 3 months. To thaw, let stand unwrapped at room temperature 30 minutes.

FRESH RASPBERRY TURNOVER

¼ cup sugar
1 tablespoon plus 1½ teaspoons cornstarch
1 pint fresh raspberries (2 cups)
Pastry (below)
Frosty Glaze (below)

Mix sugar, cornstarch and raspberries in saucepan. Cook over medium heat, stirring constantly, until mixture thickens and boils. Boil and stir 1 minute. Cool.

Heat oven to 425°. Prepare pastry; roll on lightly floured cloth-covered board into 14-inch circle. Fold pastry into quarters; unfold on ungreased baking sheet so that one half of circle is centered on sheet. Spread raspberry filling on centered half of circle to within 1½ inches of edge. Fold other half of pastry over filling. Seal edges; turn up ½ inch of edge and flute. Cut slits in top.

Bake until golden brown, about 35 minutes. Cool slightly. Spread with Frosty Glaze. Cut into wedges and serve warm.

6 servings.

Pastry
1⅓ cups all-purpose flour*
½ teaspoon salt
½ cup shortening
3 to 4 tablespoons cold water

Measure flour and salt into bowl. Cut in shortening thoroughly with pastry blender. Sprinkle in water, 1 tablespoon at a time, mixing with fork until all flour is moistened and pastry almost cleans side of bowl. Gather pastry into ball.

* If using self-rising flour, omit salt.

Frosty Glaze
Mix ½ cup confectioners' sugar, 1 tablespoon butter or margarine, softened, 1 tablespoon light cream and 1 teaspoon grated lemon peel until smooth.

Variation
FRESH STRAWBERRY TURNOVER: Substitute 2 cups sliced fresh strawberries for the raspberries.

PASTRY

9-inch One-crust Pie
1 cup all-purpose flour*
½ teaspoon salt
⅓ cup plus 1 tablespoon shortening
 or ⅓ cup lard
2 to 3 tablespoons cold water

9-inch Two-crust Pie
2 cups all-purpose flour*
1 teaspoon salt
⅔ cup plus 2 tablespoons shortening
 or ⅔ cup lard
4 to 5 tablespoons cold water

Measure flour and salt into bowl. Cut in shortening thoroughly with pastry blender. Sprinkle in water, 1 tablespoon at a time, mixing with fork until all flour is moistened and pastry almost cleans side of bowl (1 to 2 teaspoons water can be added if necessary).

Gather pastry into ball; shape into flattened round on lightly floured cloth-covered board. (For Two-crust Pie, divide pastry in half and shape into 2 flattened rounds.) With floured stockinet-covered rolling pin, roll pastry 2 inches larger than inverted pie pan. Fold pastry into quarters; place in pan. Unfold and ease into pan.

For One-crust Pie: Trim overhanging edge of pastry 1 inch from rim of pan. Fold and roll pastry under, even with pan; flute. Fill and bake as directed in recipe.

For Baked Pie Shell: Prick bottom and side thoroughly with fork. Bake at 475° for 8 to 10 minutes. Cool.

For Two-crust Pie: Turn desired filling into pastry-lined pie pan. Trim overhanging edge of pastry ½ inch from rim of pan. Roll second round of pastry 2 inches larger than inverted pie pan. Fold into quarters; cut slits so steam can escape. Place over filling and unfold. Trim overhanging edge of pastry 1 inch from rim of pan. Fold and roll top edge under lower edge, pressing on rim to seal; flute. Cover edge with 2- to 3-inch strip of alumi-

num foil to prevent excessive browning; remove foil last 15 minutes of baking. Bake as directed in recipe.

Variations
Stir one of the following into flour for 9-inch One-crust Pie. (Double the amount for 9-inch Two-crust Pie.)
☐ ½ cup shredded Cheddar cheese
☐ 1 teaspoon cinnamon
☐ 1½ teaspoons finely shredded lemon
 or orange peel
☐ 2 tablespoons finely chopped nuts

* If using self-rising flour, omit salt. Pastry made with self-rising flour differs in flavor and texture from that made with plain flour.

TART SHELLS

Prepare pastry as directed for 9-inch One-crust Pie (left) except—roll into 13-inch circle, about ⅛ inch thick.

Cut circle into 4½-inch circles. (If using individual pie pans or tart pans, cut pastry circles 1 inch larger than inverted pans; fit into pans.) Fit circles over backs of muffin cups or small custard cups, making pleats so pastry will fit closely. Prick thoroughly with fork; place on baking sheet. Bake at 475° for 8 to 10 minutes. Cool before removing from cups.

8 tart shells.

NAPOLEONS

Puff Pastry (below)
3 tablespoons granulated sugar
1 tablespoon water
1 cup confectioners' sugar
1 tablespoon milk
1 ounce melted semisweet chocolate
1 package (about 4½ ounces) chocolate or
   vanilla instant pudding and pie filling
½ cup dairy sour cream

Prepare pastry and refrigerate as directed. Heat oven to 350°. Roll one half of pastry on well-floured cloth-covered board into rectangle, 12 × 10 inches. Cut into 15 rectangles, 4 × 2 inches. Mix granulated sugar and water; brush some of the mixture over rectangles. Place on ungreased baking sheet. Bake until light brown, 15 to 18 minutes. Cool. Repeat with second half of pastry.

Mix confectioners' sugar and milk; spread over ten of the rectangles. Drizzle chocolate over frosted rectangles. Prepare pudding and pie filling as directed on package for pie filling except—substitute dairy sour cream for ½ cup of the milk. Put 3 rectangles together, sugar-glazed sides up, with about 1 tablespoon filling between each. Top layer should be a frosted one. Serve immediately or refrigerate.

10 napoleons.

Puff Pastry
1 cup butter, slightly softened
1½ cups all-purpose flour*
½ cup dairy sour cream

Cut butter into flour with pastry blender until *completely mixed* (pastry will gather together to form a soft ball). Stir in sour cream with fork until *thoroughly blended*. Divide pastry in half; wrap each half and refrigerate at least 8 hours (thorough chilling of the dough is important for ease in handling).

* Self-rising flour can be used in this recipe. Baking time may be shorter.

CHEESE-MARRON PASTRIES

Prepare Puff Pastry (left) and refrigerate as directed. Heat oven to 350°. Divide each half of pastry into thirds. Roll into 7-inch circles on well-floured cloth-covered board; place on ungreased baking sheet. Flute edges; prick with fork. Brush with mixture of 3 tablespoons sugar and 1 tablespoon water. Bake until light brown, 25 to 30 minutes. Cool.

Beat 1 package (8 ounces) cream cheese, softened, 6 whole marrons (half of 9½-ounce jar) and 1 tablespoon marron syrup 2 minutes on medium speed. Spread about 3 tablespoons marron mixture over each circle. Garnish with halved grapes or other fruits.

6 pastries.

STRAWBERRY-CHEESE TARTLETS

Prepare Puff Pastry (left) and refrigerate as directed. Heat oven to 350°. Roll one half of pastry 1/16 inch thick on well-floured cloth-covered board; cut into 2½-inch circles. In ⅔ of the circles, cut out 1-inch holes in centers. Place plain circles on ungreased baking sheet. Brush with mixture of 3 tablespoons sugar and 1 tablespoon water. Top each circle with a cut-out circle. Brush with sugar-water mixture and top with another cut-out circle. Bake until light brown, about 25 minutes. Cool. Repeat with second half of pastry.

Beat 2 packages (3 ounces each) cream cheese, softened, 1 cup dairy sour cream, 1 tablespoon sugar and ¼ teaspoon pumpkin pie spice. Spoon into tartlets; top each with a strawberry dipped in sugar or a dab of strawberry jam.

About 3 dozen tartlets.

Fruit Favorites

Mother Nature wins when it comes to planning
a dessert! Hail her fruits,
fresh, frozen, canned—warm or chilled
—in cups, cobblers, compotes.
Versatility is one of the beauties of fruit;
the combinations possible
are practically endless.

Fresh Fruits

Imagine a cool green watermelon boat—heaped with honeydew, cantaloupe, pineapple, peaches and blueberries That's Watermelon Supreme! We've got a whole crop of fresh fruit ideas, ripe and ready for picking. Our strawberries sparkle in white wine, or fold into liqueur-flavored whipped cream. Our peaches are ruby glazed with raspberry jelly. And can you picture a polka-dot melon? You'll find one on page 118. Plan these as a cool oasis for summer menus. Or count on them to end winter meals on a light note. Fresh fruit is welcome all year 'round, in every form!

GLAZED ORANGES

6 large seedless oranges
1 cup sugar
½ cup water
¼ cup light corn syrup
1 or 2 drops each red and yellow food color
1 tablespoon orange-flavored liqueur or 1
    teaspoon orange extract
2 tablespoons toasted slivered almonds

With vegetable parer or sharp knife, cut slivers of peel from one orange, being careful not to cut into white membrane; reserve peel. Pare all the oranges, cutting only deep enough to remove all the white membrane.

Stir together sugar, water and corn syrup; cook to 230 to 234° on candy thermometer or until syrup spins a 2-inch thread when dropped from a spoon. Stir in food color, reserved slivered peel and liqueur. Place pared oranges in syrup; turn to coat all sides. Remove oranges to shallow dish or pan. Spoon syrup over oranges until they are well glazed. Refrigerate, spooning syrup over oranges occasionally.

To serve, place each orange in dessert dish. Pour syrup over each serving and sprinkle with almonds.

6 servings.

Pictured on page 113: Ingredients for Fresh Fruit Plate (page 116)

GRAPEFRUIT GRENADINE

Remove seeds from 2 chilled grapefruit halves. Cut around edges and sections to loosen. Sprinkle each half with 1 to 2 teaspoons grenadine syrup.

2 servings.

BROILED GRAPEFRUIT

Cut grapefruit in half; remove seeds. Cut around edges and sections to loosen; remove centers. Sprinkle each half with 1 tablespoon brown sugar.

Set oven control at broil and/or 550°. Place grapefruit halves with tops 4 to 6 inches from heat. Broil until juice bubbles and edge of peel turns light brown, 5 to 10 minutes. Serve hot.

2 servings.

PLUGGED MELON

Cut hole 3 inches square and 3 inches deep in center of 1 ripe watermelon (about 10 pounds); pour in ¾ cup bourbon or rum. Trim pink flesh from plug, leaving ½-inch rind; replace plug in watermelon. Refrigerate until bourbon permeates melon, about 8 hours. Cut into wedges.

About 12 servings.

CHILLED MELON CUPS

Cube enough watermelon pulp to measure 6 cups; remove seeds. Divide pulp among 6 dessert dishes; refrigerate. Just before serving, sprinkle 2 to 3 teaspoons rum or white crème de menthe over each serving. Garnish with sprigs of mint.

6 servings.

WATERMELON SUPREME

1 large oblong watermelon
1 cantaloupe
1 honeydew melon
1 pineapple
2 fresh peaches or nectarines
2 cups fresh blueberries
Honey-Lime Sauce (below)
Mint leaves

Cut off lengthwise top third of watermelon; cover and refrigerate to use as desired. With ball cutter, cut balls from larger section of watermelon. Remove seeds; cover balls and refrigerate. Remove remaining pulp from watermelon to make a shell. For a decorative edge on shell, cut a saw-toothed or scalloped design. Drain shell; if necessary, cut very thin slice from bottom so shell will stand upright. Refrigerate.

Cut balls from cantaloupe and honeydew melon to measure about 3 cups each. Remove rind and core from pineapple. Cut fruit into bite-size pieces. Mix with cantaloupe and honeydew melon balls; cover and refrigerate.

Just before serving, peel and slice peaches. Drain melon balls and pineapple pieces. Combine all fruit in large bowl; pour Honey-Lime Sauce over fruit and toss. Pour fruit into watermelon shell. Garnish with mint leaves and serve immediately.

20 servings (1 cup each).

Honey-Lime Sauce
Mix thoroughly ½ cup white wine or ginger ale, 3 tablespoons honey and 2 tablespoons lime juice.

About ¾ cup.

FRUIT AND CHEESE TRAY

Arrange a variety of fresh fruit and cheese on a tray. Serve with dessert plates and small knives.

Select fresh fruit in season: apples, bananas, cherries, grapes, oranges, pears, pineapple, raspberries, strawberries, tangerines. Fill in spaces on tray with dates, figs, prunes and nuts.

As a guide to cheese selection, choose at least one soft, one semisoft and one firm-to-hard cheese, some mild and some sharp. Cheese should be served at room temperature. Try one of the following combinations:

☐ *Gourmandise (soft; cherry brandy-flavored)*
☐ *Port du Salut (semisoft; mild to robust)*
☐ *Swiss (firm to hard; mild, nutty, sweet) or Fontina (firm to hard; mellow, scattered "eyes")*
☐ *Liederkranz (soft; edible crust, pungent)*
☐ *Bel Paese (semisoft; mild)*
☐ *Cheddar (firm to hard; mild to very sharp) or Gruyère (firm to hard; nutty, sharper than Swiss)*
☐ *Camembert (soft; edible crust, pungent) or Brie (soft; edible crust, pungent)*
☐ *Roquefort (semisoft; sharp, salty)*
☐ *Edam or Gouda (firm to hard; inedible casing, mild)*

Or make substitutions or additions as desired from the following:

☐ *Club (soft; often flavored)*
☐ *Cream (soft; very mild—serve slightly chilled)*
☐ *Blue (firm to hard; tangy, sharp)*
☐ *Gorgonzola (firm to hard; piquant flavor)*
☐ *Kashkaval (firm to hard; salty)*
☐ *Neufchâtel (soft; very mild—serve slightly chilled)*

If you like, serve cheese with an assortment of crackers and a dessert wine such as cream (sweet) sherry, port, Marsala, Madeira or Tokay. Serve wine at room temperature or chilled.

FRESH FRUIT PLATE

Choose a variety of fresh fruit (below) or substitute your favorite fruit; refrigerate until well chilled. Arrange fruit on a tray, assorted plates or a lazy Susan. Serve with a selection of 2 or 3 sauces for dipping.

- [ ] *Whole strawberries with stems*
- [ ] *Orange slices*
- [ ] *Grapefruit sections*
- [ ] *Blueberries*
- [ ] *Dark sweet cherries*
- [ ] *Clusters of grapes*
- [ ] *Melon balls, cubes or slices*
- [ ] *Apple wedges**
- [ ] *Banana slices**
- [ ] *Peach, nectarine or pear slices**
- [ ] *Pineapple Tower (below)*
- [ ] *Sour Cream Sauce (below), Velvet Fruit Sauce (below), Cinnamon Sour Cream Sauce (below) or Raspberry-Currant Sauce (page 141)*

* Dip in lemon or pineapple juice to prevent discoloration of fruit.

Pineapple Tower

Cut a cone-shaped wedge around "eye" or groups of 2 "eyes," spacing cuts evenly around entire pineapple. Cut off any core from each wedge. Insert a plastic or wooden pick in each wedge; replace in pineapple. To eat, guests pull out wedges and dip in confectioners' sugar.

Sour Cream Sauce

Mix 1 cup dairy sour cream and 2 tablespoons dark brown sugar.

Velvet Fruit Sauce

Blend 1 package (8 ounces) cream cheese, softened, and ¾ cup dairy sour cream. Beat on high speed in small mixer bowl until light and smooth.

Cinnamon Sour Cream Sauce

Blend 1 cup dairy sour cream, 2 tablespoons sugar, ½ teaspoon cinnamon and ⅛ teaspoon nutmeg.

STRAWBERRIES IN WINE

1 pint fresh strawberries, cut in half
3 tablespoons sugar (optional)
½ cup white wine, champagne or ginger ale

Sprinkle strawberries with sugar; stir gently. Pour wine over berries. Cover and refrigerate at least 1 hour.

4 servings.

Variations

Try these combinations too:

- [ ] *Cantaloupe balls or mandarin orange segments and Chianti.*
- [ ] *Pineapple tidbits, seedless green grapes and Rhine wine.*
- [ ] *Peach slices and rosé.*

BERRY DIPS

Refrigerate 1 pint strawberries (with hulls) about 1 hour. Serve with compote of white wine or champagne and dish of confectioners' sugar. Dip strawberries into wine, then into sugar.

4 to 6 servings.

HONEY-SAUTERNE PEACHES

Mix ¼ cup honey and ¼ cup sauterne. Peel and slice 4 fresh peaches; divide among 4 dessert dishes. Spoon 2 tablespoons honey mixture over each serving.

4 servings.

Substitution

Fresh strawberries, pineapple or pears can be substituted for the peaches (allow about ½ cup cut-up fruit for each serving).

FRESH FRUIT WITH YOGURT

1 cup fresh blueberries
1 cup fresh raspberries
½ cup unflavored yogurt or dairy sour cream
1 tablespoon brown sugar or honey

Divide fruit among 4 dessert dishes. Mix yogurt and sugar; spoon 2 tablespoons over each serving.

4 servings.

Substitution
Pineapple chunks and pitted dark sweet cherries can be substituted for the berries.

GRAPES AND PINEAPPLE IN SOUR CREAM

2 cups fresh seedless green grapes or 1 can
   (16 ounces) seedless green grapes, drained
1 can (13¼ ounces) pineapple chunks, drained
¼ cup brown sugar (packed)
⅓ cup dairy sour cream

Mix grapes and pineapple. Reserve 1 tablespoon of the sugar; blend remaining sugar and the sour cream. Toss with fruit; refrigerate. Just before serving, sprinkle with reserved sugar.

4 servings.

Variations
PEACHES IN SOUR CREAM: Substitute 3 fresh peaches, peeled and sliced, for the grapes and pineapple. Spoon sour cream mixture over each serving. Serve immediately.

STRAWBERRIES IN SOUR CREAM: Substitute 3 cups fresh strawberry halves (about 1 pint) for the grapes and pineapple.

STRAWBERRIES TO DIP: Refrigerate 1 pint strawberries (with hulls). To serve, divide berries among dessert dishes. Pass bowls of sour cream and brown sugar to spoon on dessert plates. Dip berries first into sour cream, then into sugar.

RIVIERA PEACHES

8 fresh* or drained canned peach halves
⅓ cup raspberry jelly
1 pint vanilla or pistachio ice cream

Place 2 peach halves in each dessert dish. Melt raspberry jelly; pour over peaches. Refrigerate several hours. At serving time, top each serving with a scoop of ice cream.

4 servings.

* Dip fresh peach halves into lemon juice to prevent discoloration.

Variation
BRANDIED RIVIERA PEACHES: Use bottled brandied peaches and stir 1 tablespoon brandy syrup into melted raspberry jelly. (Any remaining brandied peach syrup can be served over ice cream or fruit.) Or mix canned peach halves (with syrup) and ⅓ cup brandy; refrigerate at least 24 hours.

STRAWBERRIES ROMANOFF

1 quart strawberries, hulled
½ cup confectioners' sugar
1 cup chilled whipping cream
¼ cup orange-flavored liqueur or orange juice

Sprinkle strawberries with confectioners' sugar; stir gently. Cover and refrigerate 2 hours.

In chilled bowl, beat whipping cream until stiff. Gradually mix in liqueur. Fold in strawberries.

6 servings.

Polka-dot Melons (page 119)

Strawberries in Melon Rings (page 119)

Sparkling Melon Compote (page 119)

POLKA-DOT MELONS

Cut ripe cantaloupe and honeydew melon into wedges; remove seeds and fibers. With ball cutter, cut balls from wedges. Replace cantaloupe balls in honeydew wedges and honeydew balls in cantaloupe wedges.

SPARKLING MELON COMPOTE

1 cantaloupe
½ honeydew melon
1 cup shredded coconut (optional)
1 pint lime, lemon or pineapple sherbet
Sparkling catawba grape juice or ginger ale, chilled

Cut melon into balls with melon ball cutter. Alternate cantaloupe and honeydew balls and the coconut in 4 parfait glasses. Top each with a scoop of sherbet; fill glasses with grape juice.

4 servings.

STRAWBERRIES IN MELON RINGS

1 honeydew melon
1 pint strawberries (with hulls)
Confectioners' sugar (optional)

Cut thin slices from ends of melon. Cut melon crosswise into 4 to 6 slices, about 1 inch thick; remove seeds and fibers. Place each ring on dessert plate. Cut around edge of rind to loosen fruit. Cut fruit into 1-inch pieces (leave rind and fruit intact). Place ⅓ to ½ cup strawberries in center of each ring. Serve with bowl of sugar for dipping strawberries.

4 to 6 servings.

CANTALOUPE WITH SHERBET BALLS

Raspberry-Currant Sauce (page 141)
3 small cantaloupes
½ pint lemon sherbet
½ pint lime sherbet
½ pint orange sherbet

Prepare Raspberry-Currant Sauce. Cut cantaloupes in half; remove seeds and fibers. Make small balls of sherbet with scoop or spoon; divide among cantaloupe halves. Serve with Raspberry-Currant Sauce.

6 servings.

CANTALOUPE WITH PORT AND FRUIT

2 cantaloupes
½ cup fresh, frozen or canned pineapple chunks, drained
½ cup fresh strawberries
½ cup fresh or thawed frozen blueberries
½ to 1 cup port or cranberry cocktail

Cut cantaloupes lengthwise in half, making a sawtoothed edge with sharp small knife. Remove seeds and fibers. Divide pineapple chunks, strawberries and blueberries among cantaloupe halves. Just before serving, spoon 2 to 4 tablespoons port over each serving.

4 servings.

FRESH FRUIT MEDLEY

1 cup fresh seedless green grapes
1 cup cantaloupe balls or pineapple cubes
1 cup fresh strawberries
1 can (6 ounces) frozen fruit juice concentrate (pineapple, orange, lemonade or cranberry juice cocktail), partially thawed

Divide fruit among 6 dessert dishes. Just before serving, spoon 1 to 2 tablespoons fruit concentrate over each serving.

6 servings.

MINTED PINEAPPLE SPEARS

Cut a thick slice from top and bottom of 1 pineapple. Remove rind by cutting down length of pineapple in long wide strokes; remove eyes. Cut pineapple lengthwise into spears; discard core. Place 2 or 3 spears on each dessert plate. Sprinkle each serving with 1 teaspoon crème de menthe. Refrigerate.

4 to 6 servings.

NOTE

Ripe fresh pineapples are great favorites; knowing what to look for will help you get the most flavor for your money. They don't ripen after they're harvested—so what you select is what you'll eat. Pineapples won't improve with storage! The peak season for pineapples is between April and June. To find a good one, look for a pineapple that's plump, of a fairly good size, and is fresh in appearance. Skip bruised fruits or those with soft spots. If the pips (eyes) look slightly separated, that's another sign of ripeness. For the final test: Pick one up and sniff it. If it's ripe, it will have an aromatic fragrance. In other words, it will smell like pineapple. Once you've brought your choice home, refrigerate it or store it in a cool place; enjoy it as soon as possible.

AMBROSIA FRUIT BOATS

1 medium pineapple
1 large orange, pared and sectioned, or 1 can (11 ounces) mandarin orange segments, drained
½ cup shredded coconut
½ cup mandarin orange-, lemon- or pineapple-flavored yogurt
Maraschino cherries

Cut pineapple lengthwise in half through green top. Remove fruit from halves by cutting around curved edges with grapefruit knife. Reserve pineapple shell. Cut fruit into chunks; discard core. Mix pineapple chunks, orange sections, coconut and yogurt. Serve in pineapple shells. Garnish with maraschino cherries.

4 servings.

PINEAPPLE-BERRY BASKET

1 medium pineapple
1 pint fresh strawberries
1 cup dairy sour cream or unflavored yogurt
½ cup brown sugar (packed)

Remove top from pineapple. Cut 2 quarter sections from long side of pineapple, leaving a 1-inch band in center for "basket handle." Remove fruit from basket and handle by cutting around curved edges with grapefruit knife. Cut fruit into chunks; discard core. Cut skin and eyes from quarters and cut fruit into chunks.

Mix pineapple chunks and strawberries; spoon into basket. Serve with a dish each of sour cream and brown sugar. Spear fruit with wooden pick; dip into sour cream and then into sugar.

6 servings.

STRAWBERRY LUSCIOUS

1 cup vanilla wafer or graham cracker
   crumbs (about 16 wafers or 14 squares)
2 tablespoons confectioners' sugar
¼ cup butter or margarine, melted
2 egg whites
6 tablespoons granulated sugar
1 pint strawberries, cut in half
1 cup chilled whipping cream or 1 envelope
   (about 2 ounces) dessert topping mix
3 tablespoons confectioners' sugar
½ teaspoon vanilla

Mix crumbs, 2 tablespoons confectioners' sugar and the butter thoroughly. Press mixture firmly and evenly in bottom of ungreased square pan, 8×8×2 inches. Or divide mixture among 6 to 8 dessert dishes and press in bottoms and halfway up sides of dishes. Refrigerate while preparing topping.

Beat egg whites in small mixer bowl until foamy. Beat in granulated sugar, 1 tablespoon at a time; continue beating until stiff and glossy. Do not underbeat. Spread meringue evenly over crumb mixture in pan. Top meringue with strawberry halves, reserving a few halves for garnish.

In chilled bowl, beat whipping cream, 3 tablespoons confectioners' sugar and the vanilla until stiff. (If using dessert topping mix, prepare as directed on package; omit sugar and fold vanilla into topping.) Spread over strawberries. Garnish with reserved berries. Serve immediately or refrigerate no longer than 2 hours.

6 to 8 servings.

Variations

BLUEBERRY LUSCIOUS: Substitute 2 cups fresh blueberries for the strawberries.

RASPBERRY LUSCIOUS: Substitute 2 cups fresh raspberries for the strawberries.

COMPOTES AND BAKED FRUITS

Think of serving fruit cooked instead of raw, for a change. And think of these for times other than after dinner—what about for a beautiful beginning to brunch? You needn't be limited by season; our recipes call for canned and frozen as well as fresh fruit. So take your choice—sweet or tangy, warm or chilled—there's something here for every mood.

SPICED PLUMS IN PORT

2 cans (16 ounces each) whole plums,
   drained (reserve syrup)
1 cup port or cranberry juice
4 whole cloves
3-inch cinnamon stick
1 orange, pared and cut into thin slices

Heat reserved plum syrup, the port, cloves and cinnamon stick to boiling. Reduce heat; simmer uncovered about 15 minutes. Remove cloves and cinnamon stick. Add plums and orange slices. Serve warm, in dessert dishes.

6 to 8 servings.

HOT CARAMEL FRUITS

1 can (30 ounces) fruits for salad or fruit
   cocktail, drained
1 tablespoon lemon juice
¼ cup brown sugar (packed)
2 tablespoons butter or margarine

Heat oven to 325°. Mix fruit, lemon juice and sugar in ungreased 1½-quart casserole. Dot with butter. Bake uncovered until hot and bubbly, 35 to 40 minutes. If desired, top with vanilla ice cream.

4 to 6 servings.

FRUIT AND WINE COMPOTE

¾ cup sugar
¾ cup dry red wine
3 tablespoons lemon juice
3 fresh peaches, peeled and cut into quarters
4 fresh large red plums, cut into quarters

Heat all ingredients in large saucepan to boiling, stirring occasionally. Reduce heat; cover and simmer until fruit is tender, about 5 minutes. Serve warm or chilled.

4 servings.

WINTER FRUIT COMPOTE

1 jar (17 ounces) figs, drained (reserve syrup)
1 jar (16 ounces) prunes, drained (reserve syrup)
3-inch cinnamon stick
1 can (29 ounces) peach halves, drained
1 lime, cut into wedges

Heat reserved syrup and the cinnamon stick to boiling; boil 5 minutes. Add figs, prunes and peach halves; heat through. Remove cinnamon stick. Serve fruit warm, in dessert dishes. Garnish with lime wedges.

6 to 8 servings.

ROSY CINNAMON FRUIT

Drain 1 can (16 ounces) peaches or pears; reserve ½ cup syrup. Heat reserved syrup and ¼ cup red cinnamon candies in small saucepan to boiling. Boil 1 minute. Remove from heat. Cover; let stand until candies are dissolved, about 10 minutes. Stir in fruit. Serve warm or chilled.

4 servings.

CRIMSON PEARS

¼ cup sugar
¼ cup water
2 tablespoons lemon juice
6 fresh pears
1 package (10 ounces) frozen raspberries, thawed

Heat oven to 350°. Mix sugar, water and lemon juice in ungreased 2-quart casserole until sugar is dissolved. Pare pears (do not core or remove stems). Arrange pears in casserole, turning pears to coat with sugar mixture. Cover and bake until pears are tender when pierced with fork, 45 to 60 minutes.

Carefully remove pears; pour off sugar mixture. Replace pears in casserole. Sieve raspberries over pears; turn to coat with raspberry syrup. Cool 30 minutes. Refrigerate about 12 hours, turning pears occasionally to coat evenly with raspberry syrup. To serve, place pears upright in dessert dishes or serving dish. Pour raspberry syrup over each pear.

6 servings.

MIXED FRESH FRUIT COMPOTE

1 jar (10 ounces) currant jelly
½ cup water
4 fresh plums, cut in half and pitted
2 fresh pears, cut in half, pared and cored
2 fresh peaches, cut in half, peeled and pitted

Mix all ingredients in large saucepan. Cover and heat to boiling. Reduce heat; simmer until fruit is tender, about 10 minutes. Serve warm.

4 to 6 servings.

Crimson Pear (page 122), Mixed Fresh Fruit Compote (page 122)

RUM POT

1 can (16 ounces) sliced peaches, drained
1 can (13½ ounces) pineapple chunks,
    drained
2 cups sugar
1 cup golden rum
1 can (about 16 ounces) sliced pears,
    drained
1 can (about 17 ounces) apricot halves,
    drained
2 cups sugar
1 package (10 ounces) frozen raspberries,
    thawed

Place peaches and pineapple chunks in 2- to 3-quart sterilized glass or glazed pottery container. Add 2 cups sugar and the rum. (Fruit should be completely covered with rum; add more rum if necessary.) Cover container loosely. Let stand at room temperature 2 weeks, stirring several times to dissolve sugar. (Stir carefully to avoid breaking up fruit.)

After 2 weeks, add pears, apricots and remaining 2 cups sugar. (Fruit should always be completely covered; add rum if necessary.) Let stand at room temperature 2 weeks longer, stirring several times to dissolve sugar.

After 2 weeks, stir in raspberries. Use as a topping for ice cream, cake or pudding. The rum pot will keep for several weeks if stored in refrigerator. For best flavor, serve at room temperature.

15 to 20 servings.

NOTE

Rum pot dates back to pre-Revolutionary days. Ingenious colonial housewives found it an easy way to preserve fresh fruits, and have them ready to serve as fall and winter desserts. Since our recipe calls for canned fruits, you can start your rum pot any time of year. Just remember to allow at least 4 weeks before serving so that you can keep supplementing it with additional fruit and sugar.

OLD-FASHIONED APPLESAUCE

4 medium apples, pared, quartered and
    cored
1 cup water
⅓ to ½ cup granulated or brown sugar
    (packed)

Heat apples and water in 3-quart saucepan to boiling over medium heat. Reduce heat; simmer, stirring occasionally to break up apples, until apples are tender, 5 to 10 minutes. Stir in sugar; heat to boiling. Serve warm or chilled.

About 4 cups.

Variation

SPICED APPLESAUCE: Add ¼ teaspoon cinnamon and ⅛ teaspoon nutmeg with the sugar.

BAKED BANANAS

2 firm large bananas
Lemon juice
2 teaspoons grated lemon peel
2 tablespoons brown sugar
2 tablespoons butter or margarine, melted
½ teaspoon rum flavoring (optional)
Ice cream (optional)

Heat oven to 375°. Peel bananas; cut lengthwise in half. Place halves cut sides down in greased baking dish, 8×8×2 inches. Brush with lemon juice. Sprinkle each half with ½ teaspoon lemon peel and ½ tablespoon sugar; drizzle with butter and rum flavoring. Bake uncovered 20 minutes. Serve warm, with ice cream.

4 servings.

BAKED PRUNE WHIP

1 cup cut-up cooked prunes
3 egg whites
⅓ cup sugar
¼ teaspoon salt
1 tablespoon lemon juice
¼ cup chopped pecans
Sweetened whipped cream or soft custard

Heat oven to 350°. Beat prunes, egg whites, sugar and salt in small mixer bowl until stiff. Fold in lemon juice and pecans. Pour into ungreased 1½-quart casserole. Place in pan of hot water (1 inch). Bake until mixture is puffed and thin film has formed on top, 30 to 35 minutes. Serve warm, with whipped cream.

4 to 6 servings.

PEARS IN SOUR CREAM SAUCE

6 egg yolks
1 cup dairy sour cream
1 cup granulated sugar
3 tablespoons rum, brandy or sherry
1 can (29 ounces) pear halves, well drained
¼ cup brown sugar (packed)

Blend egg yolks, sour cream and granulated sugar in saucepan. Cook over low heat, stirring constantly, until mixture simmers. Simmer until thickened, about 3 minutes, stirring constantly. Remove from heat; stir in rum.

Arrange pear halves cut sides down in ungreased baking dish, 8×8×2 inches, or individual ramekins. Pour sour cream sauce over pears. Sprinkle with brown sugar.

Set oven control at broil and/or 550°. Place pears with tops 6 to 8 inches from heat. Broil until brown sugar is melted, 1 to 2 minutes. Serve warm or chilled.

8 to 10 servings.

CARAMELIZED PEARS DELUXE

4 firm fresh d'Anjou pears, pared,
   quartered and cored
½ cup sugar
2 tablespoons butter or margarine
½ cup whipping cream

Heat oven to 500°. Arrange pear quarters round sides up in single layer in ungreased baking dish, 8×8×2 inches. Sprinkle with sugar; dot with butter. Bake uncovered until sugar melts and turns golden brown, 20 to 30 minutes. Pour whipping cream evenly over pears. Gently stir cream and syrup with fork until blended. Serve hot, in dessert dishes.

4 to 6 servings.

APRICOT-GLAZED PEARS

⅓ cup orange juice
⅓ cup apricot jam
4 fresh pears, cut in half, pared and cored

Heat oven to 350°. Mix orange juice and jam in ungreased baking dish, 8×8×2 or 9×9×2 inches, or 2-quart casserole. Place pears cut sides down in sauce. Cover and bake until pears are tender, 25 to 30 minutes. Serve warm or chilled. If desired, garnish each serving with a dollop of whipped topping and a dash of nutmeg.

4 servings.

Variation
APRICOT-GLAZED PEACHES: Substitute 4 fresh peaches, peeled and cut in half, for the pears.

CINNAMON-BAKED APPLES

Heat oven to 375°. Core and remove 1-inch strip of skin around middle of each apple or pare upper half to prevent skin from splitting. Place apples upright in ungreased baking dish. Spoon 1 to 2 tablespoons granulated or brown sugar, 1 teaspoon butter or margarine and ⅛ teaspoon cinnamon into center of each apple. Pour water (¼ inch) into baking dish.

Bake until apples are tender when pierced with fork, 30 to 40 minutes. (Time will vary with size and variety of apple.) If desired, spoon syrup in pan over apples several times during baking. Serve plain or with light cream or sweetened whipped cream.

Note: Choose baking apples such as Rome Beauty, Wealthy, Winesap, Northern Spy, Golden Delicious or Greening.

Variations

BAKED APPLES GRENADINE: Substitute grenadine syrup for the sugar. Spoon syrup in pan over apples several times during baking.

BAKED APPLES VERMONT: Substitute maple-flavored syrup for the sugar.

BAKED HONEY APPLES: Substitute honey for the sugar.

ROSY CINNAMON APPLES: Omit butter and cinnamon; spoon 1 tablespoon red cinnamon candies into each apple. Spoon syrup in pan over apples several times during baking.

STUFFED BAKED APPLES: Add 1 tablespoon raisins, chopped nuts or mincemeat to center of each apple.

Dumplings and Cobblers

For those who love fruit and those who love baked desserts—the perfect solution. Dumplings with creamy sauces, biscuit-topped cobblers, crunchy crisps and kuchens—this is a warmhearted group, best-served "right from the oven."

PEAR DUMPLINGS WITH NUTMEG SAUCE

4 fresh pears
1½ cups all-purpose flour*
⅓ cup confectioners' sugar
¾ cup butter or margarine, softened
Nutmeg Sauce (below)

Heat oven to 375°. Pare pears, leaving stems intact. Core from blossom ends. Blend flour, sugar and butter thoroughly; divide into 4 equal parts. With floured hands, flatten each part; place pear in center. Carefully mold dough evenly around pear, leaving only stem exposed. Place 2 inches apart on ungreased baking sheet. Bake until light brown, 25 to 30 minutes. Serve warm, with Nutmeg Sauce.

4 servings.

* Do not use self-rising flour in this recipe.

Nutmeg Sauce
½ cup chilled whipping cream
1 egg
3 tablespoons butter or margarine, melted
1 cup confectioners' sugar
½ teaspoon nutmeg
⅛ teaspoon salt

In chilled bowl, beat whipping cream until stiff. Beat egg in small mixer bowl until foamy. Blend in butter, sugar, nutmeg and salt. Fold in whipped cream. Serve immediately or refrigerate no longer than 1 hour.

1½ cups.

APPLE DUMPLINGS WITH BRANDY SAUCE

Pastry for 9-inch Two-crust Pie (page 111)
6 medium baking apples, pared and cored
½ cup brown sugar (packed)
¼ teaspoon cinnamon
2 tablespoons butter or margarine
1 egg, beaten
Brandy Sauce (below) or Creamy Stirred
  Custard (page 15)

Heat oven to 425°. Prepare pastry as directed except—divide into 6 equal parts. Roll each part into 8-inch circle. If necessary, trim edge of each to make even. Reserve trimmings. Place an apple on each circle.

Mix sugar and cinnamon. Fill center of each apple with 1 teaspoon butter and 2 tablespoons sugar-cinnamon mixture. Bring sides of pastry up; dampen edges and press pastry firmly around apple. Press edges *firmly* to seal. Arrange dumplings seam sides down in ungreased baking dish, 11¾ × 7½ × 1¾ inches. Brush the dumplings with part of the beaten egg.

Roll any remaining pastry trimmings about ⅛ inch thick. Cut into ½-inch strips with pastry wheel. Crisscross 2 strips on each dumpling, tucking ends under dumpling. Brush strips with remaining beaten egg. Bake until crust is golden brown and apples are tender, 40 to 45 minutes. Serve warm, with Brandy Sauce.

6 servings.

Brandy Sauce
½ cup chilled whipping cream
1 egg or 2 egg yolks
¼ cup sugar
2 tablespoons brandy or 1 teaspoon brandy
  flavoring

In chilled bowl, beat whipping cream until stiff. Beat egg, sugar and brandy until blended; fold into whipped cream. Serve immediately or refrigerate no longer than 1 hour.

About 1 cup.

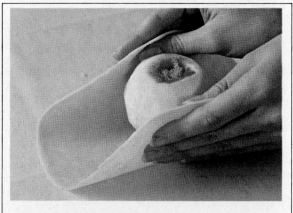

Fold pastry up over apple.

Lay pastry strips crisscross on top.

Apple Dumpling with Brandy Sauce

Royal Fresh Fruit Cobbler (page 129)

ROYAL FRESH FRUIT COBBLER

1 cup sugar
3 tablespoons cornstarch
¾ teaspoon cinnamon
3 cups sliced peeled fresh peaches or
  nectarines (5 or 6 medium)
2 cups unpeeled sliced red plums (6 to 8
  large)
1 cup fresh blueberries
1 cup all-purpose flour*
2 tablespoons sugar
1½ teaspoons baking powder
½ teaspoon salt
⅓ cup shortening
3 tablespoons milk
1 egg

Heat oven to 375°. Mix 1 cup sugar, the cornstarch and cinnamon in 3-quart saucepan. Stir in peaches and plums. Cook, stirring constantly, until mixture thickens and boils. Boil and stir 1 minute. Stir in blueberries. Pour into ungreased baking dish, 8 × 8 × 2 inches.

Measure flour, 2 tablespoons sugar, the baking powder and salt into bowl. Cut in shortening thoroughly. Mix in milk and egg. Drop dough by 9 spoonfuls onto hot fruit mixture. Bake until topping is golden brown, 25 to 30 minutes. Serve warm, and if desired, with light cream or ice cream.

9 servings.

* If using self-rising flour, omit baking powder and salt.

Note: Other combinations of fresh fruit to total 6 cups can be substituted (purple plums, berries, cut-up rhubarb, cherries).

STRAWBERRY-RHUBARB PUFF

1 package (16 ounces) frozen rhubarb, thawed
1 package (10 ounces) frozen strawberries,
  thawed
½ cup sugar
2 cups all-purpose flour*
2 tablespoons sugar
3 teaspoons baking powder
1 teaspoon salt
⅓ cup salad oil
⅔ cup milk
Butter or margarine
2 tablespoons sugar
1 teaspoon cinnamon

Heat oven to 450°. Mix rhubarb, strawberries (with syrup) and ½ cup sugar in ungreased square pan, 9 × 9 × 2 inches. Heat in oven while preparing biscuit topping.

Measure flour, 2 tablespoons sugar, the baking powder and salt into bowl. Pour oil and milk into measuring cup (do not stir); pour all at once into flour mixture. Stir until mixture cleans side of bowl and forms a ball.

Drop dough by 9 spoonfuls onto hot fruit. Make an indentation in top of each spoonful of dough; dot with butter. Mix 2 tablespoons sugar and the cinnamon; sprinkle over dough. Bake until topping is golden brown, 20 to 25 minutes. Serve warm, and if desired, with light cream or sweetened whipped cream.

9 servings.

* If using self-rising flour, omit baking powder and salt.

CHERRY SKILLET COBBLER

1 can (21 ounces) cherry pie filling
½ cup orange juice
1 cup biscuit baking mix
1 tablespoon shredded orange peel
1 tablespoon sugar
¼ cup milk

Heat pie filling and orange juice in 8-inch skillet or large saucepan to boiling, stirring occasionally. Stir baking mix, orange peel, sugar and milk to a soft dough. Drop dough by 6 spoonfuls onto boiling cherry mixture. Cook uncovered over low heat 10 minutes; cover and cook 10 minutes. Serve warm. Top with light cream or sweetened whipped cream if you wish.

6 servings.

PEACH COBBLE-UP

1 package (18.5 ounces) yellow cake mix
¼ to ½ teaspoon nutmeg (optional)
½ cup water
2 eggs
2 cans (16 ounces each) sliced peaches
Sweetened whipped cream or ice cream

Heat oven to 375°. Grease and flour oblong pan, 13×9×2 inches. Blend cake mix (dry), nutmeg, water and eggs until moistened. (Batter will be slightly lumpy.) Spread in pan. Pour peaches (with syrup) over batter. Bake until cake springs back when touched lightly in center, about 40 minutes. While warm, spoon into dessert dishes. Serve with whipped cream.

10 to 12 servings.

Note: Cover and refrigerate leftover dessert. Reheat covered in 350° oven about 30 minutes or until warm.

APRICOT COBBLE-UP

1 cup biscuit baking mix
⅓ cup milk
1 tablespoon brown sugar
1 tablespoon butter or margarine, softened
¼ teaspoon nutmeg
1 can (17 ounces) apricot halves

Heat oven to 400°. Mix all ingredients except apricot halves to a soft dough. Spread in ungreased square pan, 8×8×2 inches. Pour apricots (with syrup) over dough. Bake 25 to 30 minutes. Serve warm, and if desired, with light cream.

4 to 6 servings.

QUICK BLUEBERRY COBBLER

1 can (21 ounces) blueberry pie filling
1 teaspoon grated orange peel
1 cup biscuit baking mix
1 tablespoon sugar
¼ cup orange juice
1 tablespoon butter or margarine, softened

Heat oven to 400°. Mix pie filling and orange peel in ungreased 1½-quart casserole. Heat in oven 15 minutes while preparing topping.

Stir remaining ingredients to a soft dough. Drop dough by 6 spoonfuls onto hot blueberry mixture. Bake until topping is light brown, 20 to 25 minutes. Serve warm, and if desired, with light cream.

6 servings.

Variation
CHERRY-ALMOND COBBLER: Substitute 1 can (21 ounces) cherry pie filling for the blueberry pie filling, ½ teaspoon almond extract for the orange peel and ¼ cup milk for the orange juice. Stir 2 tablespoons toasted slivered almonds into the dough.

APPLE CRISP

4 cups sliced pared tart apples (about 4 medium)
⅔ to ¾ cup brown sugar (packed)
½ cup all-purpose flour
½ cup uncooked rolled oats
¾ teaspoon cinnamon
¾ teaspoon nutmeg
⅓ cup butter or margarine, softened

Heat oven to 375°. Grease square pan, 8×8×2 inches. Spread apple slices in pan. Mix remaining ingredients thoroughly; sprinkle over apples.

Bake until apples are tender and topping is golden brown, about 30 minutes. Serve warm, and if desired, with light cream, ice cream or hard sauce.

6 servings.

Variations

APRICOT CRISP: Substitute 2 cans (16 ounces each) apricot halves, drained, for the apples and use ⅔ cup sugar.

CHERRY CRISP: Substitute 1 can (21 ounces) cherry pie filling for the apples and use ⅔ cup sugar.

PEACH CRISP: Substitute 1 can (29 ounces) peach slices, drained, for the apples and use ⅔ cup sugar.

CHEERY CHERRY CRUNCH

½ cup butter or margarine, softened
1 package (18.5 or 19.5 ounces) yellow or cherry chip cake mix
2 cans (21 ounces each) cherry pie filling
½ cup chopped walnuts

Heat oven to 350°. Cut butter into cake mix (dry) until crumbly. Reserve 1½ cups crumbly mixture; pat remaining mixture lightly in ungreased oblong pan, 13×9×2 inches, building up ½-inch edges. Spread pie filling over mixture in pan to within ½ inch of edges. Mix walnuts and reserved crumbly mixture; sprinkle over top.

Bake 45 to 50 minutes. Serve warm, and if desired, with sweetened whipped cream or ice cream.

12 to 15 servings.

Note: For a thinner, crisper dessert, use 1 can (21 ounces) cherry pie filling; bake 35 to 40 minutes.

Variations
Try one of these combinations:
☐ Butter pecan cake mix and apple pie filling.
☐ Chocolate fudge supreme cake mix and cherry pie filling.
☐ Devils food cake mix and apricot pie filling.
☐ Lemon cake mix and peach pie filling.
☐ White cake mix and blueberry pie filling.
☐ Yellow cake mix and mince pie filling.

NOTE

Choose apples that feel firm and have a good color. Store apples in the refrigerator to protect their crispness and tangy flavor. To keep pared apples from discoloring, sprinkle them with lemon juice or put them in water mixed with a little lemon juice. Good cooking apples include the Rome Beauty, Rhode Island Greening, Starr and Jersey Red varieties. Apples good for both eating and cooking include the Newtown Pippin, Golden Delicious, Cortland, Winesap and Northern Spy. Most of these varieties are widely available.

RHUBARB MERINGUE DESSERT

½ cup butter or margarine, softened
1 cup all-purpose flour
1 tablespoon sugar
3 egg yolks
1 cup sugar
2 tablespoons flour
¼ teaspoon salt
½ cup light cream (20%)
2½ cups cut-up rhubarb
3 egg whites
⅓ cup sugar
1 teaspoon vanilla
¼ cup flaked coconut

Heat oven to 350°. Blend butter, 1 cup flour and 1 tablespoon sugar. Press evenly in ungreased square pan, 9×9×2 inches. Bake 10 minutes.

Blend egg yolks, 1 cup sugar, 2 tablespoons flour, the salt and cream; mix in rhubarb. Pour over hot crust. Bake 45 minutes.

Beat egg whites until foamy. Beat in ⅓ cup sugar, 1 tablespoon at a time; continue beating until stiff and glossy. Do not underbeat. Beat in vanilla. Spread over rhubarb mixture; sprinkle with coconut. Bake until light brown, about 10 minutes.

9 servings.

NOTE

Rhubarb is a vegetable, but we cook, eat and enjoy it as a fruit. Select it almost as you would celery: Look for fresh, firm, crisp and tender stalks. Color? Usually pink or cherry red, although some good-quality stems will be predominantly light green. Rhubarb wilts rapidly at room temperature so you should always refrigerate it. From a nutrition standpoint, rhubarb contributes to the daily ration of vitamins A and C. From a taste standpoint, rhubarb ranks high on the list of dessert winners. The Rhubarb Meringue Dessert above, for example, combines a tangy rhubarb filling with a buttery base and a fluffy meringue topping. A flavor sensation!

PEACH-CUSTARD KUCHEN

1 cup all-purpose flour*
2 tablespoons sugar
¼ teaspoon salt
⅛ teaspoon baking powder
¼ cup butter or margarine, softened
1½ cups drained sliced peaches (fresh, canned or thawed frozen)
¼ cup plus 2 tablespoons sugar
1 teaspoon cinnamon
2 egg yolks
1 cup whipping cream

Heat oven to 400°. Stir together flour, 2 tablespoons sugar, the salt and baking powder. Work in butter until mixture is crumbly. Pat mixture firmly and evenly in bottom and halfway up sides of ungreased square pan, 8×8×2 inches. Arrange peach slices in pan. Mix ¼ cup plus 2 tablespoons sugar and the cinnamon; sprinkle over peach slices. Bake 15 minutes.

Blend egg yolks and whipping cream; pour over peaches. Bake until custard is set and edges are light brown, 25 to 30 minutes. Serve warm.

9 servings.

* If using self-rising flour, omit salt and baking powder.

Variations
APPLE-CUSTARD KUCHEN: Substitute 2 cups sliced pared tart apples or 1 can (20 ounces) pie-sliced apples, well drained, for the peaches.

PEAR-CUSTARD KUCHEN: Substitute 1 can (16 ounces) sliced pears, well drained, for the peaches; omit cinnamon. If desired, substitute 1 cup dairy sour cream for the whipping cream. Before baking, sprinkle with nutmeg and slivered almonds.

Fast Finales

These are the jet set of
the contemporary dessert world—sleek as
modern glass, fast as flight in the making.
The dazzling variety here includes everything from
brandied Alexanders to a
peanut butter sundae that should be
the junior set's idea of a dream come true.

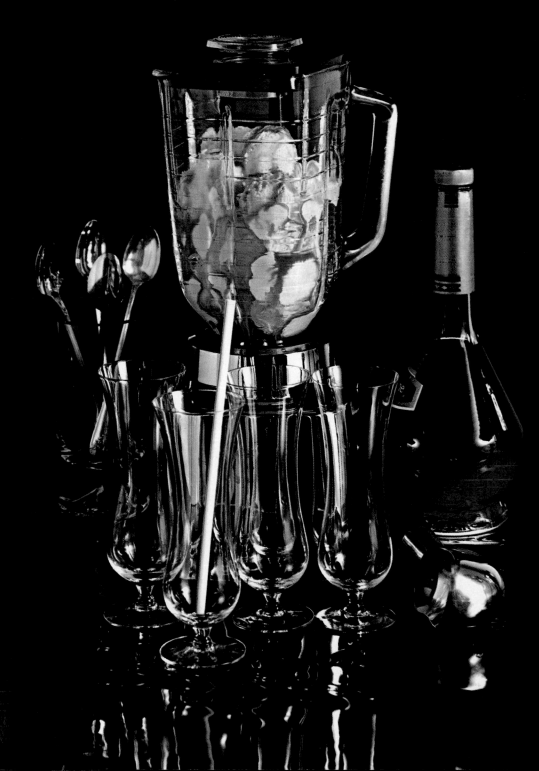

DESSERT BEVERAGES

Here's a thought: Serve California Coffee at the next big buffet you give. It's dessert, coffee and an after-dinner drink all in one. And therein lies the advantage of these more-than-beverages. Another advantage: They really shine in the spur-of-the-moment department. They're ideal for quick desserts, late-night parties, snack-time refreshers; in other words, they make a lot of sense for today's busy life-style.

COFFEE A LA MODE

For each serving, fill mug about ¾ full with hot strong coffee. Top with small scoop of vanilla, chocolate or coffee ice cream.

MOCHA COOLER

1 cup strong coffee, chilled
1 pint chocolate ice cream, softened
1 teaspoon vanilla
½ teaspoon cinnamon
¼ teaspoon salt

Mix all ingredients thoroughly in blender or small mixer bowl. Serve over ice cubes in tall glasses.

3 or 4 servings.

FROSTY MOCHA

2½ cups chilled strong coffee
1 pint vanilla ice cream, softened
¼ cup chocolate syrup
½ teaspoon aromatic bitters

Beat all ingredients in small mixer bowl until smooth. Pour into small ice-frosted glasses.

8 servings.

Pictured on page 133: Ingredients for Grasshopper (this page)

CALIFORNIA COFFEE

For each serving, pour 1 ounce (2 tablespoons) brandy into mug. Fill ⅔ full with hot strong coffee. Top with scoop of chocolate ice cream.

DELUXE DESSERT BEVERAGES

Slightly soften 1 pint vanilla ice cream. Mix in any of the following in blender or small mixer bowl just until smooth. Pour into glasses or dessert cups. Serve with cocktail straws and dessert spoons.

2 or 3 servings.

Brandy Alexander: 2 tablespoons white crème de cacao and 2 tablespoons brandy.

Brandy Ice: ¼ cup brandy.

Cherry Frost: 2 tablespoons white crème de cacao and 2 tablespoons cherry-flavored liqueur.

Grasshopper: 2 tablespoons white crème de cacao and 2 tablespoons green crème de menthe.

Orange Ice: ¼ cup thawed frozen orange juice concentrate.

Velvet Frost: 2 tablespoons white crème de cacao and 2 tablespoons orange-flavored liqueur.

FRESH FRUIT SLUSH

1 pint vanilla ice cream, softened
1 teaspoon lemon juice
1 cup fresh strawberries, raspberries, pineapple cubes, sliced peaches or sliced
   bananas

Mix all ingredients in blender or small mixer bowl just until smooth. Pour into glasses or dessert cups. Serve with cocktail straws and dessert spoons.

3 or 4 servings.

Mix-Quick Desserts

Dessert from a mix—but no ordinary dessert. Mix and match cake and frosting flavors, top warm cake squares with the sauce or ice cream of your choosing, make Jiffy Tarts and fill with what you will. Once you've got the knack, there's a world of almost-instant custom-designed desserts you can serve.

YELLOW CAKE VARIATIONS

Prepare 1 package (18.5 ounces) yellow cake mix as directed except—try one of the following:

Maple-Nut: Add 2 teaspoons maple flavoring and ⅓ cup finely chopped nuts before beating.

Nutmeg-Mace: Add ½ teaspoon each nutmeg and mace before beating.

Orange: Add 2 tablespoons grated orange peel before beating.

Toasted Coconut: Stir 1 to 1½ cups toasted flaked coconut into batter.

WHITE CAKE VARIATIONS

Prepare 1 package (18.5 ounces) white cake mix as directed except—try one of the following:

Cherry: Stir ½ cup drained finely chopped maraschino cherries into batter.

Cherry-Nut: Stir ½ cup finely chopped nuts and ½ cup drained finely chopped maraschino cherries into batter.

Coconut: Stir 1 to 1½ cups flaked coconut into batter.

Mint: Add ¼ teaspoon peppermint extract before beating; stir few drops red or green food color into batter.

Orange: Add 2 tablespoons grated orange peel before beating.

DEVILS FOOD CAKE VARIATIONS

Prepare 1 package (18.5 ounces) devils food cake mix as directed except—try one of the following variations:

Cherry-Chocolate: Stir ½ cup drained finely chopped maraschino cherries into batter.

Chocolate-Banana: Use ¼ cup less water; add ¾ cup mashed banana (1½ to 2 medium) and ⅛ teaspoon baking soda before beating. Stir ½ cup chopped nuts into batter.

Fudge-Nut: Stir ½ cup chopped nuts into batter.

Mocha: Use 1 cup cold strong coffee for part of the water; add 3 tablespoons instant coffee before beating.

Orange: Add 2 tablespoons grated orange peel before beating.

Peppermint: Add ¼ teaspoon peppermint extract before beating.

Spice: Add 1 teaspoon cinnamon, ¼ teaspoon cloves and ¼ teaspoon ginger before beating.

POUND CAKE VARIATIONS

Prepare 1 package (16 ounces) golden pound cake mix as directed except—try one of the following variations:

Chocolate-Nut: Stir 2 squares (1 ounce each) unsweetened chocolate, grated, and ½ cup chopped nuts into batter.

Fruit-Nut: Stir ½ cup finely cut-up mixed candied fruit and ½ cup finely chopped nuts into batter.

Lemon: Stir 1 tablespoon grated lemon peel into batter.

Pecan: Stir 1 cup finely chopped pecans into batter.

Raisin-Nut: Stir ½ cup finely chopped raisins and ½ cup chopped nuts into batter.

CHOCOLATE FROSTING VARIATIONS

Prepare 1 package (15.4 ounces) chocolate fudge frosting mix as directed except—try one of the following variations:

Mocha: Add 1 tablespoon powdered instant coffee before beating.

Peppermint: Sprinkle top of frosted cake with ½ cup crushed peppermint candy.

Peppermint Fudge: Stir in ¼ to ½ teaspoon peppermint extract after beating.

Rocky Road: Stir in ½ cup miniature marshmallows and ½ cup chopped nuts after beating.

CREAMY WHITE FROSTING VARIATIONS

Prepare 1 package (15.4 ounces) creamy white frosting mix as directed except—try one of the following variations:

Cocoa Mocha: Substitute strong coffee for the water; add ½ cup cocoa before beating.

Lemon, Orange or Lime: Substitute lemon, orange or lime juice for the water.

Peppermint: Stir in ½ teaspoon peppermint extract and 3 or 4 drops red or green food color after beating.

Raisin-Nut: Stir in ½ cup chopped raisins and ½ cup finely chopped nuts after beating.

Raspberry or Strawberry: Substitute crushed fresh or thawed frozen raspberries or strawberries for the water.

NOTE

Microwave magic. These electronic marvels are ideal for reheating desserts (pie, for instance) as well as quick cooking. Since each brand is a little different, your best bet is to refer to the manufacturer's instruction book for specific directions.

FLUFFY WHITE FROSTING VARIATIONS

Prepare 1 package (7.2 ounces) fluffy white frosting mix as directed except—try one of the following variations:

Almond: Fold in ½ teaspoon almond extract after beating.

Cherry-Nut: Fold in ⅓ cup drained chopped maraschino cherries and ½ cup chopped nuts after beating.

Chocolate Chip: Fold in ½ cup semisweet chocolate pieces after beating.

Cinnamon: Add 1 teaspoon cinnamon before beating.

Clove: Add ¼ teaspoon cloves before beating.

Coffee: Add 2 teaspoons powdered instant coffee before beating.

Lemon: Fold in ½ teaspoon lemon extract after beating.

Maple-Nut: Fold in ½ teaspoon maple flavoring and ½ cup chopped pecans after beating.

Nutmeg: Add ½ teaspoon nutmeg before beating.

Orange-Coconut: Fold in 1 tablespoon grated orange peel and ½ cup flaked coconut after beating.

Orange-Raisin: Fold in ½ cup chopped nuts, 1½ cups raisins and 2 tablespoons coarsely grated orange peel after beating.

Peppermint: Fold in ¼ teaspoon peppermint extract and few drops red or green food color after beating.

Spice: Add ½ teaspoon cinnamon, ¼ teaspoon nutmeg and ¼ teaspoon cloves before beating.

ANGEL FOOD CAKE VARIATIONS

Prepare 1 package (15 or 16 ounces) white angel food cake mix as directed except—try one of the following variations:

Apricot: Substitute apricot nectar for the water.

Orange: Substitute frozen orange juice concentrate (reconstituted) for the water.

Pineapple: Substitute unsweetened pineapple juice for the water.

Pink Lemonade: Substitute frozen pink lemonade concentrate (reconstituted) for the water.

Pink Peppermint: Add ½ teaspoon peppermint extract and 6 drops red food color to the water.

Root Beer: Substitute root beer-flavored carbonated beverage for the water.

Strawberry: Substitute strawberry-flavored carbonated beverage for the water.

TOASTED CAKE QUICKIES

Cut pound cake into ½-inch slices. Toast in toaster or under broiler. Top each slice with one of the following:

- [ ] *1 canned peach half, drained, and ¼ cup frozen raspberries, thawed.*
- [ ] *Lemon sherbet and ¼ cup frozen strawberries, thawed.*
- [ ] *Ice cream and ice-cream topping.*
- [ ] *Spread with butter and sprinkle with mixture of cinnamon and sugar.*
- [ ] *Spread with dairy sour cream and sprinkle with brown sugar.*
- [ ] *Spread with mixture of cream cheese, softened and grated lemon peel.*

GINGERBREAD VARIATIONS

Prepare 1 package (14.5 ounces) gingerbread mix as directed except—try one of these variations:

Ambrosia Gingerbread: Stir 1 cup flaked coconut into batter. Nice served with orange sauce.

Applesauce Gingerbread: Decrease water to ¼ cup; add 1 cup canned applesauce. Bake about 35 minutes. Serve warm, with sweetened whipped cream, lemon sauce, hard sauce or applesauce.

Chocolate Gingerbread: Stir 1 ounce melted unsweetened chocolate (cool) into batter.

Lemon Gingerbread: Add 1 teaspoon grated lemon peel before beating.

Orange Gingerbread: Add 1 tablespoon grated orange peel before beating.

QUICK SHORTCAKE ALASKAS

1 package sponge shortcakes (4)
1 pint any flavor ice cream or sherbet
1 package (7.2 ounces) fluffy white frosting mix

Cover baking sheet with aluminum foil; place shortcakes on baking sheet. Place scoop of ice cream in each shortcake. Freeze at least 1 hour (or up to 24 hours).

Move oven rack to lowest position. Heat oven to 500°. Prepare frosting mix as directed on package. Completely cover shortcake and ice cream with frosting, sealing it to foil.

Bake until frosting is light brown, 3 to 5 minutes. Serve immediately. If desired, top each serving with ice-cream topping.

4 servings.

CHOCOLATE PUDDING CAKE VARIATIONS

Prepare 1 package (11 ounces) chocolate pudding cake mix as directed except—try one of these variations:

Chocolate-Marshmallow Pudding Cake: Sprinkle 1 cup miniature marshmallows over batter in pan.

Milk Chocolate Pudding Cake: Substitute 1½ cups hot milk for the boiling water. Bake about 35 minutes.

Mocha Pudding Cake: Add 2 teaspoons instant coffee to Pudding Mix (dry) and substitute 1½ cups hot milk for the boiling water. Bake about 30 minutes.

LEMON PUDDING CAKE VARIATIONS

Prepare 1 package (11 ounces) lemon pudding cake mix as directed except—try one of these variations:

Ambrosia Pudding Cake: Stir 1 tablespoon grated orange peel into batter and sprinkle ½ cup flaked coconut over batter in pan.

Lemon-Blueberry Pudding Cake: Sprinkle ½ cup unthawed frozen blueberries over batter in pan and decrease hot water to 1⅓ cups. Bake 25 to 30 minutes.

Lemon-Date Pudding Cake: Sprinkle ¼ cup chopped nuts and ¼ cup cut-up dates over batter before adding Pudding Mix. Bake 30 to 35 minutes.

CHOCOLATE-CHERRY PUDDING CAKE

Prepare 1 package (11 ounces) chocolate pudding cake mix as directed except—stir ¼ cup well-drained chopped maraschino cherries and ¼ cup chopped nuts into batter. Sprinkle Pudding Mix evenly over batter. Do not mix. Combine ¼ cup maraschino cherry syrup and 1¼ cups boiling water; pour slowly over mix to moisten entire top. Do not stir. Bake about 25 minutes.

9 servings.

BROWNIE SUNDAE PIE

Prepare 1 package (15.5 ounces) fudge brownie mix as directed except—spread in greased round layer pan, 9 × 1½ inches. Bake 30 to 35 minutes. Cool. Cut into wedges; serve with ice cream and chocolate sauce.

8 to 10 servings.

JIFFY TARTS

Prepare pastry for Two-crust Pie as directed on 1 package (11 ounces) pie crust mix or sticks except—divide pastry into 16 equal parts; roll each part into 4-inch circle. (Or divide pastry in half; roll each half into rectangle, 11 × 8 inches. Cut into six 3½-inch squares.) Prick circles or squares thoroughly with fork. Stack, placing 4-inch squares of aluminum foil between them. Wrap stack in foil; freeze.

To bake, heat oven to 475°. Remove desired number of pastry circles or squares from freezer and unwrap. Place on backs of alternating muffin cups or inverted custard cups; place on baking sheet. (Pastry shapes itself around cups during baking.) Bake 8 to 10 minutes. Cool. Remove from cups. Fill tart shells with one of the fillings below.

12 or 16 tarts.

Fillings
- [ ] *Ice cream and fresh or thawed frozen fruit.*
- [ ] *Ice cream and favorite ice-cream topping.*
- [ ] *Canned fruit pie filling; garnish with dollop of frozen whipped topping.*
- [ ] *Sweetened fresh or well-drained canned fruit; dot with jelly for color and flavor*
- [ ] *Sliced bananas and prepared vanilla pudding.*

Ambrosia Pudding Cake (page 138)

Applesauce Gingerbread (page 137)

Brownie Sundae Pie (page 138)

Ice Creams and Puddings

Creamy, dreamy desserts—your choice is wide, your time-to-make fast, fast, fast. A few for-instances: Cherry Pudding Parfaits, Cranberry Sundaes, a luscious Quick Lemon-Cheese Dessert. Or mix-match sauces with puddings and ice creams. Then have a fling with coconut, candy, cookie garnishes!

RICH CHOCOLATE SAUCE

8 ounces sweet cooking chocolate or 1 package (6 ounces) semisweet chocolate pieces
¼ cup sugar
¼ cup water
¼ cup light cream or evaporated milk

Heat chocolate, sugar and water in saucepan over low heat, stirring constantly, until chocolate and sugar are melted. Remove from heat; blend in cream. Serve warm or cool.

About 1 cup.

FUDGE SAUCE

1 can (14½ ounces) evaporated milk
2 cups sugar
4 ounces unsweetened chocolate
¼ cup butter or margarine
1 teaspoon vanilla
½ teaspoon salt

Heat milk and sugar to rolling boil, stirring constantly. Boil and stir 1 minute. Add chocolate, stirring until melted. Beat over heat until smooth. (If sauce has slightly curdled appearance, beat until smooth.) Remove from heat; blend in butter, vanilla and salt. Serve warm or cool.

About 3 cups.

BUTTERSCOTCH SAUCE

1½ cups brown sugar (packed)
½ cup light corn syrup
¼ cup butter or margarine
½ cup whipping cream
1 teaspoon vanilla

Heat sugar, syrup and butter to boiling over low heat, stirring constantly. Remove from heat; stir in whipping cream and vanilla. Stir just before serving. Serve warm or cool.

About 1 cup.

BUTTER PRALINE SAUCE

½ cup butter or margarine
1 cup confectioners' sugar
¼ cup corn syrup
¼ cup water
⅔ cup raisins (optional)
½ cup chopped pecans
1 teaspoon rum flavoring or vanilla

Heat butter in saucepan over medium heat until golden brown. Cool. Mix in sugar until smooth. Stir in syrup and water; heat to boiling. Boil and stir 1 minute. Cool slightly. Stir in raisins, pecans and flavoring. Serve warm, over vanilla ice cream or chocolate cake.

About 1⅔ cups.

TANGY MINCEMEAT SAUCE

Heat 1 cup prepared mincemeat and ½ cup port or, if desired, ½ cup cranberry cocktail. Serve warm.

About 1½ cups.

AMBER SAUCE

1 cup brown sugar (packed) or granulated
  sugar
½ cup light corn syrup
¼ cup butter or margarine
½ cup light cream (20%)

Combine ingredients in small saucepan. Cook over low heat 5 minutes, stirring occasionally. Serve warm, over vanilla ice cream, gingerbread or yellow cake.

About 2 cups.

HONEY-RUM SAUCE

1 cup light brown sugar (packed)
½ cup honey
¼ cup butter or margarine
¼ cup light or dark rum

Heat sugar, honey and butter to rolling boil in small saucepan; remove from heat. Cool. Stir in rum. Serve over ice cream, cake or baked apples.

About 2 cups.

RASPBERRY-CURRANT SAUCE

1 package (10 ounces) frozen raspberries,
  thawed, or 1 cup fresh raspberries
½ cup currant jelly
1½ teaspoons cornstarch
1 tablespoon water

Heat raspberries (with syrup) and jelly to boiling. Mix cornstarch and water; stir into raspberries. Heat to boiling, stirring constantly. Boil and stir 1 minute. Cool; if desired, press through a sieve to remove seeds.

About 1⅓ cups (with frozen berries) or about ¾ cup (with fresh berries).

TART CHERRY SAUCE

¾ cup sugar
2 tablespoons cornstarch
¼ teaspoon cinnamon
⅛ teaspoon salt
1 can (16 ounces) pitted red tart cherries,
  drained (reserve liquid)
1 tablespoon lemon juice
Few drops red food color

Stir together sugar, cornstarch, cinnamon and salt in saucepan. Add enough water to reserved cherry liquid to measure ¾ cup; stir into cornstarch mixture. Stir in cherries, lemon juice and food color. Cook over medium heat, stirring constantly, until mixture thickens and boils. Boil and stir 1 minute. Serve warm, over vanilla ice cream or yellow cake.

About 2 cups.

CINNAMON-BLUEBERRY SAUCE

2 tablespoons sugar
1 teaspoon cornstarch
1 cup fresh or thawed frozen blueberries
2 tablespoons water
1 tablespoon lemon juice
¼ teaspoon cinnamon

Stir together sugar and cornstarch in saucepan. Stir in remaining ingredients. Cook, stirring constantly, until mixture boils. Reduce heat; simmer 5 minutes, stirring occasionally. Serve warm.

About ⅔ cup.

STRAWBERRY SAUCE

Crush 1 pint fresh strawberries; stir in 3 tablespoons sugar. Spoon over ice cream.

About 2 cups.

CRANBERRY SUNDAES

Heat 1 package (10 ounces) frozen cranberry-orange relish or 1 can (8 ounces) whole cranberry sauce, stirring occasionally. Scoop 1 pint vanilla ice cream into 4 balls; place each ball in a serving dish. Spoon hot relish over ice cream.

4 servings.

PEANUT BUTTER SUNDAES

Blend ½ cup chocolate syrup or honey and ¼ cup peanut butter. Scoop 1 pint vanilla ice cream into 4 balls; place each ball in a serving dish. Spoon sauce over ice cream.

4 servings.

COCONUT ICE-CREAM BALLS

Place 1 cup flaked coconut and 1 teaspoon red or green colored sugar in plastic bag or jar. Close tightly and shake until coconut is uniformly colored. Scoop 1 pint vanilla or chocolate ice cream into 4 balls; roll each in tinted coconut.

4 servings.

Substitution
One-half cup cookie wafer crumbs and 1 tablespoon confetti decorators' candies can be substituted for the tinted coconut.

NOTE

More speedy ideas for desserts with sparkle. For a fancy finale (adult style), add zing to scoops of vanilla ice cream or lemon sherbet with 1 to 2 tablespoons of crème de menthe, grenadine syrup or fruit-flavored liqueur. Bring sparkle to the children's eyes by topping their servings with honey, maple syrup or jam.

CHERRY PUDDING PARFAITS

1 cup dairy sour cream or unflavored yogurt
1 cup milk
1 package (about 3½ ounces) vanilla instant pudding and pie filling
1 can (21 ounces) cherry pie filling

Beat sour cream and milk with rotary beater until smooth. Add instant pudding; beat until smooth and slightly thickened, about 2 minutes. Alternate layers of pudding and cherry pie filling in parfait glasses. Refrigerate at least 15 minutes.

6 servings.

QUICK EGGNOG PUDDING

Prepare 1 package (about 3½ ounces) vanilla instant pudding and pie filling as directed for pudding. Stir in 1 to 1½ teaspoons brandy or rum flavoring. Pour into dessert dishes. Sprinkle with nutmeg. Serve with light cream if desired.

4 servings.

PEANUT BUTTER PUDDING

Prepare 1 package (about 3½ ounces) vanilla or butterscotch instant pudding and pie filling with 2 cups milk as directed for pudding. Beat in ¼ cup peanut butter with rotary beater. Pour into dessert dishes.

4 servings.

LIME YOGURT DESSERT

1 cup boiling water
1 package (3 ounces) lime-flavored gelatin
4 to 6 ice cubes
1 carton (8 ounces) lime-flavored yogurt
  (1 cup)

Pour boiling water over gelatin in large bowl; stir until gelatin is dissolved. Add ice cubes; stir until gelatin begins to thicken. Remove any remaining unmelted ice.

Add yogurt; beat with rotary beater until smooth. Pour into dessert dishes, parfait glasses or molds. Refrigerate until firm, about 45 minutes. If desired, serve with a dollop of whipped topping on each.

5 or 6 servings.

RASPBERRY CREAM

1 cup boiling water
1 package (3 ounces) raspberry-flavored
  gelatin
1 package (10 ounces) frozen raspberries
1 cup vanilla ice cream

Pour boiling water over gelatin in large bowl; stir until gelatin is dissolved. Stir in frozen raspberries; break up raspberries with fork. Stir in ice cream. Pour into dessert dishes, parfait glasses or molds. Refrigerate until set, 20 to 30 minutes.

6 servings.

Variation

STRAWBERRY CREAM: Substitute 1 package (3 ounces) strawberry-flavored gelatin for the raspberry-flavored gelatin and 1 package (10 ounces) frozen strawberries for the raspberries.

Raspberry Cream

QUICK LEMON-CHEESE DESSERT

1 package (8 ounces) cream cheese, softened
1½ cups milk
1 package (about 3½ ounces) lemon instant
  pudding and pie filling
1 to 2 tablespoons grated lemon peel

Blend cream cheese and ½ cup of the milk in small mixer bowl; add remaining milk, the pudding and pie filling and lemon peel. Beat on low speed just until blended, 1 to 2 minutes. (Do not overbeat.) Pour into dessert dishes. Refrigerate at least 15 minutes. If desired, serve with vanilla wafers.

6 servings.

MOCK ZABAGLIONE

1 package (about 3½ ounces) vanilla instant
  pudding and pie filling
1 cup whipping cream
2 egg whites
¼ cup sugar
¼ cup sherry

Prepare pudding and pie filling as directed on package for pudding except—decrease milk to 1 cup and substitute the whipping cream for the remaining milk. Beat egg whites until foamy in small mixer bowl. Beat in sugar, 1 tablespoon at a time; continue beating until soft peaks form. Fold into pudding. Refrigerate about 1 hour.

Just before serving, stir in sherry. Spoon into dessert dishes or use as a topping for fruit or angel food cake.

6 or 7 servings.

DELUXE CHOCOLATE PUDDING

Beat 2 cups milk and 1 envelope (about 2 ounces) dessert topping mix in small mixer bowl until mixture begins to thicken, about 2 minutes. Gradually add 1 package (about 4½ ounces) chocolate instant pudding and pie filling; beat until soft peaks form, about 3 minutes. Pour into dessert dishes. Refrigerate at least 15 minutes.

6 to 8 servings.

FRUIT AND PUDDING PARFAITS

1 package (about 3½ ounces) vanilla instant
  pudding and pie filling
1 cup milk
1 cup chilled whipping cream
¾ teaspoon almond extract
1 to 1½ cups sliced fresh* fruit or 1 can
  (17 ounces) sliced peaches, pears or fruits
  for salad, drained

Mix pudding and pie filling and milk in small mixer bowl on low speed until smooth. Add whipping cream and extract; beat on medium speed until soft peaks form, 2 to 3 minutes.

Alternate layers of fruit and pudding, beginning and ending with fruit, in parfait glasses or dessert dishes. Refrigerate at least 15 minutes. Garnish with toasted flaked coconut or finely chopped nuts if desired.

6 servings.

* If using fresh peaches, pears, nectarines or bananas, dip slices for top layer into lemon juice to prevent discoloration.

Substitutions
Substitute one of the following for the almond extract:
☐ ½ teaspoon cinnamon
☐ ¼ teaspoon nutmeg
☐ ¾ teaspoon cardamom
☐ 1 tablespoon rum or brandy

Worldwide Winners

Rome, Paris, Vienna—where do you
want to travel tonight? Our "continentals"
can add an intriguing foreign atmosphere
to the good meals you cook right at home.
Difficult to make? Not really.
Often the cooking skills are familiar;
it's the taste that's new!

TORTES AND CAKE DESSERTS

These are the intriguing internationals—desserts with flair. Time and effort are needed, but what rewards —a rich Linzer Torte, delicate Bûche de Noël or brandy-syruped Savarin, to name a few.

PECAN TORTE

½ pound broken pecans
1 tablespoon flour
1 teaspoon baking powder
⅛ teaspoon salt
3 eggs, separated
¾ cup granulated sugar
1 cup chilled whipping cream
¼ cup confectioners' sugar
1 teaspoon rum flavoring or vanilla
Chocolate curls or grated chocolate

Heat oven to 350°. Line bottom of round layer pan, 9 × 1½ inches, with waxed paper. Grease waxed paper and side of pan. Chop nuts to the consistency of cornmeal, or place nuts in a blender. Cover and blend just long enough to chop pecans to proper consistency. (You should have 1½ cups of finely chopped pecans, packed.) Mix nuts, flour, baking powder and salt.

Beat egg whites until foamy. Beat in granulated sugar, 1 tablespoon at a time; continue beating until stiff and glossy. Beat egg yolks until light and lemon colored. Fold into whites. Fold in nut mixture; pour into pan.

Bake until top springs back when touched lightly, about 30 minutes. Invert pan on rack; remove waxed paper. Turn layer right side up. Cool.

In chilled bowl, beat whipping cream, confectioners' sugar and flavoring until stiff. Spread whipped cream on side and top of layer. Garnish with chocolate curls.

8 servings.

Pictured on page 145: Baklava (page 152)

LINZER TORTE

1 cup all-purpose flour
1 cup confectioners' sugar
¾ cup finely chopped blanched almonds
½ teaspoon cinnamon
⅛ teaspoon cloves
1 tablespoon grated lemon peel
¾ cup butter or margarine, softened
1 egg, slightly beaten
½ cup red raspberry jam
2 tablespoons red raspberry jam
½ cup chilled whipping cream

Mix flour, sugar, almonds, spices, lemon peel, butter and egg until dough forms a ball. Cover; refrigerate until firm, about 3 hours.

Heat oven to 375°. Press ⅔ of the dough evenly in bottom of ungreased round layer pan, 8 × 1½ inches. Spread with ½ cup jam.

Shape remaining dough on floured surface with floured hands into pencil-like rolls. Make a lattice design on jam by crisscrossing ten of the rolls. Place a long roll around edge. Bake until golden brown, about 40 minutes. Cool 10 minutes in pan.

Run knife around edge of pan to loosen torte. Invert on cloth-covered wire rack, then turn right side up on another rack and cool. Fill squares of lattice design with 2 tablespoons jam. In chilled bowl, beat whipping cream until stiff. Make a border of whipped cream on edge of torte or, if desired, top each serving with a dollop of whipped cream.

10 servings.

CINNAMON-APPLE TORTE

Pastry for 9-inch Two-crust Pie (page 111)
2 teaspoons cinnamon
6 tablespoons sugar
1 cup applesauce
Custard Filling (below)
½ cup chilled whipping cream

Heat oven to 425°. Prepare pastry as directed except—stir cinnamon into flour. Divide pastry into 6 equal parts. Roll each into a 7-inch circle; place on ungreased baking sheets. Prick circles with fork; sprinkle each with 1 tablespoon sugar. Bake until almost firm, 6 to 8 minutes. Cool on wire racks.

Stack circles, spreading alternately with ⅓ cup applesauce and ⅓ cup Custard Filling. In chilled bowl, beat whipping cream until stiff; fold in reserved filling. Spread over top. If desired, garnish with toasted slivered almonds. Refrigerate at least 2 hours before serving.

8 servings.

Custard Filling
¼ cup sugar
1 tablespoon cornstarch
¼ teaspoon salt
1 cup milk
1 egg yolk, slightly beaten
1 tablespoon butter or margarine
1 teaspoon vanilla

Mix sugar, cornstarch and salt in small saucepan. Gradually stir in milk. Cook over medium heat, stirring constantly, until mixture thickens and boils. Boil and stir 1 minute. Gradually stir at least half of the hot mixture into egg yolk. Blend into hot mixture in pan. Boil and stir 1 minute. Remove from heat; stir in butter and vanilla. Press plastic wrap on filling; cool. Reserve ⅓ cup filling for top of cake.

BUCHE DE NOEL

Old-fashioned Jelly Roll (page 89) or
*   Quick Jelly Roll (page 88)*
1 cup chilled whipping cream
2 tablespoons sugar
1½ teaspoons instant coffee
Cocoa Frosting (below)
Chopped pistachio nuts or red and green
*   candied cherries*

Prepare jelly roll as directed except—omit jelly. In chilled bowl, beat whipping cream, sugar and instant coffee until stiff. Unroll cake; remove towel. Spread whipped cream over cake. Roll up; frost with Cocoa Frosting. With tines of fork, make strokes in frosting to resemble bark. Sprinkle with pistachio nuts.

10 servings.

Cocoa Frosting
⅓ cup butter or margarine, softened
⅓ cup cocoa
2 cups confectioners' sugar
1½ teaspoons vanilla
1 to 2 tablespoons hot water

Mix butter and cocoa thoroughly. Blend in sugar. Stir in vanilla and water; beat until frosting is smooth and spreading consistency.

NOTE

Bûche de Noël—a charming way to gather around a Yule log at holiday time! And you don't even have to have a fireplace; this traditional French delicacy comes to the table for your enjoyment. It's a delicate cake roll, frosted and decorated to look like a log. Our recipe is based on the jelly roll, a variation of the basic yellow sponge cake. There's no trick to the making—just remember to roll the baked cake (while it's still hot) in a towel sprinkled with confectioners' sugar. Another hint: Cut off any crisp edges so the cake won't crack when you roll it. Follow these tips and your Yule log will do you proud indeed!

BABA AU RHUM

1 package active dry yeast
½ cup warm water (105 to 115°)
3 tablespoons sugar
2 cups all-purpose flour*
½ teaspoon salt
4 eggs, slightly beaten
½ cup raisins
¾ cup butter or margarine, softened
Rum Syrup (below)
1 jar (12 ounces) apricot preserves
Juice of 1 lemon (about 3 tablespoons)
Sweetened whipped cream

Dissolve yeast in warm water in large bowl. Stir in sugar, flour, salt, eggs and raisins. Beat vigorously until batter is smooth, elastic and slightly sticky, about 5 minutes. Cover; let rise in warm place until double, about 45 minutes.

Generously grease 8- or 9-cup metal mold with tube or 9-cup bundt pan. Stir down batter by beating 25 strokes. Stir in butter; beat until batter is sticky and elastic, about 5 minutes. Spread batter evenly in mold. Cover; let rise until double, about 45 minutes.

Heat oven to 375°. Bake until golden brown, about 30 minutes. Immediately remove from mold; cool slightly on wire rack.

Place warm baba on serving tray or plate with a rim. Drizzle ¾ cup Rum Syrup on baba; let stand 15 minutes. Repeat until all syrup is used.

Heat preserves and lemon juice over medium heat, stirring occasionally; cool slightly. Spoon off excess Rum Syrup from baba. Spread preserves mixture over baba. Serve with whipped cream.

12 to 16 servings.

* If using self-rising flour, omit salt.

Rum Syrup

Heat 2 cups water and 1½ cups sugar to boiling, stirring occasionally. Cool to lukewarm; stir in ½ cup dark rum.

Variations

INDIVIDUAL BABAS AU RHUM: Generously grease 24 muffin cups or twelve 6-ounce custard cups. Divide batter among cups. Cover; let rise until double, about 40 minutes. Bake in 375° oven until golden brown, about 20 minutes. Remove from cups; cool on wire rack.

Place babas on serving tray or plate with a rim. Spoon about 1 tablespoon Rum Syrup over each baba; let stand 15 minutes. Repeat until all syrup is used.

SAVARIN: Omit raisins and substitute Brandy Syrup (below) for the Rum Syrup. Substitute 1 jar (12 ounces) cherry preserves for the apricot preserves. Use 6½-cup metal ring mold and two 6-ounce custard cups; fill custard cups ½ full and spread remaining batter evenly in mold. Bake until golden brown, custard cups about 20 minutes, mold 30 minutes. Drizzle ⅔ cup Brandy Syrup over large savarin and 2 tablespoons syrup on each individual savarin; let stand 15 minutes. Repeat until all syrup is used. If you prefer a slightly smoother glaze, break up cherries with fork before you spread them on the savarin.

Brandy Syrup

Heat 2 cups water and 1½ cups sugar to boiling, stirring occasionally. Cool to lukewarm; stir in ½ cup cherry-flavored brandy.

NOTE

Like bread, Baba au Rhum is leavened with yeast; like cake, it's sweet. This delectable dessert is well worth the time taken to make it—its special-look appearance is confirmed by its taste. Saturated with a rum syrup after it's baked, then spread with apricot preserves, your creation can't help but find an appreciative audience. Try the Savarin variation, too—and for a further change of pace, serve it with fresh berries or with a topping of fluffy custard sauce, whipped cream or vanilla ice cream.

Pictured from bottom, clockwise: Individual Baba au Rhum, Baba au Rhum, Savarin (page 148)

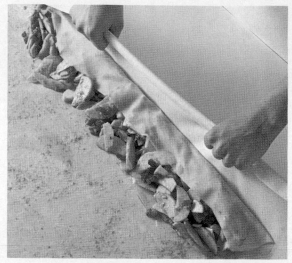

Gently lift and stretch dough with backs of hands.

Lift cloth; roll strudel as for a jelly roll.

Apple Strudel (page 151)

Pastry, Pudding and Fruit Desserts

You meet such interesting desserts when you travel! Apple Strudel in Germany, Zabaglione in Italy, flaky Baklava in Greece. You can't make a trip? Then make these great desserts at home.

APPLE STRUDEL

1½ cups all-purpose flour*
½ teaspoon salt
2 tablespoons salad oil
½ cup lukewarm water
¼ cup butter or margarine, melted
Filling (right)
2 tablespoons dry bread crumbs
¾ cup blanched almonds, ground
Confectioners' sugar

Measure flour, salt, oil and water into bowl. Mix with fork until all flour is moistened and dough cleans bowl. Turn dough onto lightly floured surface; knead until dough does not stick to surface and is satiny smooth, about 10 minutes. If necessary, sprinkle surface with small amount of flour while kneading. Shape dough into ball; brush with melted butter and cover with warm bowl. (To warm bowl, rinse with hot water, drain and dry.) Let rest about 30 minutes—dough will be easier to handle.

While dough is resting, cover a space on counter or table about 3 feet square with large dish towel or tablecloth. Tuck ends of cloth under and secure with tape. Sprinkle cloth with small amount of flour. Assemble ingredients for Filling but do not mix.

Heat oven to 425°. Roll dough on cloth to ⅛-inch thickness. Place hands palms down and close together under dough; gently lift and move hands apart until dough is paper thin and is stretched evenly to form a 30- to 36-inch square. Trim thick edges with kitchen scissors.

Brush square with melted butter and sprinkle with bread crumbs. Sprinkle almonds in a 3-inch strip along one edge. Mix Filling; spread over strip of almonds to within 2 inches of each end. Lift edge of cloth nearest apples with both hands; roll up square as for a jelly roll. Place roll seam side down on greased baking sheet in a horseshoe shape. Brush with melted butter.

Bake 15 minutes. Decrease oven temperature to 375°. Bake until golden brown, about 15 minutes. Remove from oven; sieve confectioners' sugar over top. Serve warm or cool. Cut into 1-inch slices, and if desired, serve with ice cream or sweetened whipped cream.

16 to 18 servings.

* Do not use self-rising flour in this recipe.

Filling
6 cups thinly sliced pared tart apples
   (about 6 medium)
¾ cup sugar
⅔ cup golden raisins
1 tablespoon cinnamon
1 tablespoon grated lemon peel

NOTE

Paper-thin layers of flaky pastry coupled with a spicy-sweet fruit filling combine to form this glorious treat. Apple Strudel is a great finale to a meal, but it's so special you may want to feature it some time all on its own. The next time you're having a kaffeeklatsch at your place, why not serve your own homemade strudel? Or bring it out for a dessert and coffee party; the only accompaniment needed will be guests' oohs and aahs. Maybe some whipped cream, too, if you really want to gild the lily.

BAKLAVA

Honey Syrup (right)
4 cups finely chopped walnuts, almonds,
   pecans or combination of nuts (1 pound
   shelled)
2 teaspoons cinnamon
1 teaspoon nutmeg
½ teaspoon cloves
1 pound butter
1 package (16 ounces) frozen filo leaves,
   thawed

Prepare syrup; set aside to cool. Mix nuts and spices. Clarify butter by melting slowly over low heat and skimming off foam as it rises to surface. Remove from heat and let stand 2 or 3 minutes. Spoon off clear butter; discard milky liquid in bottom of pan.

Heat oven to 350°. Brush bottom and sides of jelly roll pan, 15½ × 10½ × 1 inch, with some of the clarified butter. Unfold filo leaves; cover completely with damp towel to prevent them from drying out. Gently separate one leaf; place in pan, folding edges over to fit pan if necessary. Brush lightly with butter. Repeat 9 times. Sprinkle 2 cups of the nut mixture evenly over top. Layer 10 more filo leaves in pan, buttering each leaf. Sprinkle remaining nut mixture over top. Layer remaining 10 filo leaves over nuts, buttering each leaf.

With a sharp knife, cut pastry in pan ½ inch deep into 6 lengthwise strips, about 1¾ inches wide. Make diagonal cuts across strips ½ inch deep and 2 inches wide. Pour remaining butter over top. Bake until golden brown, 1 to 1¼ hours. Place pan on wire rack; pour cooled syrup over top. Cool. Cut along scored lines to bottom.

About 42 pieces.

Honey Syrup

2 cups sugar
2 cups water
3 tablespoons lemon juice
3-inch cinnamon stick
6 whole cloves
½ cup honey

Heat all ingredients except honey in medium saucepan to boiling, stirring until sugar is dissolved. Boil 5 minutes or to 220° on candy thermometer. Remove from heat; discard cinnamon stick and cloves. Stir in honey. Cool.

ZABAGLIONE

4 egg yolks
¼ teaspoon salt
¼ cup sugar
¼ cup sherry or Marsala
½ cup chilled whipping cream

Beat egg yolks in small mixer bowl on high speed until thick and lemon colored, 3 to 5 minutes. Add salt; gradually beat in sugar, scraping bowl occasionally. Blend in sherry on low speed.

Pour mixture into top of double boiler. Place enough hot water in bottom part of double boiler so that top part does not touch water. Cook over medium heat, stirring constantly, until thick, 5 to 7 minutes. (Water in double boiler should not boil.) Place top of double boiler in bowl of ice and water; stir mixture constantly until it is cool.

In chilled bowl, beat whipping cream until stiff. Fold whipped cream into pudding. Serve immediately or refrigerate.

4 servings.

Note: Zabaglione is delicious as a topping over fruit (strawberries, raspberries, pears, peaches). If you wish, omit the whipped cream; serve hot in demitasse cups or chilled.

DANISH PUFF

½ cup butter or margarine, softened
1 cup all-purpose flour
2 tablespoons water
½ cup butter or margarine
1 cup water
1 teaspoon almond extract
1 cup all-purpose flour
3 eggs
Confectioners' Sugar Glaze (below)
Chopped nuts

Heat oven to 350°. Cut ½ cup butter into 1 cup flour. Sprinkle 2 tablespoons water over mixture; mix. Round dough into ball; divide in half. On ungreased baking sheet, pat each half into strip, 12 × 3 inches. Strips should be about 3 inches apart.

Heat ½ cup butter and 1 cup water to rolling boil in saucepan. Remove from heat and quickly stir in almond extract and 1 cup flour. Stir vigorously over low heat until mixture forms a ball, about 1 minute. Remove from heat. Add eggs; beat until smooth.

Divide batter in half; spread each half evenly over strips. Bake until topping is crisp and brown, 55 to 60 minutes. Cool. Spread with Confectioners' Sugar Glaze and sprinkle generously with nuts.

10 to 12 servings.

Confectioners' Sugar Glaze

Mix 1½ cups confectioners' sugar, 2 tablespoons butter or margarine, softened, 1½ teaspoons vanilla and 1 to 2 tablespoons warm water until smooth.

Variation

INDIVIDUAL DANISH PUFFS: Pat dough into 3-inch circles, using a rounded teaspoonful (1½ teaspoons) for each. Spread rounded tablespoonful (1½ tablespoons) batter over each circle, extending batter just beyond edge of circle. (Topping will shrink slightly when baked.) Bake 30 minutes.

2 dozen puffs.

DANISH APPLE PUDDING

1⅓ cups finely crushed zwieback crumbs
½ cup butter or margarine
½ cup brown sugar (packed)
1 teaspoon cinnamon
1 can (16 ounces) applesauce (2 cups)
½ cup chilled whipping cream

Heat oven to 325°. Cook and stir zwieback crumbs in butter until brown. Mix in sugar and cinnamon. Pour applesauce into ungreased 9-inch pie pan; top with crumb mixture. Bake 30 minutes. In chilled bowl, beat whipping cream until stiff. Serve dessert warm or chilled, with whipped cream.

6 servings.

CARAMEL FLAN

½ cup sugar
3 eggs, slightly beaten
⅓ cup sugar
Dash of salt
1 teaspoon vanilla
2½ cups milk, scalded

Heat ½ cup sugar in small heavy skillet over low heat, stirring constantly, until sugar melts and is golden brown. Divide syrup among six 6-ounce custard cups; tilt and rotate each cup to coat the bottom. Allow syrup to set in cups about 10 minutes.

Heat oven to 350°. Blend eggs, ⅓ cup sugar, the salt and vanilla. Gradually stir in milk. Pour custard mixture over syrup in cups. Place cups in oblong pan, 13 × 9 × 2 inches; pour very hot water into pan to within ½ inch of tops of cups.

Bake until knife inserted halfway between center and edge comes out clean, about 45 minutes. Remove cups from water. Let cool to room temperature and invert custard cups to unmold, or chill and unmold at serving time.

6 servings.

SCANDINAVIAN FRUIT SOUP

1 package (about 12 ounces) mixed dried
    fruit such as prunes, apricots, peaches,
    pears, raisins (2 cups)
1½ cups water
1½ cups grape juice or cranberry juice
    cocktail
2 tablespoons quick-cooking tapioca
¼ teaspoon salt
½ cup sugar
3-inch cinnamon stick
2 or 3 thin slices lemon (optional)
1 can (8 ounces) pitted dark sweet cherries

Measure all ingredients except cherries into large
saucepan. Heat to boiling, stirring occasionally.
Reduce heat; cover and simmer until fruit is tender,
30 to 40 minutes. Stir in cherries (with syrup) and
heat. Serve warm or cold.

6 servings.

POT DE CREME AU CHOCOLAT

⅔ cup semisweet chocolate pieces
1 cup light cream (20%)
2 eggs
3 tablespoons sugar
Dash of salt
1½ tablespoons rum (optional)

Heat oven to 350°. Heat chocolate pieces and
cream, stirring constantly, until chocolate is melted
and mixture is smooth. Cool slightly. Beat remaining ingredients; gradually stir into chocolate mixture. Pour into 4 ungreased 6-ounce custard cups
or 4 or 5 small ovenproof pots.

Place cups in baking pan on oven rack; pour boiling water into pan to within ½ inch of tops of
cups. Bake 20 minutes. Remove cups from water.
Cover and refrigerate at least 4 hours.

4 servings.

RASPBERRY ROSETTES

1 egg
1 tablespoon sugar
½ teaspoon salt
1 tablespoon salad oil
½ cup water or milk
½ cup all-purpose flour*
Sweetened whipped cream
Fresh or thawed frozen raspberries

Heat oil or fat (3 to 4 inches) in small deep saucepan to 400°. Beat egg, sugar and salt in small deep
bowl. Beat in oil, water and flour until smooth.

Heat rosette iron by placing in hot oil 1 minute.
Tap excess oil from iron; dip hot iron in batter
just to top edge (be careful not to go over the top).
Fry until golden brown, about ½ minute. Immediately remove rosette (use a fork if necessary); invert on paper towel to cool. (If rosette is not crisp,
batter is too thick—stir in small amount of water
or milk.)

Heat iron in hot oil before making each rosette.
(If iron is not hot enough, batter will not stick to
iron.) Just before serving, top rosettes with whipped
cream and raspberries.

18 rosettes.

* If using self-rising flour, omit salt.

Variations

FRUIT ROSETTES: Substitute sweetened fresh strawberries or other fresh or thawed frozen fruit for
the raspberries.

TIMBALES: Substitute timbale form for rosette iron;
invert iron each time to drain oil. Just before serving, fill Timbales with fresh fruit, ice cream, pudding or fruit pie filling.

Note: Rosettes can be stored in waxed paper-lined
containers in cool dry place up to 2 weeks. Or
you can wrap and freeze them up to 2 months.

Dip hot rosette iron in batter just to top edge.   Fry until golden brown, about ½ minute.

Raspberry Rosette (page 154)

INDEX